MORE Easy Everyday FAVORITES

by MarkCharles Misilli

© 2019 Cogin, Inc. All rights reserved. Photos ©Cogin, Inc.
No part of this publication may be reproduced or transmitted in any form or by any means, electronic or mechanical, including duplication, recording, or by any information storage or retrieval system, without the prior written permission from the Publisher.

Author, MarkCharles Misilli. *Editors*, Jodi Flayman, Merly Mesa, Carol Ginsburg; *Recipe Development and Food Styling*, Patty Rosenthal; *Photographers*, Kelly Rusin and Freedom Martinez; *Post Production*, Hal Silverman of Hal Silverman Studio; *Cover and Page Design*, Lorraine Dan of Grand Design.
Special thanks to *Business Partners*, Steve Lichter and Lisa Matz.

The paper in this printing meets the requirements of the ANSI Standard Z39.48-1992.

While every care has been taken in compiling the recipes for this book, the publisher, Cogin, Inc., or any other person who has been involved in working on this publication assumes no responsibility or liability for any errors or omissions, inadvertent or not, that may be found in the recipes or text, nor for any problems or damages that may arise as a result of preparing these recipes.

If food allergies or dietary restrictions are a concern, it is recommended that you carefully read ingredient product labels as well as consult a nutritionist or your physician to determine if a particular recipe meets your dietary needs.

We encourage you to use caution when working with all kitchen equipment and to always follow food safety guidelines.

To purchase this book for business or promotional use or to purchase more than 50 copies at a discount, or for custom editions, please contact Cogin, Inc. at the address below.

Inquiries should be addressed to:
Cogin, Inc.
1770 NW 64 Street, Suite 500
Fort Lauderdale, FL 33309

ISBN: 978-0-9981635-8-1

Printed in the United States of America
First Edition

INTRODUCTION

As I sit here writing this introduction, I'm overwhelmed with mixed emotions. Before I go any further, I want to personally thank all of you who not only picked up a copy of my last book, *Easy Everyday Favorites*, but who also shared personal stories about how much you enjoy using it. If you've ever wondered whether an author actually reads the comments and reviews you write about their book, the answer is YES (at least I do!). In fact, it was the hundreds of positive comments and stories that encouraged me to set out and create another great cookbook for you, and this one is full of even *MORE Easy Everyday Favorites*.

While reading your comments, I made sure to take notes. So yes, there are lots and lots of full-page photos and large, easy-to-read print with only a handful of easy-to-follow instructions for each recipe. And of course, all the ingredients that I used can be found in your local supermarket.

I'm even sharing a few photos from get-togethers that I've hosted over the last year. As you'll see, I think it's just as important to present food in an appealing way, as it is to prepare it. I hope these pictures and tips throughout the book encourage you to have fun "tablescaping" (that's when you sort of landscape your table, so it looks extra-special).

For those of you who wrote that you wanted more space for writing down your own recipe notes, I heard you. There's plenty of white space throughout the book, so you can write down all your family's favorite tweaks and changes. I also suggest jotting down the date and who you made the dish for (like a diary to look back on). Yes, I encourage you to write in the book and dog-ear the pages! It's one of the best indicators that a book is well-loved.

INTRODUCTION

If you're wondering whether I've repeated any recipes from the last book, the answer is no. They're all new, all tasty, and all ready for you to share them with your friends and family. (I still have lots more, so who knows, maybe there'll be another book in the future?!)

As I started saying, I'm writing this with mixed emotions; of joy and sadness. The joy comes from knowing that I can once again share with you the recipes that are part of my life. Every recipe in this book has a special meaning. It might be a recipe that I serve year after year during the holidays or a weeknight go-to favorite that I rely on when time is super limited.

On the other hand, I'm also saddened that my Grandmother or "Meme," isn't here to celebrate with me. After all, she was my greatest inspiration in the kitchen, as well as in life in general. While I worked on these recipes, I often felt her beautiful spirit looking over my shoulder, guiding me with her lifetime of wisdom. I know that Meme would've been proud of what we've put together for you, and I hope your food is as full of love as she was.

So once you've made your first few recipes, would you do me a favor and share your experiences with me? After working on this cookbook for more than a year, tweaking and tasting everything until it was just perfect, I hope it brings as much happiness to you, your friends, and family, as it did to me.

As my dear Meme used to say in her broken English when dinner was ready…"DEEG-IN!"

MarkCharles Misilli

MY TIPS FOR ENTERTAINING

As you might already know, I love to entertain. Yes, even with my busy schedule, I find nothing more rewarding than hosting meals and celebrations with friends and family. For those of you who have seen my posts on Facebook, you know that when I say I entertain, I mean I like to go all out.

I want to help you be an even better host by sharing some of my favorite tips for entertaining, whether you're hosting four people or the whole neighborhood.

What's the occasion? You'll be making your plans based on the reason for the celebration. Is it a birthday or anniversary party? Are you having friends over to watch the big game? Is everyone getting together for a bridal shower, a holiday or New Year's Eve? Or maybe, it's a Sunday family dinner or a celebration "just because." Once you know the occasion, you can plan the details around it.

How many guests and who are they? Knowing this will help you select the perfect place to host your celebration, as well as how much food you'll need (check out the following tips on Planning a Perfect Buffet and Sit-Down Meals). It's important to know who your guests are, as it will make planning the details of location, time, and menu a little easier.

Where will you host it? You want to make sure you've got enough room and seating for the number of people you plan to invite. It's also important to think about whether your chosen location can accommodate your kitchen needs. If it's an outdoor party, consider making an alternate plan in case the weather doesn't cooperate. Try thinking outside the box, like maybe turning your driveway into the setting for a party if you don't have enough room for the number of folks coming over on your porch or deck, or maybe set up a cozy dining experience for four in front of your fireplace on a winter's evening, just to mix it up.

When will you host it? The day, time, and season can really impact your celebration. Remember, most parties last for 3 to 4 hours, so you probably won't want yours to start too late in the evening—unless it's New Year's Eve or some other time when you want to be up really late! A 75th birthday and a 50th anniversary party would be the perfect occasions for a Sunday brunch because it's the best party time for people of all ages. An end-of-the-year holiday party is great to schedule on a Saturday evening, so that families can join and enjoy your twinkling holiday lights. If it's an outdoor barbecue, you obviously want to schedule it when the weather is most likely to be agreeable for an outdoor event (but as I said, make sure you have a backup plan!).

What should you serve? The type of food and how you should plan to serve it will be determined by the answers to the above questions. Will you need a special menu to accommodate any dietary restrictions? Does your guest list include kids with pickier taste buds? You should also consider how much time you have to plan and prepare.

If you use even a few of the tips here, along with my recipes, you'll be done preparing before you know it—and entertaining will be fun!

MY TIPS FOR ENTERTAINING

PLANNING A PERFECT BUFFET

If you're looking for an easy way to serve food to a lot of people, then you might want to consider a buffet. Typically, a buffet includes a larger variety of foods than what'd you'd generally serve for a sit-down meal. The better you know your guests and their food likes, the easier it'll be to know what to serve, but even if you don't know them too well, you can still offer enough choices to please everyone without it getting too complicated.

Develop a "traffic pattern." You want to make sure everyone can get to and through your buffet line as quickly and smoothly as possible, which is why it's important to consider where you're going to set up your buffet spread. For example, you don't want to put a buffet table in the corner of your kitchen. Try to keep it in the dining room or somewhere out of the main flow of party traffic. You'll want to be able to get in and out of the kitchen without having to maneuver around extra people.

Consider your layout. Place the plates at the beginning of the buffet table, where the guests will start serving themselves. Next should come a salad, followed by a main course, side dishes, and bread. For dessert, I suggest bringing that out later or setting it out in a separate area, if the room permits. And don't forget the silverware! Before your party, roll individual sets of utensils in napkins and place them at the end of the buffet table, so that your guests don't have to balance them all the way through the buffet line.

It's all about variety. When it comes to food, who doesn't love having lots of options? I like to serve both cold and hot foods, so that I'm not worrying about heating up too many dishes with a limited amount of oven and stovetop space. I also serve foods that vary in flavor and texture. For example, you might want to consider offering two contrasting main dishes like a chicken and a fish. No matter what you serve, try not to put food out too soon before serving time, and refill frequently to keep things fresh!

Don't forget the serving pieces. Every bowl or platter of food should have at least one serving piece—and be sure it's one that's appropriate, like a large spoon for meatballs, a slotted spoon for coleslaw, tongs for salad, a fork for cold cuts, etc.

Label your food. I like to use place card holders to label each dish and let my guest know what's in each one. This helps people make smart decisions while they help themselves, plus it's especially helpful for those who need to avoid certain foods due to allergies.

> "When it comes to food, who doesn't love having lots of options?"

TIPS FOR SIT-DOWN MEALS

Family-style or sit-down meals are still popular for smaller gatherings. Your sit-down meal can be anything from a weeknight dinner to a grand formal feast. My favorite way to serve is when you can dish out some of everything onto individual plates in the kitchen (the way most restaurants serve), but another way to serve is "family-style" where you set everything out in bowls or on platters and let everyone serve themselves.

Sit in the seat closest to the kitchen. That way, when you need to get up during the meal you won't disturb your guests.

Make space. If you don't have enough room at your kitchen or dining room table, it might be time to bring out your folding table. (We always called that extra table the "kids' table," and now I think it's flattering if I get to sit there!)

Use place settings. Whether you use your everyday dishes, your fine china for a special occasion, or disposable paper plates and plasticware for casual events, there should be a place setting for each guest. Be sure to have extras on hand, because you're bound to need something extra. You don't have to have multiple sets. You can be creative and mix and match dishes. Often, after a holiday, you can find holiday-themed dishes and accessories at a deep discount.

Consider your tableware options.
You can choose not to cover your table (depending upon what your table is made of, of course), use a tablecloth, multiple table runners, or use colorful place mats. Use table pads (if you need them) to protect your table from heat and moisture. There are loads of different kinds, textures, and colors of paper and plastic plates, utensils, napkins, cups, tablecloths, and place mats available now. Some paper napkins even feel like linen. And if you want to use cloth napkins (they'll make your guests feel really special!), they're available in all kinds of colors and patterns. It's easy to give your table a festive look!

> *"I believe that a beautifully set table makes everybody smile!"*

Don't forget the silverware. When setting your table, be sure to put out the right silverware for what you're serving—you know, a soup spoon if your serving soup, a salad fork if you don't want your guests to use the same fork they'll use for dinner, etc.

Check out my suggestion for a proper place setting. (If you're more comfortable doing it a different way, that's fine too! Anything goes…it's your table. Have fun with it!)

Official rules say that utensils are placed in the order of use; that is, from the outside in. A second rule, with only a few exceptions, is: Forks go to the left of the plate, and knives and spoons go to the right. And finally, only set the table with utensils you will use. No soup; no soup spoon.

MY TIPS FOR ENTERTAINING

WE EAT WITH OUR EYES!

There's an expression that says we "eat with our eyes." I happen to agree with that! No matter how good food tastes, it has to look good too, or people won't want to eat it. Now I'm not saying we need to spend hours making fancy decorations or buying expensive centerpieces. I just think there's something to be said about making our food and our tables look colorful whenever company's invited.

Fresh greens make great garnishes. Use fresh herbs, scallions, or different types of lettuces or greens (the heartier types like endive, leaf lettuce, kale, and romaine are the best) for garnishing platters and individual plates. For example, it's easy to place a bit of green around a serving bowl and then place potato or macaroni salad in the bowl. Finish your garnish with a few cherry tomatoes, sliced hard-boiled eggs, and some black or green olives.

Decorate with colorful fruits and veggies. Decorate with strawberries or radishes by cutting thin slices three quarters of the way through and fanning them out. After cutting radishes this way, it's best to store them in icy cold water for about an hour so they really get a chance to "blossom."

Get creative with a melon baller. You can use a melon baller or small scoop to make scoops of butter to top pancakes, fish, steak, or even for piling on a serving plate to go along with your favorite bread or rolls. Butter balls can be made in advance, laid out on a baking sheet, covered with plastic wrap, and kept frozen until ready to use.

> "Go ahead and have fun making your party table special. I bet your guests will be surprised by what you can do!"

Create a "tablescape." Besides dressing up your food, you can create a visually appealing landscape for your spread (a tablescape!). You can buy an arrangement of flowers for a centerpiece or put a bunch of flowers loose in a vase (this is usually less expensive). Be sure the flowers aren't so tall that people can't see one another across a sit-down dinner table, or use very tall, clear vases that hold the flowers higher up. You may even want to make your own novelty decorations for placing around the house—and you can do this by using things that you've already got on hand. Drape a Mexican shawl over a chair near your buffet table or put a piñata in the center of your Mexican buffet. Pumpkins, gourds, and baskets of apples sure say "Happy harvest time!" on an autumn buffet. How about putting party hats and streamers around the back edge of a New Year's or birthday buffet—or serve right from a wok on a Chinese buffet and add a few decorative Chinese fans around the back of the table? Dollar and craft stores are great places to get started.

Don't forget the candles! They can create almost any mood—classy, romantic, or even festive. Just be sure to put something under them to catch drips, and place them safely out of the reach of little AND big guests (pets too), and away from curtains, furniture, and other flammables. I like to use flameless candles, too. They can be placed anywhere and you never have to worry about them. You can even turn some wine glasses upside-down and place the candles on top of the bases of the glasses to elevate the candles off the table. You can use varying heights of glasses to add even more visual appeal. Now, all that's left to do is to enjoy!

> *I hope you have as much fun cooking from this book as I had creating it. Now as my Meme always said It's time to....'DEEG-IN!'*

TABLE OF CONTENTS

Introduction	iii
My Tips for Entertaining	vi
Breakfast & Brunch	1
Starters	27
Soups & Salads	55
Chicken & Turkey	83
Beef & Pork	113
Seafood, Pasta, & More	141
Side Dishes	169
Desserts	193
Index	231
My Favorite Recipes	239
Notes	240

"I don't believe in skipping breakfast, especially when there are homemade blueberry muffins involved! And can you believe they're made in an air fryer?"

BREAKFAST & BRUNCH

Sheet Pan Eggs & Corned Beef Hash 2

"Classy Café" Avocado Toast 4

Overstuffed Omelet for Two 6

Cheesy Sausage & Tots Bake 7

Bun-less Egg Sandwich 8

Hot 'n' Hearty Breakfast Casserole 10

Cereal-Crusted French Toast 12

Banana Pancakes with Banana Syrup 13

Bite-Sized Berry Dutch Babies 14

Ham 'n' Egg Rollups 16

Blueberry-Lemon Air Fryer Muffins 18

Banana-Walnut Overnight Oats 19

Make-Your-Own Oatmeal Cookie Pizza 20

Peachy-Keen Cinnamon Bun Bake 22

Paradise Pineapple Fritters 24

SHEET PAN EGGS & CORNED BEEF HASH

Don't know what to serve your family for breakfast? Instead of sitting there for (what feels like) hours trying to "hash" things out with yourself, I'm suggesting you make this tasty New England-style hash. It's a homestyle favorite that makes enough to feed everyone, but also doesn't leave you with a huge pile of pots and pans in the sink. That's a win/win in my book!

Serves 3 to 6

2 tablespoons vegetable oil

½ teaspoon garlic powder

½ teaspoon salt

¼ teaspoon black pepper, plus extra for sprinkling

2 (½-inch-thick) slices deli corned beef, cut into ¼-inch cubes

3 cups refrigerated diced potatoes

½ cup diced onion

6 eggs

- Preheat oven to 425 degrees F. Coat a rimmed baking sheet with cooking spray

- In a large bowl, combine oil, garlic powder, salt, and pepper; mix well. Add corned beef, potatoes, and onion; toss until evenly coated. Place mixture in a single layer on baking sheet. Bake 30 minutes or until potatoes begin to brown.

- Remove from oven and form 6 wells in the hash. (Check out the picture to see what I mean!) Gently crack an egg into each well. Bake an additional 5 to 7 minutes or until egg whites are firm and yolks are cooked to your liking. Sprinkle with black pepper and serve immediately.

Sometimes I like to serve this on individual salad plates rather than bringing the sheet pan to the table. It gives everyone a feeling of individual attention. And, did you know that you can freeze fresh thyme and defrost it in seconds? That way you always have some on hand. MCM

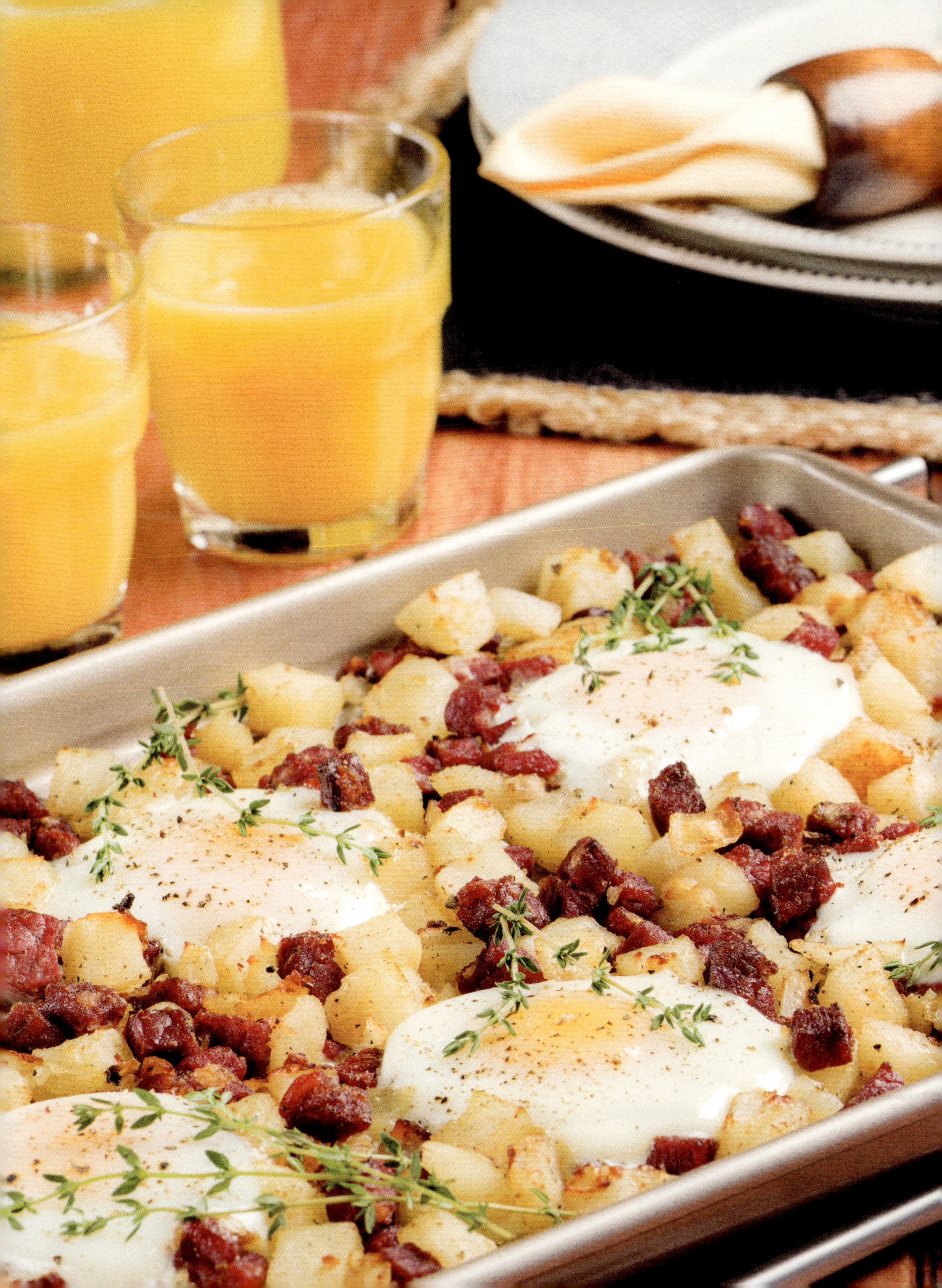

"CLASSY CAFÉ" AVOCADO TOAST

In my last book, I introduced you to my "Hotel Breakfast" Eggs Benedict. Now it's time for your taste buds to meet my "Classy Café" Avocado Toast. No matter where I go, avocado toast is on practically every breakfast or brunch menu, so I thought I'd give my twist to share with you. My version has a lot of texture, flavor, and style, so serve it up when you want to impress your friends!

Makes 4

- 4 cups water
- ¼ cup white vinegar
- 4 eggs
- 3 ripe avocados, halved, pitted, and skin removed
- 1 tablespoon lemon juice
- ¼ teaspoon salt
- 4 slices multigrain bread
- ¼ cup coarsely chopped, peeled and cooked shrimp
- 4 slices cooked bacon, each slice cut in half
- Black pepper for sprinkling

- In a medium saucepan over medium-high heat, bring water and vinegar to a boil. (The vinegar helps the egg stay together when you poach it.) Reduce heat so that water is vigorously simmering. Crack eggs one at a time, and gently drop each into the water. Cook 4 to 6 minutes or until egg whites are firm and the yolks are to your liking.

- Meanwhile, in a small bowl, mash avocados with a fork until desired consistency. Stir in lemon juice and salt; set aside.

- Toast bread and place on a platter. Spread evenly with avocado mixture and top with shrimp. Using a slotted spoon, remove eggs from water and place 1 egg on each piece of toast. Top with bacon and sprinkle with black pepper. Serve immediately.

If you really want to take things up a notch and go from "classy" to "extravagant" you can substitute cooked lobster tail for the shrimp. Just make sure you cut it into chunks. (I haven't found toast big enough for a whole tail yet!) MCM

BREAKFAST & BRUNCH

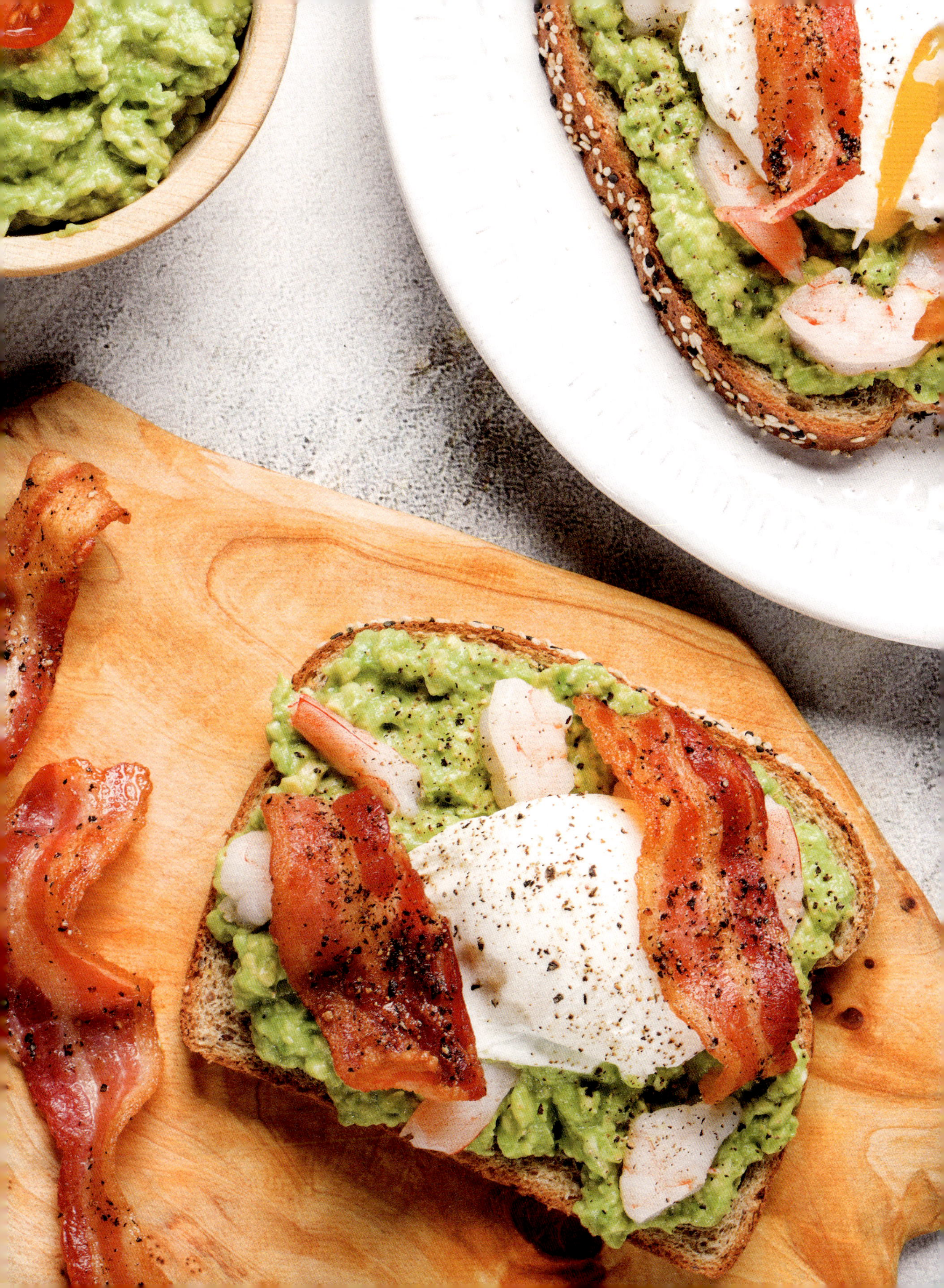

OVERSTUFFED OMELET FOR TWO

Get a head start on your day with an overstuffed omelet that's perfectly-sized for you and that lucky someone. I load mine up with tomatoes, onion, and spinach before smothering it in lots of cheese. This one is so easy, it's perfect for a busy weekday morning.

Serves 2

2 teaspoons olive oil

2 tablespoons diced sweet onion

¼ cup cherry tomatoes, cut in half

½ teaspoon garlic powder

¼ teaspoon salt

1 cup fresh baby spinach

4 eggs

2 tablespoons water (see note)

½ cup shredded Swiss cheese

■ In an 8- to 10-inch nonstick skillet over medium heat, heat oil until hot. Add onion, tomatoes, garlic powder, and salt. Sauté 4 to 5 minutes or until vegetables are tender. Stir in spinach and cook 1 minute or until wilted. Remove vegetables from skillet and set aside.

■ Coat skillet with cooking spray and place over medium heat. In a medium bowl, beat eggs with water. Add eggs to skillet, and with a spatula, gently stir, pushing the cooked portion of the eggs to the center of the pan.

■ When eggs are firmed up, but not dry, sprinkle with cheese and top one half of the omelet with the vegetable mixture. Cook until cheese is melted. To serve, slide the omelet out of the pan and onto a platter, folding it in half over the filling. Cut in half and serve.

One thing I've learned over the years is that adding a bit of room temperature water to eggs makes them nice and fluffy. If the water is too cold, it tightens up the eggs and if it's too hot, it cooks them. Tap water should be perfect. MCM

Breakfast & Brunch

CHEESY SAUSAGE & TOTS BAKE

This bake delivers all the goodness. I'm talking cheesy, meaty, eggy, creamy, potato tot-y deliciousness that's so mouthwatering-good you have to invite all your friends over just so you don't eat it all by yourself. Nothing about this is low calorie, and that's fine by me. Some mornings, you just have to go all out!

Serves 6 to 8

16 ounces bulk or tube pork breakfast sausage

½ cup chopped onion

½ red bell pepper, diced

1-½ cups shredded sharp cheddar cheese, divided

6 eggs

1-½ cups milk

½ teaspoon onion powder

⅛ teaspoon salt

½ teaspoon black pepper

½ (32-ounce) bag potato tots

- Preheat oven to 375 degrees F. Coat a 9- x 13-inch baking dish with cooking spray.

- In a large skillet over medium-high heat, cook sausage, onion, and bell pepper 5 to 6 minutes or until sausage is browned, stirring occasionally to make sure sausage is crumbled; drain. Place sausage mixture in baking dish and sprinkle evenly with 1 cup cheese.

- In a large bowl, whisk eggs, milk, onion powder, salt, and black pepper. Pour over the egg and cheese mixture and top with potato tots.

- Bake 30 to 35 minutes or until eggs are set. Sprinkle remaining cheese over top and cook an additional 5 minutes or until cheese is melted. Serve immediately.

Potato tots are all the rage, and like the "Taco Tuesday Totchos" in my previous book, this recipe uses potato tots in a new way. Also, I love to keep sausage in my freezer as a staple that can be added to many recipes. MCM

BUN-LESS EGG SANDWICH

It only makes sense that I follow up the hearty breakfast bake on page 7 with a tasty, low-carb idea. I came up with this one when I was trying to cut down on carbs (and it was so easy and delicious, I still make it every once in a while). Rather than using a bagel, biscuit, or bun, I use turkey sausage patties to sandwich my fluffy egg and cheese omelet. It's a great, protein-packed way to start your day.

Makes 2

- 2 eggs
- 1 tablespoon milk
- 1/8 teaspoon salt
- 1/8 teaspoon black pepper
- 1 tablespoon butter, divided
- 1/4 cup shredded cheddar cheese
- 4 frozen turkey sausage patties, heated according to package directions

- In a small bowl, whisk together eggs, milk, salt, and pepper.

- In a small skillet over medium heat, melt 1/2 tablespoon butter. Pour half of the egg mixture into the skillet and stir gently with a spatula until it just starts to set up.

- Sprinkle half of the cheese in the middle of egg and let cook until the cheese is melted and egg is no longer runny. Fold the sides of the egg over the cheese, then repeat with the other two sides, creating a pillow of egg filled with cheese. Place egg between two warmed sausage patties and secure with a toothpick. Repeat with remaining egg mixture and sausage. Serve piping hot.

If you want to serve these to a group of friends, feel free to make them in advance. Then when everyone is ready to eat, just reheat them on a baking sheet in a 300 degree oven for 10 to 12 minutes. MCM

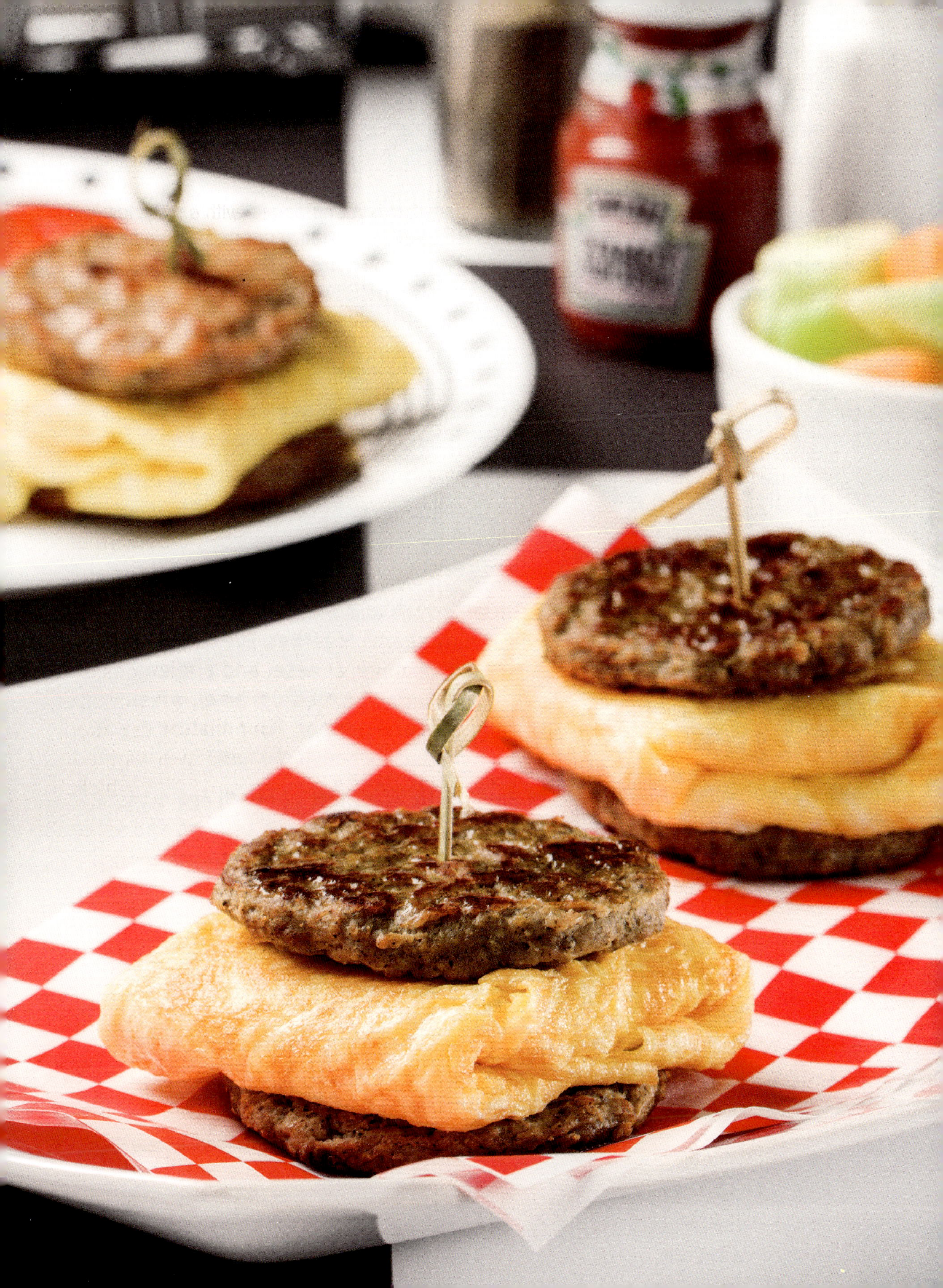

HOT 'N' HEARTY BREAKFAST CASSEROLE

If they say they're still hungry after eating this hearty breakfast casserole … they're probably lying. (It's either that or you tried to make this feed way more than suggested.) From the sausage and eggs to the crescent roll base, everything about this casserole will leave you feeling full and satisfied.

Serves 6 to 8

16 ounces bulk or tube pork breakfast sausage

1 (8-ounce) can refrigerated crescent rolls

1-½ cups shredded Colby Jack cheese

1 (2-ounce) jar diced pimientos, drained well

6 eggs

¾ cup milk

½ teaspoon salt

¼ teaspoon black pepper

- Preheat oven to 375 degrees F. Coat a 9- x 13-inch baking dish with cooking spray.

- In a large skillet over medium heat, cook sausage 5 to 6 minutes or until browned, stirring occasionally to crumble; drain liquid and set aside.

- Unroll dough and place in baking dish, pinching seams together. Evenly sprinkle cooked sausage, cheese, and pimientos on top of dough. In a medium bowl, whisk eggs, milk, salt, and pepper. Pour mixture evenly over meat and cheese mixture.

- Bake 30 to 35 minutes or until egg mixture sets up in center. Cut into squares and serve.

At times when I don't have breakfast sausage in the house, I just crumble a few cooked hamburgers or some super-crispy bacon into the casserole dish. There really are no rules to this casserole, so you can get creative! MCM

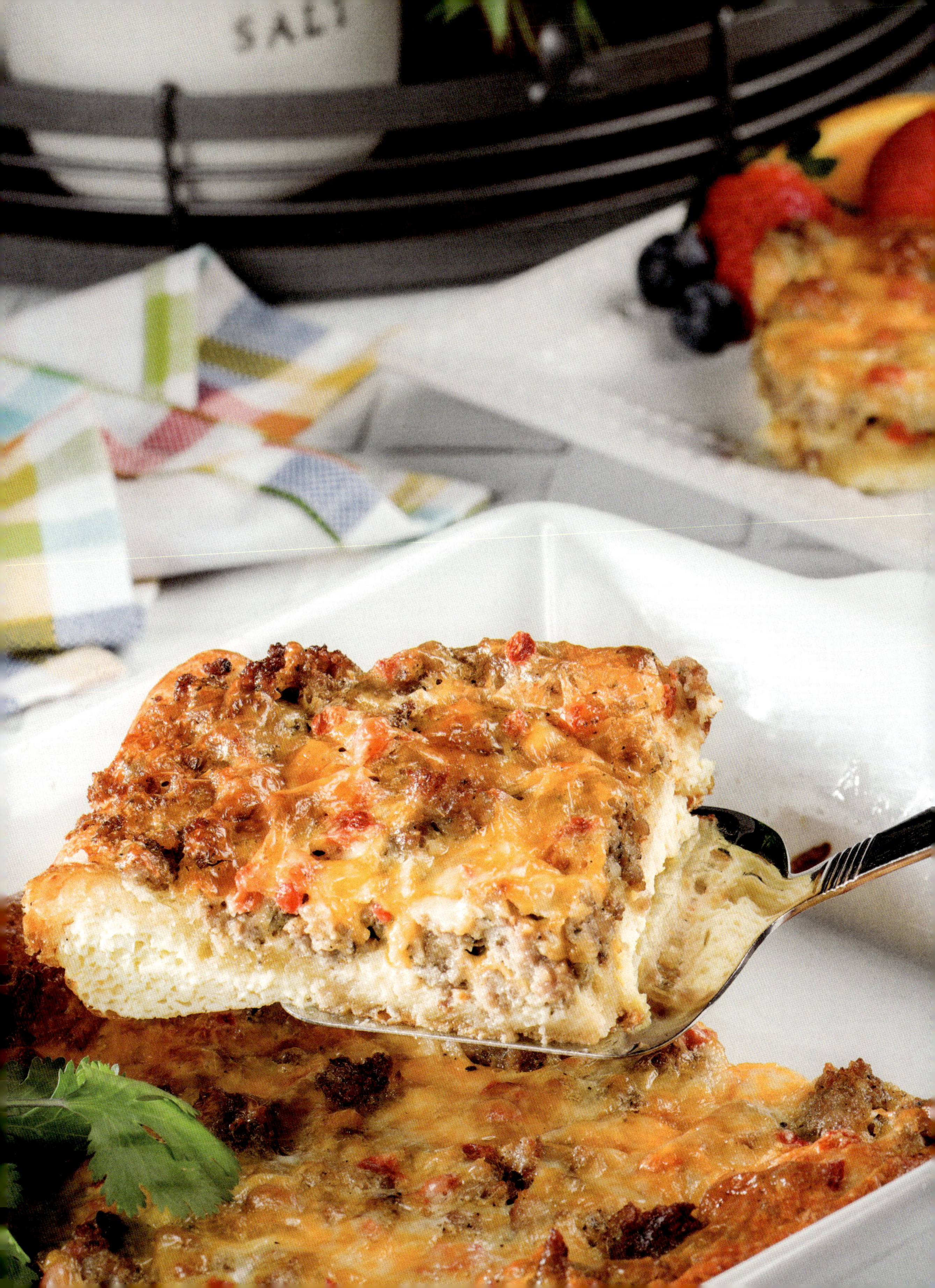
SALT

CEREAL-CRUSTED FRENCH TOAST

When you can't decide whether you want a big bowl of cereal or mouthwatering French toast ... have both! As you might've learned about me by now, I'm a big fan of crispy-crunchy textures, so French toast with an extra-crispy crust is a real favorite. You can even get creative by making it with different kinds of cereal!

Serves 4

- 4 cups coarsely crushed cornflakes
- ¼ cup sugar
- 1 teaspoon ground cinnamon
- 7 eggs
- ¼ cup milk
- 1 teaspoon vanilla extract
- 1 (1-pound) loaf egg bread (challah), cut into 8 (1-inch) slices
- ⅓ cup vegetable oil
- Syrup and fresh fruit for serving

- In a shallow dish, combine crushed cereal, sugar, and cinnamon; mix well and set aside.

- In another shallow dish, beat eggs, milk, and vanilla.

- Dip one slice of bread in egg mixture, coating both sides, then place in cereal mixture, coating both sides; gently pat coating onto bread, so it stays when cooked.

- In a large skillet over medium heat, heat oil until hot. Cook bread slices, 2 to 4 minutes on each side or until golden. Remove to a paper towel-lined platter and cover to keep warm. Repeat with remaining bread. Serve immediately with syrup or your favorite fresh fruit.

The easiest way to crush cornflakes is to add them to a resealable plastic bag and crunch away with your hands. But don't get too carried away when you're crushing them! You want them to give the French toast some texture. And forget about using store-bought cornflake crumbs; they're way too fine for this recipe. MCM

Breakfast & Brunch

BANANA PANCAKES WITH BANANA SYRUP

Do you go bananas for bananas? I hope so, because these pancakes deliver double the dose of banana goodness. There's banana in the batter and in the syrup. If that doesn't sound a-peel-ing to you, just flip the page for a berry-good, banana-less treat! (By the way, parents, this one goes over really well with kids!)

Makes 12

3 large bananas, divided

½ cup maple syrup

1 tablespoon butter

2 eggs

1 tablespoon sugar

1 cup buttermilk

2 cups pancake and baking mix

- Peel and cut 2 bananas into ¼-inch-thick slices. Combine syrup and butter in a medium saucepan; bring to a simmer. Stir in sliced bananas and remove from heat; set banana syrup aside.

- Mash the remaining banana in a medium bowl; whisk in eggs, sugar, and buttermilk. Whisk in baking mix until blended.

- Coat a griddle or skillet with cooking spray and heat over medium heat. Pour about ¼ cup batter for each pancake onto hot griddle. (I like to use a ¼ cup dry measuring cup, so that all my pancakes come out the same size.) Cook pancakes until bubbles begin to form on top; flip and cook until golden. Repeat procedure with remaining batter. Serve pancakes with warmed banana syrup.

Rather than throwing out bananas that might be starting to brown or have too many spots, you can put them in the freezer and thaw as needed. I suggest peeling them and wrapping each in plastic wrap first. (Many people use thawed bananas for banana bread, but they're just as good for this recipe!) MCM

BREAKFAST & BRUNCH

BITE-SIZED BERRY DUTCH BABIES

I don't know why a Dutch Baby is named that way, but I assure you that no babies were involved in the making of this recipe. Now that I've got that out of the way, a Dutch Baby is just a big pancake that's baked in the oven. Because I love finding new ways to make and serve things, I went ahead and shrunk the big Baby into 12 bite-sized ones that are perfect for serving at a brunch with friends.

Makes 12

½ stick butter, melted

2 eggs

½ cup milk

⅛ teaspoon salt

½ teaspoon vanilla extract

½ cup all-purpose flour

¼ cup strawberry jam

Fresh berries and mint for garnish

Powdered sugar for sprinkling

- Preheat oven to 375 degrees F. Evenly divide melted butter into 12 muffin cups.

- In a blender, combine eggs, milk, salt, and vanilla; blend until frothy. Add flour and blend until smooth. Pour batter evenly into muffin cups.

- Bake 13 to 15 minutes or until puffy and edges are golden brown. Remove from oven and allow to cool for a few minutes. Remove Dutch Babies from muffin cups and place on a serving platter.

- Fill each Dutch Baby with a teaspoon of strawberry jam, top with fresh berries and mint, and sprinkle with powdered sugar.

If you've got a lot to do before everyone comes over for brunch, make these ahead of time. Then when you're ready to serve, just reheat them in a warm oven. Once they're heated through you can add the finishing touches (that's the jam, berries, and powdered sugar!). MCM

Breakfast & Brunch

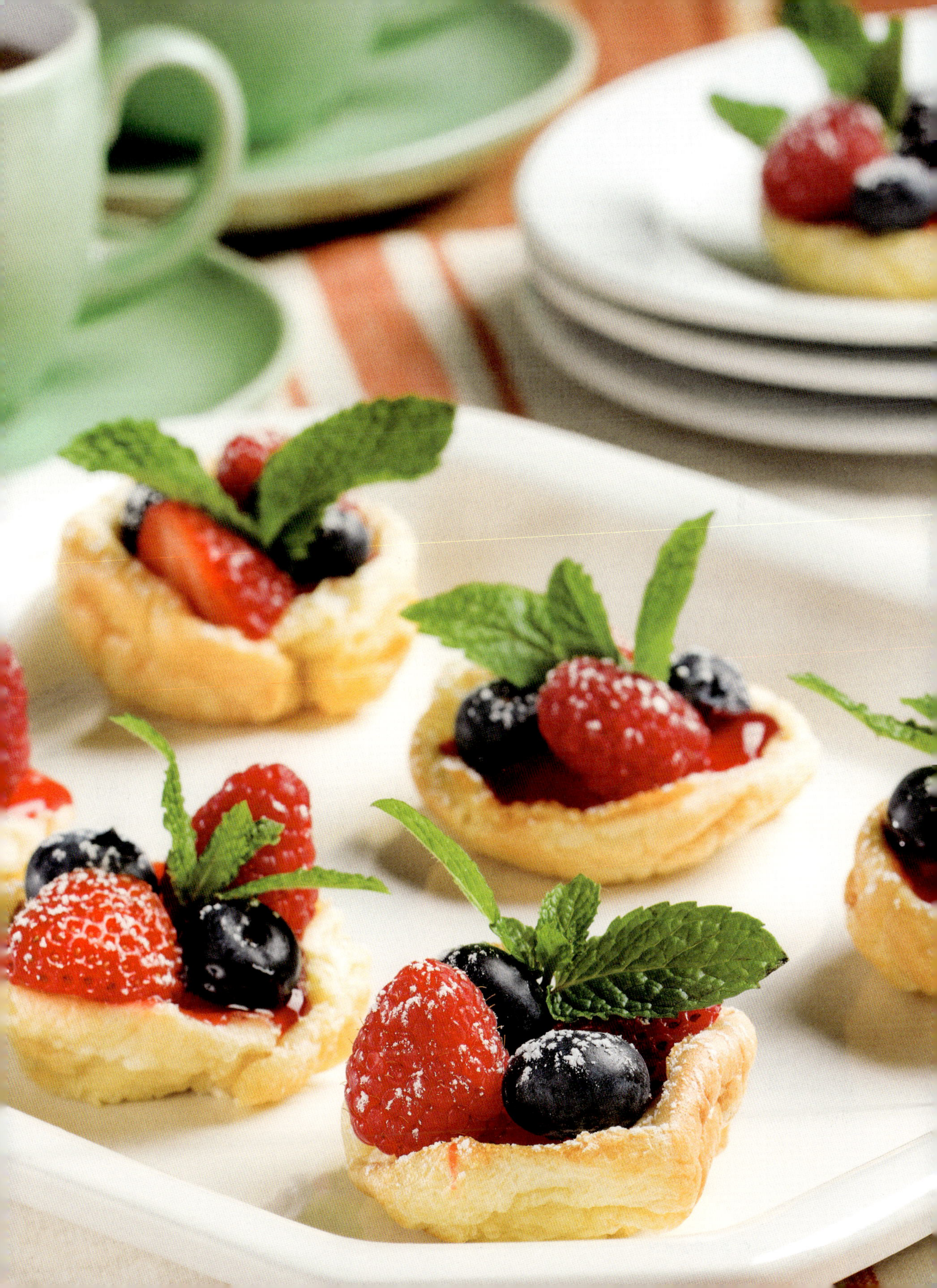

HAM 'N' EGG ROLLUPS

Here's a fun new way for you to serve ham and eggs for breakfast. Most of the time the ham is chopped up and mixed with the scrambled eggs or served on the side, like in the case of a ham steak. But here, the ham is what keeps it all together. These are like fancy crepes, except the ham replaces the delicate crepe. And it's a great way to lower the carbs too!

Serves 4 to 8

- ½ cup mayonnaise
- 2 teaspoons Dijon mustard
- 1 teaspoon lemon juice
- ⅛ teaspoon plus ¼ teaspoon salt, divided
- 6 eggs
- 2 tablespoons water
- ¼ teaspoon onion powder
- ⅛ teaspoon black pepper
- 1 tablespoon butter
- 1 cup finely diced cooked broccoli
- 8 (⅛-inch-thick) slices deli baked ham
- 1 cup shredded Swiss cheese, divided

- Preheat oven to 375 degrees F. Coat a 9- x 13-inch baking dish with cooking spray.

- In a small bowl, whisk together mayonnaise, Dijon mustard, lemon juice, and 1/8 teaspoon salt; set aside. (This will be your shortcut Hollandaise sauce.)

- In a medium bowl, whisk together eggs, water, onion powder, remaining ¼ teaspoon salt, and black pepper. In a medium skillet over medium heat, melt butter and add egg mixture; scramble until set. Remove from heat and gently stir in broccoli.

- Place ham slices on a cutting board. Divide egg mixture evenly onto each slice of ham and top with half of the Swiss cheese. Roll up and place seam-side down in baking dish. Spoon shortcut Hollandaise sauce evenly over the top of ham rolls and sprinkle with remaining Swiss cheese. Bake 5 to 8 minutes or until warmed through. Serve immediately.

I love adding a sprinkle of chopped fresh chives to make these look even more breakfast-special. MCM

Breakfast & Brunch

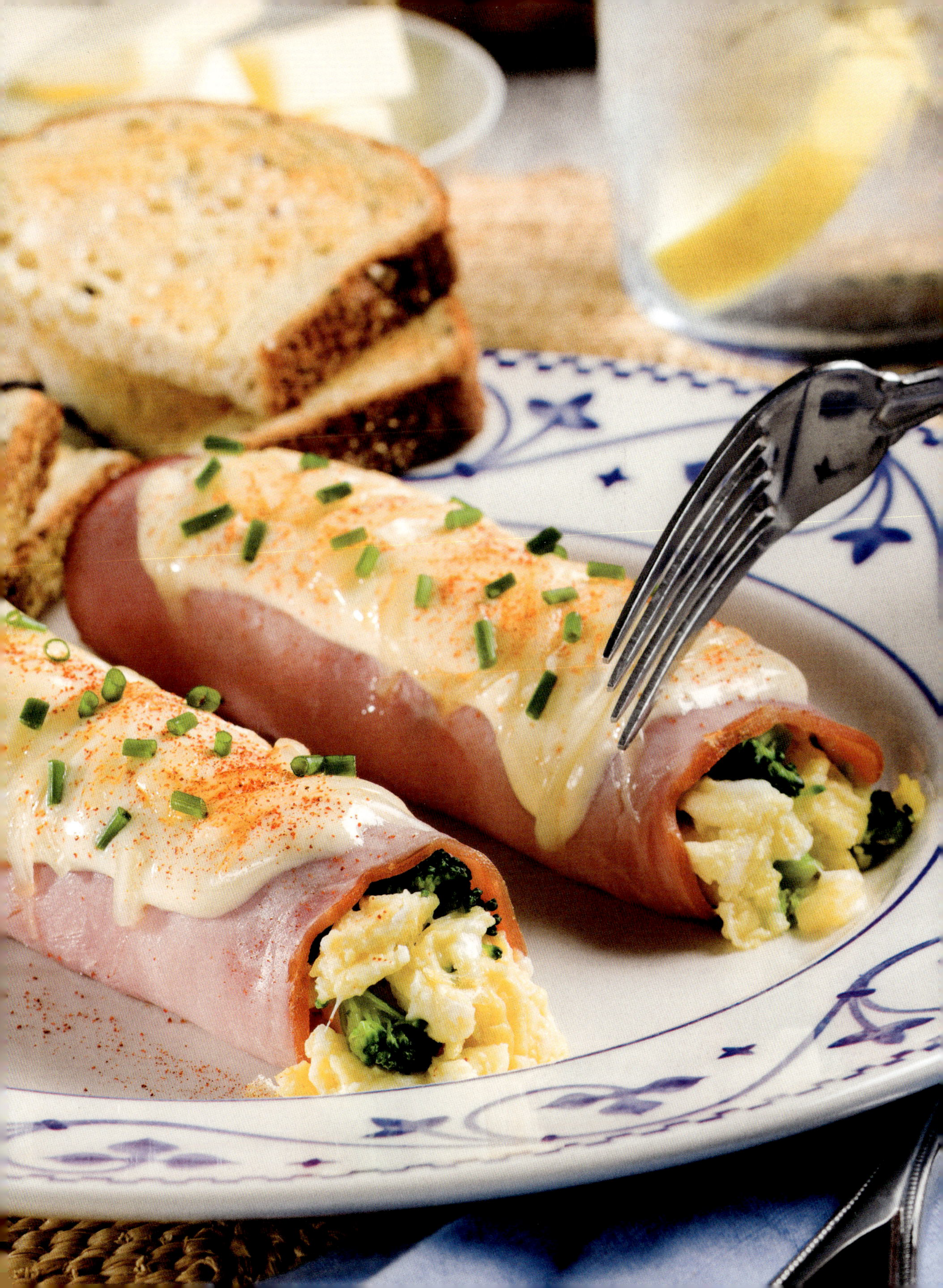

BLUEBERRY-LEMON AIR FRYER MUFFINS

If you would've told me a couple of years ago that I'd be able to bake muffins without having to turn on my oven, I wouldn't have believed you. But ever since the air fryer started gaining popularity on QVC, things have changed. Now I love experimenting with air fryer recipes. These muffins are one of my favorite air-fried creations, featuring one of my favorite fruits – blueberries!

Makes 6

½ stick butter, softened

½ cup plus 1 tablespoon sugar, divided

1 egg

1 tablespoon lemon juice

¾ cup all-purpose flour

½ teaspoon baking soda

⅓ cup blueberries

1-½ teaspoons lemon zest

¼ cup chopped walnuts

- Coat 6 foil baking cups with cooking spray.

- In a large bowl with an electric mixer, beat butter and ½ cup sugar until creamy. Add egg and lemon juice and beat until light and fluffy. Slowly add flour and baking soda, mixing just until moistened. (If you add all the dry ingredients at one time you'll end up with a mess in your kitchen; trust me on this one – I've done it.) Stir in blueberries and lemon zest. Spoon batter evenly into baking cups.

- In a small bowl, combine walnuts and remaining 1 tablespoon sugar; mix well. Sprinkle mixture evenly over batter.

- Preheat air fryer to 350 degrees F. Place 3 baking cups in air fryer basket and air-fry 15 to 17 minutes or until a toothpick inserted in center comes out clean; let cool. Repeat with remaining 3 muffins, if need be. (If you have a bigger air fryer and they all fit without being crowded, go ahead and make them all at once.)

In order to get more traditional-shaped muffins, I like to put each baking cup in a ramekin, then fill with batter. This will help them hold their shape. And you only need 3 ramekins for this recipe since you're baking these in batches! MCM

BANANA-WALNUT OVERNIGHT OATS

While I wish every morning included eggs benedict, a hearty breakfast casserole, or crispy French toast, there are a lot of mornings where I'm rushing out the door to get to a business meeting or run some errands. Fortunately, I have a few grab 'n' go breakfast ideas up my sleeve, including these overnight oats. They're called overnight oats because you combine all the ingredients the day before and in the morning, they're ready for digging into.

Serves 1

½ cup old-fashioned oats

½ cup milk

2 tablespoons vanilla yogurt

2 teaspoons honey

½ teaspoon vanilla extract

1 banana, diced

1 tablespoon chopped walnuts

- In a small bowl or canning jar, combine oats, milk, yogurt, honey, and vanilla extract; mix well. Cover and refrigerate overnight.

- Stir banana into the oat mixture, top with walnuts, and serve.

While I typically chop my walnuts the night before, I don't add them or the banana until I'm ready to eat my oats -- otherwise the walnuts will lose their crunch and the banana will get mushy. I love walnuts -- that's why I always keep a big bag of raw, shelled walnuts as a staple in my pantry. I use them to top yogurt, cereal, salads, and even on cut-up fruit. They're also one of my favorite things to snack on. MCM

BREAKFAST & BRUNCH

MAKE-YOUR-OWN OATMEAL COOKIE PIZZA

Cookie? Pizza? For breakfast? Yes, and also not exactly. I call this a cookie pizza because it's sweet and about the size of a large cookie, but also gets a bunch of toppings added on to it, like a pizza. This breakfast treat is both crispy-crunchy and chewy-delicious. The oats make it really filling so you could share it if you wanted to ... or you could dress it up however you like best, and enjoy it on your own.

Serves 1 to 2

1 cup old-fashioned oats

1 egg

¼ cup applesauce

½ teaspoon almond extract

¼ teaspoon salt

TOPPING OPTIONS

Yogurt

Fresh fruit for garnish

Sliced almonds for garnish

Honey for drizzling

- Preheat oven to 350 degrees F.
- In a medium bowl, combine oats, egg, applesauce, almond extract, and salt; mix well. Spoon oat mixture onto a baking sheet and shape into a 4-inch round circle, about ½-inch thick. (See photo.) Bake 10 to 15 minutes or until it holds its shape.
- While still warm, add your choice of toppings.

This is another great one for kids! Just make a few of these cookie pizzas and set out a topping bar, so that everyone can customize their own. MCM

Breakfast & Brunch

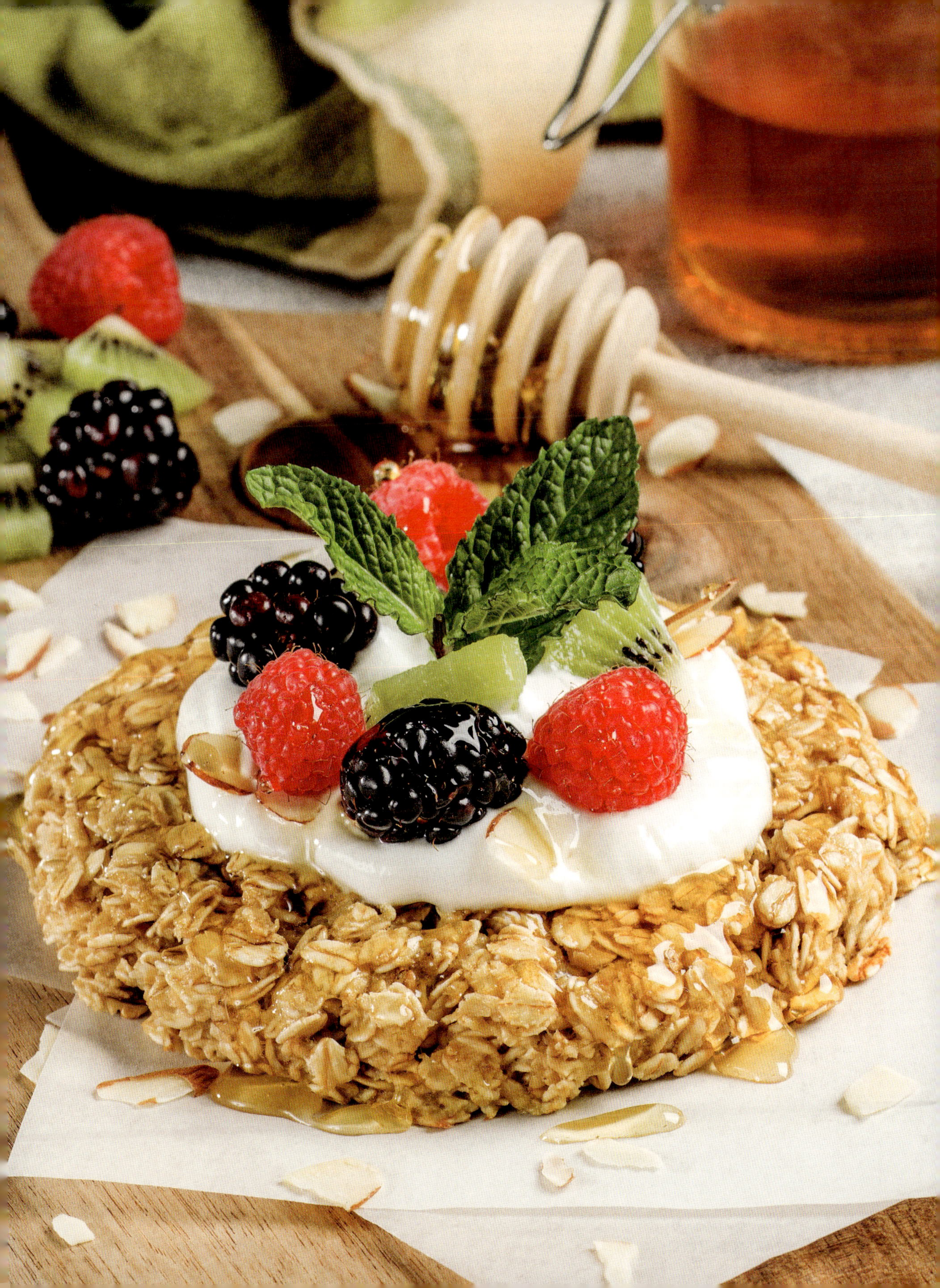

PEACHY-KEEN CINNAMON BUN BAKE

No matter how hectic things get, I always take the time to remember how lucky I am to be doing what I love to do and sharing it with all of you. In other words, it's fair to say that most of the time life's peachy keen. Celebrate a sweet moment in your life by baking up this indulgent and peachy breakfast treat. It's sure to become a family favorite.

Serves 8 to 12

- 2 (17.5-ounce) cans refrigerated cinnamon rolls with icing
- 1/3 cup sugar
- 1 teaspoon ground cinnamon
- 1/2 stick butter, melted
- 1 (21-ounce) can peach pie filling
- 1/2 cup chopped nuts

- Preheat oven to 350 degrees F. Coat a 9- x 13-inch baking dish with cooking spray.

- Remove icing from cinnamon roll packages; set aside. Cut each cinnamon roll into 6 pieces and place in a large bowl. In a small bowl, combine sugar and cinnamon; mix well. Pour melted butter over cinnamon roll pieces, sprinkle with cinnamon sugar mixture, and toss gently until evenly coated. Arrange cinnamon roll pieces in baking dish.

- Using a spoon, break up peach slices slightly and drop tablespoons of pie filling evenly onto cinnamon roll pieces. Bake 30 to 35 minutes or until dough is baked through in center. Let cool 10 minutes.

- Drizzle icing on top and sprinkle with nuts; serve warm.

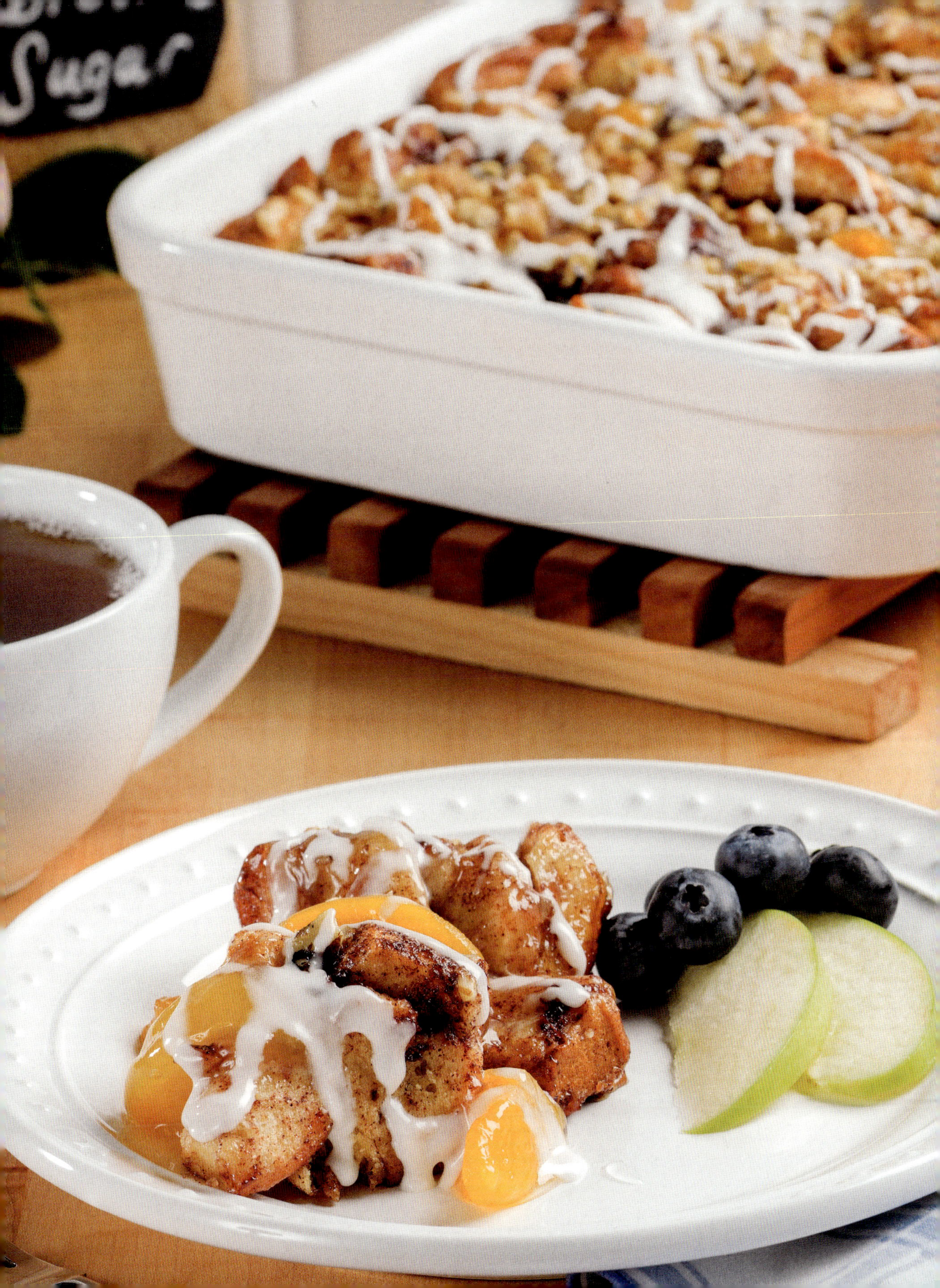
Sugar

PARADISE PINEAPPLE FRITTERS

You may not be able to take the whole family on an all-inclusive vacation to Hawaii right now, but you can bring some of the flavors of paradise to your breakfast table. These fritters are bursting with the sweet and tangy taste of pineapple. I love serving these all summer long as a way to get into my tropical groove.

Makes 12

- 1-¾ cups all-purpose flour
- 3 tablespoons granulated sugar
- 2 teaspoons baking powder
- ¼ teaspoon salt
- 1 (20-ounce) can crushed pineapple, drained and juice reserved
- ½ cup milk
- 1 egg
- ½ teaspoon vanilla extract
- ¾ cup vegetable oil
- ½ cup powdered sugar

- In a large bowl, whisk together flour, granulated sugar, baking powder, and salt. Add pineapple, milk, egg, and vanilla; mix well.

- In a large skillet over medium heat, heat oil until hot, but not smoking. Drop batter by 2 heaping tablespoonfuls into skillet, a few at a time. Cook 2 to 3 minutes per side or until golden and crispy. Drain on a wire rack.

- To make the glaze, in a small bowl, whisk powdered sugar and 3 teaspoons of reserved pineapple juice together until smooth. Drizzle glaze over fritters and serve warm.

If you want to make these in advance, after frying and draining them, store until ready to serve. When ready to serve, place them on a baking sheet and warm them in a 300 degree oven for about 5 minutes. Then glaze them, set them out, and watch them disappear. And here's a presentation tip: place each fritter on top of a slice of pineapple. That little extra step can really elevate this recipe! MCM

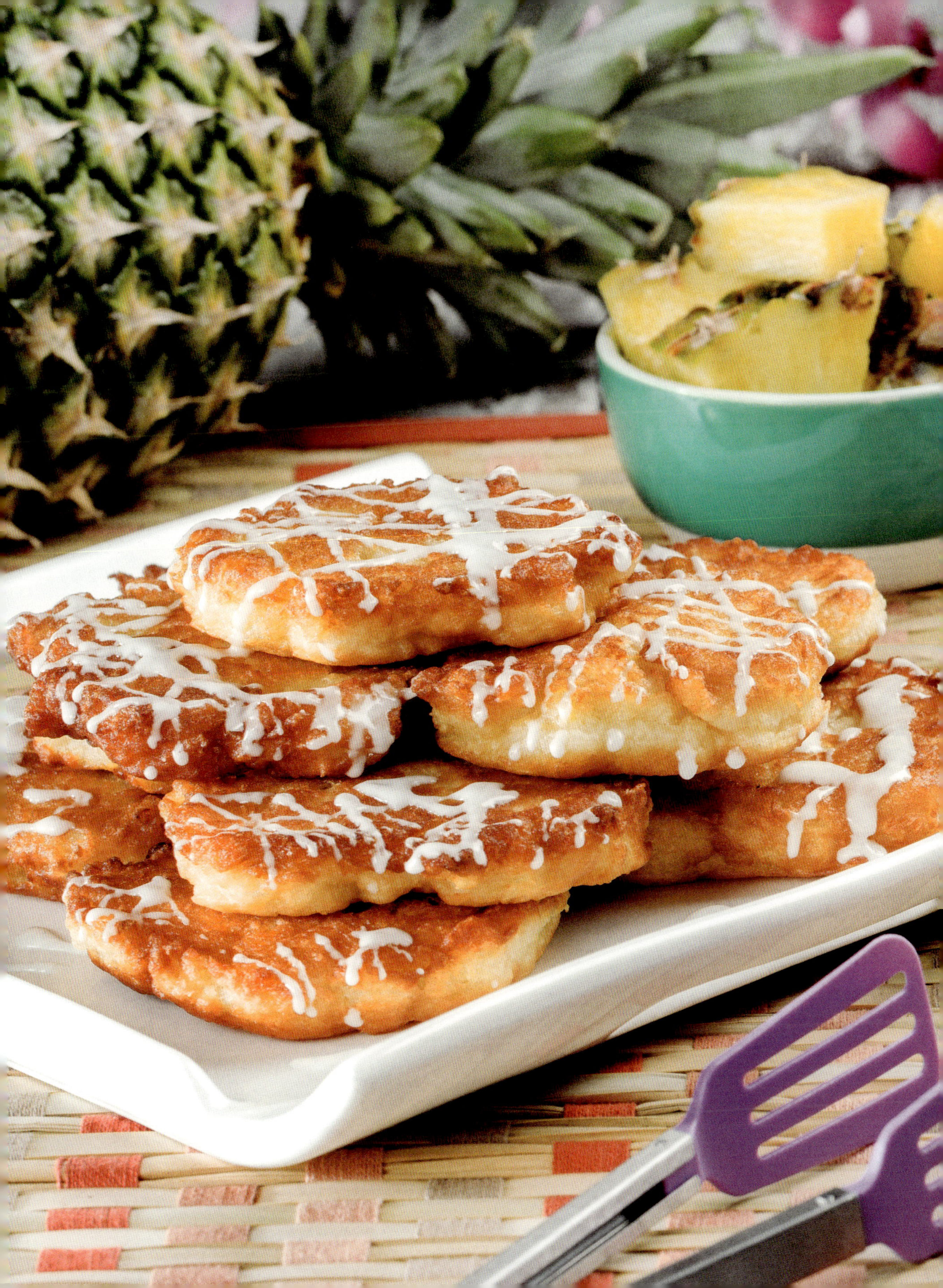

> "I can't think of a better way to bring family and friends together than with a simple, throw-together meat-and-cheese board or some fancied-up deviled eggs (both are low-carb and keto-friendly!). Of course, you can't forget the wine. I know it's not low-carb, but it's a must-have!"

STARTERS

Little Italy Antipasto Stack	28
Fantastic Philly Cheesesteak Dip	30
BBQ-Style Deviled Eggs	32
Pepperoni Pizza Poppers	33
Pimiento Cheese Lollipops	34
Garlicky Lemon Chicken Wings	36
Black Bean Tex-Mex Hummus	38
Loaded Potato Bites	39
Roasted Eggplant Spread	40
Wine & Dine Goat Cheese Bites	42
Popular Party Meatballs	44
Keep-it-Simple Shrimp Scampi	45
Bread Bowl Buffalo Chicken Dip	46
Wrapped-Up Cranberry Brie	48
Creamy Swiss Fondue Bread	49
Barbecue Chicken Flatbread	50
Munch Madness Snack Mix	52

LITTLE ITALY ANTIPASTO STACK

This is an easy way to fancy up a cheese or charcuterie board, and the best part is, you can make it days ahead. So if you've got company coming over on, let's say Friday, you can get this done as early as Tuesday. It's also pretty fun to think of this as a salami and cheese cake where each layer is "frosted" with homemade pesto. You just know your friends are going to have something to say about this one!

Serves 10 to 12

1/3 cup olive oil

1/3 cup fresh parsley, stems removed

2 tablespoons grated Parmesan cheese

2 cloves garlic

1/4 teaspoon salt

12 thin slices provolone cheese

33 thin slices Genoa salami (about 3/4 pound)

10 to 12 assorted pitted olives for garnish

10 to 12 toothpicks

This is impressive enough to serve on its own, on a really nice wood board, but you could also serve it as the centerpiece to an array of other yummy antipasto ingredients, like chopped artichokes, roasted red peppers, and pepperoncinis.

MCM

■ To make my homemade pesto, in a food processor or blender, pulse oil, parsley, Parmesan cheese, garlic, and salt until smooth; set aside.

■ Place 1 slice of provolone cheese on a large piece of plastic wrap; lightly brush with pesto. Evenly top cheese with 3 slices of salami, overlapping the slices. (These should cover the cheese, rather than simply being stacked.) Brush salami lightly with more pesto. Repeat layers, using all of the cheese, pesto, and salami, and ending with the cheese. (Check out the photo for reference!)

■ Wrap the plastic wrap tightly around the stack, making sure it's sealed. Then place the wrapped stack on a plate and top with a heavy object (like a small cast-iron skillet) to compress the layers. Chill overnight or up to 3 days.

■ Right before serving, remove plastic wrap. Place an olive on each toothpick and insert into cheese, as shown in photo. Using a sharp knife, cut cheese stack into wedges and serve.

STARTERS

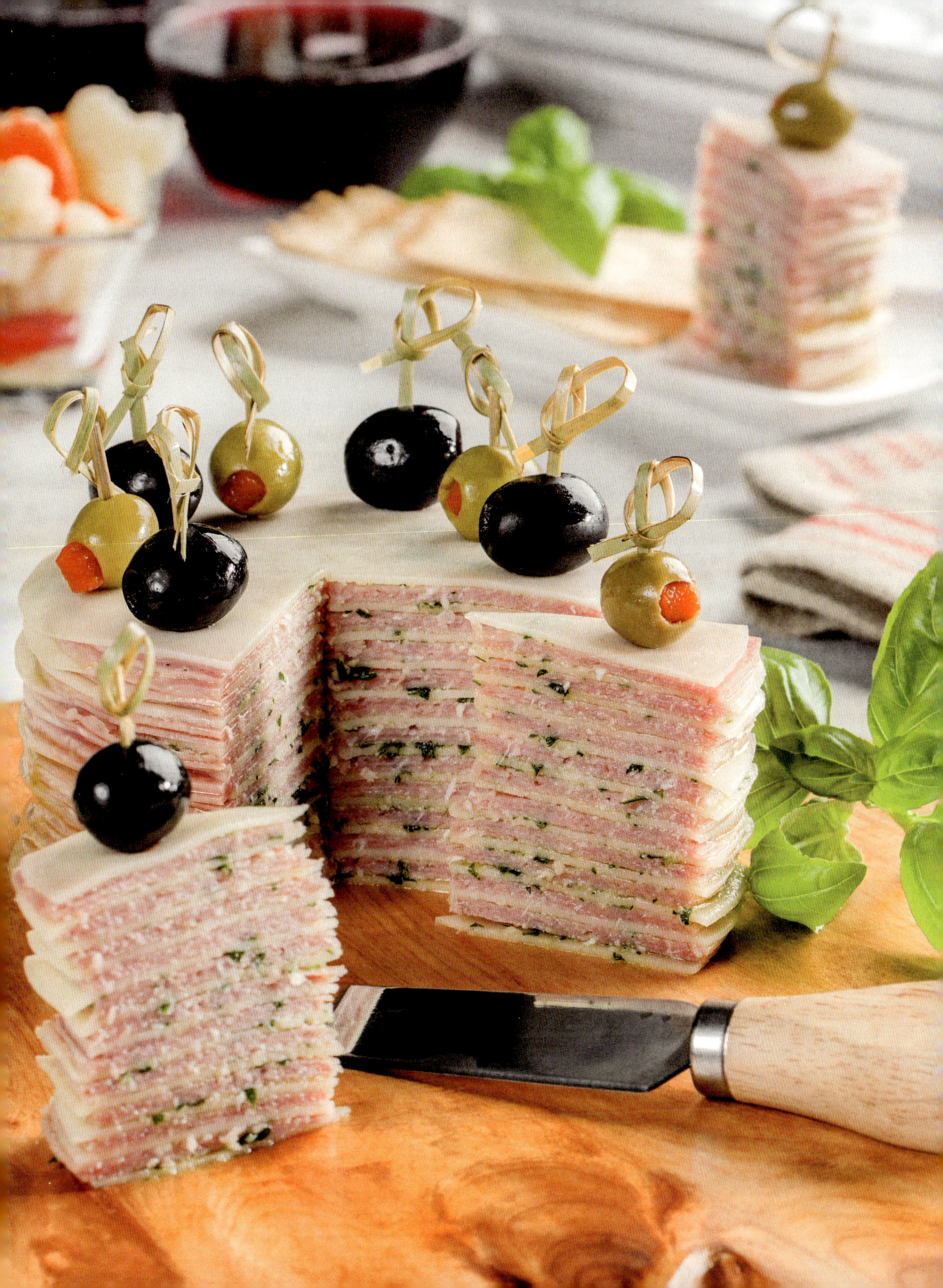

FANTASTIC PHILLY CHEESESTEAK DIP

I'm not going to weigh in on who has the best Philly cheesesteak in town. I'll just say, there are a lot of good contenders and a lot of people who are really passionate about them. If you're one of them, then this recipe is just for you (and all of your friends). It's a dip that combines some of the classic Philly cheesesteak flavors – beefy, cheesy, and loaded with peppers and onions.

Serves 8 to 10

2 tablespoons butter

¾ cup chopped onion

¾ cup chopped green bell pepper

6 slices frozen thin sliced beef steaks (the kind used to make Philly cheesesteaks)

1 (8-ounce) package cream cheese, softened

¼ cup mayonnaise

1 teaspoon garlic powder

½ teaspoon salt

¼ teaspoon black pepper

1 cup chopped provolone cheese

1 cup shredded white cheddar cheese

■ Preheat oven to 375 degrees F.

■ In a large skillet over medium heat, melt butter; sauté onion and bell pepper 5 to 7 minutes or until tender. Remove vegetables to a bowl; set aside. Add steak slices, in batches, to skillet and cook 1 minute per side or until no longer pink, shredding beef with 2 forks.

■ In a large bowl, combine cream cheese, mayonnaise, garlic powder, salt, and black pepper; mix well. Stir in provolone and cheddar cheeses, vegetables, and steak until thoroughly combined. Spoon mixture into a 1-½ quart baking dish.

■ Bake 30 to 35 minutes or until bubbly and heated through.

Sure, I guess you could eat this dip with a spoon, but that would make a really awkward party. So instead, make sure you have an array of dippers to serve alongside. As an ode to Philly, I suggest soft pretzels. You can find them in the freezer aisle. All you have to do is warm them up and cut them into 2-inch dunkable pieces. Or if you're more traditional, slice up a crusty French bread and go to town. MCM

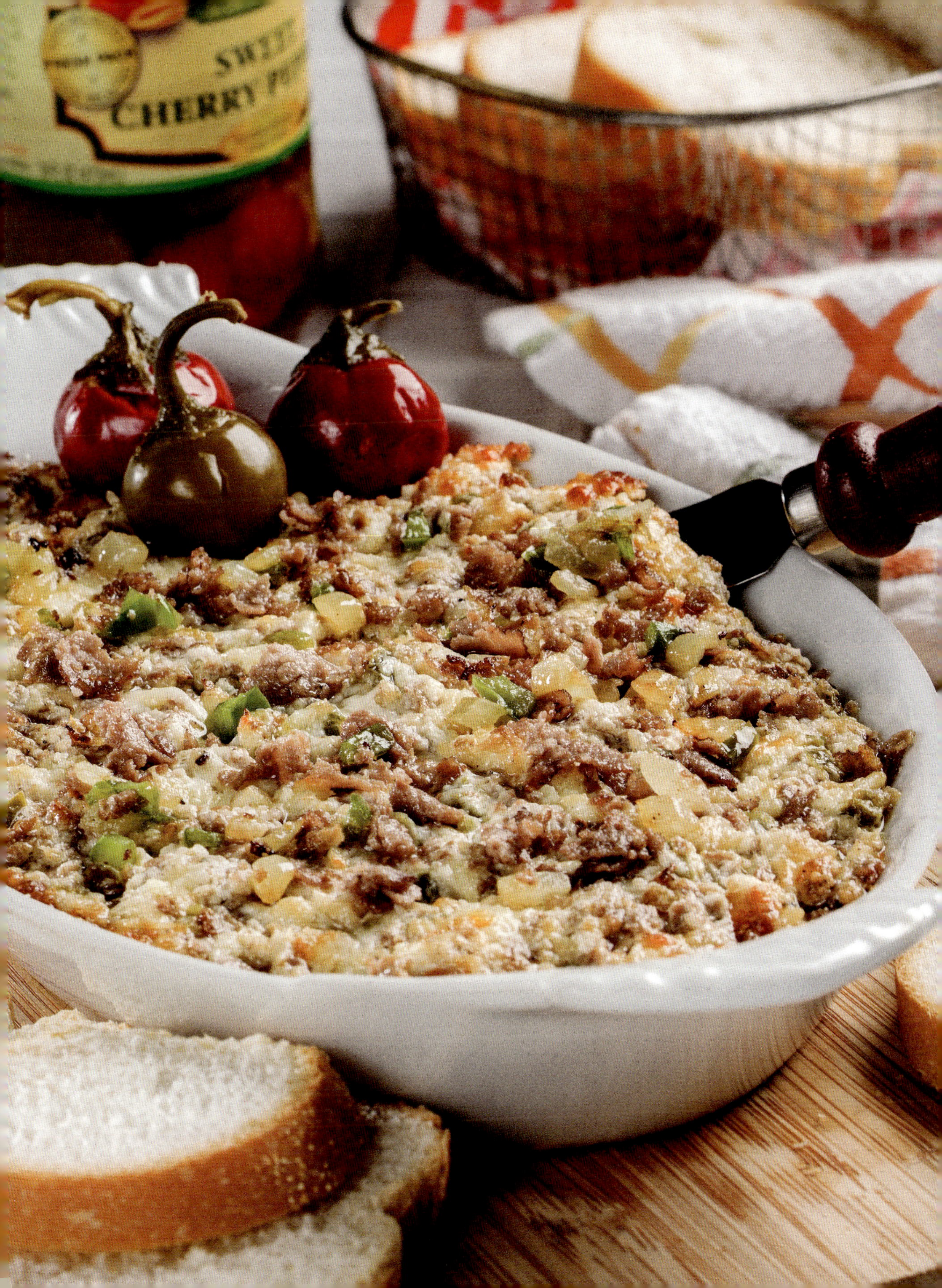
CHERRY

BBQ-STYLE DEVILED EGGS

In my *Easy Everyday Favorites* cookbook, I shared a recipe for classic deviled eggs that everyone loves. But this time around, I wanted to show you how easy it is to make another "egg-cellent" and flavor-packed version. These deviled eggs are perfect for game day, especially when paired with some BBQ chicken wings. All that smoky goodness!

Makes 12

6 hard-boiled eggs, peeled and cut in half lengthwise

3 tablespoons barbecue sauce

1 tablespoon mayonnaise

1 to 2 tablespoons French-fried onions, chopped

1 scallion, thinly sliced

- Remove yolks and place in a small bowl, setting egg whites aside. Mash egg yolks and combine with barbecue sauce and mayonnaise; mix well.

- Fill egg white halves with yolk mixture and place on a platter. Sprinkle each egg with French-fried onions and sliced scallion. Cover with plastic wrap and refrigerate until ready to serve.

There are a few ways to fill your eggs. You can keep things simple and use a spoon or you can add some style by using a pastry bag with a special tip. Another method is to take a plastic storage bag, snip off a corner, and pipe the mixture on. MCM

STARTERS

PEPPERONI PIZZA POPPERS

It's hard to grow up in New York and not be a pizza snob. (I'm sorry, but we just really know how to make good pizza!) Just thinking of pizza makes me happy, so when I came up with these "poppable" pizza bites, I knew I had to share them with you. They're easy to make, serve, and eat, which is what makes them such a great party food!

Makes 10

1 (7.5-ounce) can refrigerated biscuits (10 biscuits)

Garlic powder for sprinkling

3 (1-ounce) mozzarella string cheese sticks, cut into 1-inch pieces

2 tablespoons chopped pepperoni slices

Cooking Spray

½ cup pizza or spaghetti sauce

- Preheat oven to 375 degrees F. Coat a baking sheet with cooking spray.

- Separate biscuit dough into 10 pieces. Using your thumb, make an indentation in the center of each biscuit. Lightly sprinkle each with garlic powder, then top with a piece of cheese and evenly divide the chopped pepperoni onto each piece of cheese. Pull dough over filling, pinching it together so that filling is completely enclosed. Place seam-side down on baking sheet and lightly spray tops with cooking spray.

- Bake 10 to 12 minutes or until golden. Serve with warmed pizza sauce.

STARTERS

PIMIENTO CHEESE LOLLIPOPS

I love getting creative with simple recipes and that's just what happened here! Pimiento cheese balls are really popular in the South and I wanted to come up with an even easier way for my guests to enjoy them. So I made bite-sized balls and popped in a pretzel stick to make them look like a lollipop. Now this favorite Southern appetizer is more fun to eat than ever.

Makes 36

¾ cup finely chopped pecans

1 (8-ounce) package cream cheese, softened

1 teaspoon Worcestershire sauce

½ teaspoon garlic powder

¼ teaspoon salt

⅛ teaspoon cayenne pepper

1 (8-ounce) block sharp cheddar cheese, shredded

1 (4-ounce) jar diced pimientos, well drained

½ cup bacon bits

36 pretzel sticks

- Place pecans in a shallow dish; set aside.
- In a large bowl with an electric mixer, beat cream cheese until smooth. Add Worcestershire sauce, garlic powder, salt, and cayenne pepper; mix well. Stir in cheddar cheese, pimientos, and bacon bits until thoroughly combined.
- Form mixture into 36 bite-sized balls. Roll each ball in pecans, pressing gently until evenly coated. Refrigerate at least 1 hour or until ready to serve. Just before serving, insert a pretzel stick into center of each ball, just like you would with a toothpick.

The balls can be made the day before, so you have less to worry about the day of. Right before serving, insert the pretzel stick and you're good to go. When it comes to entertaining, I believe that if you choose the right menu, you can enjoy the party as much as your guests. MCM

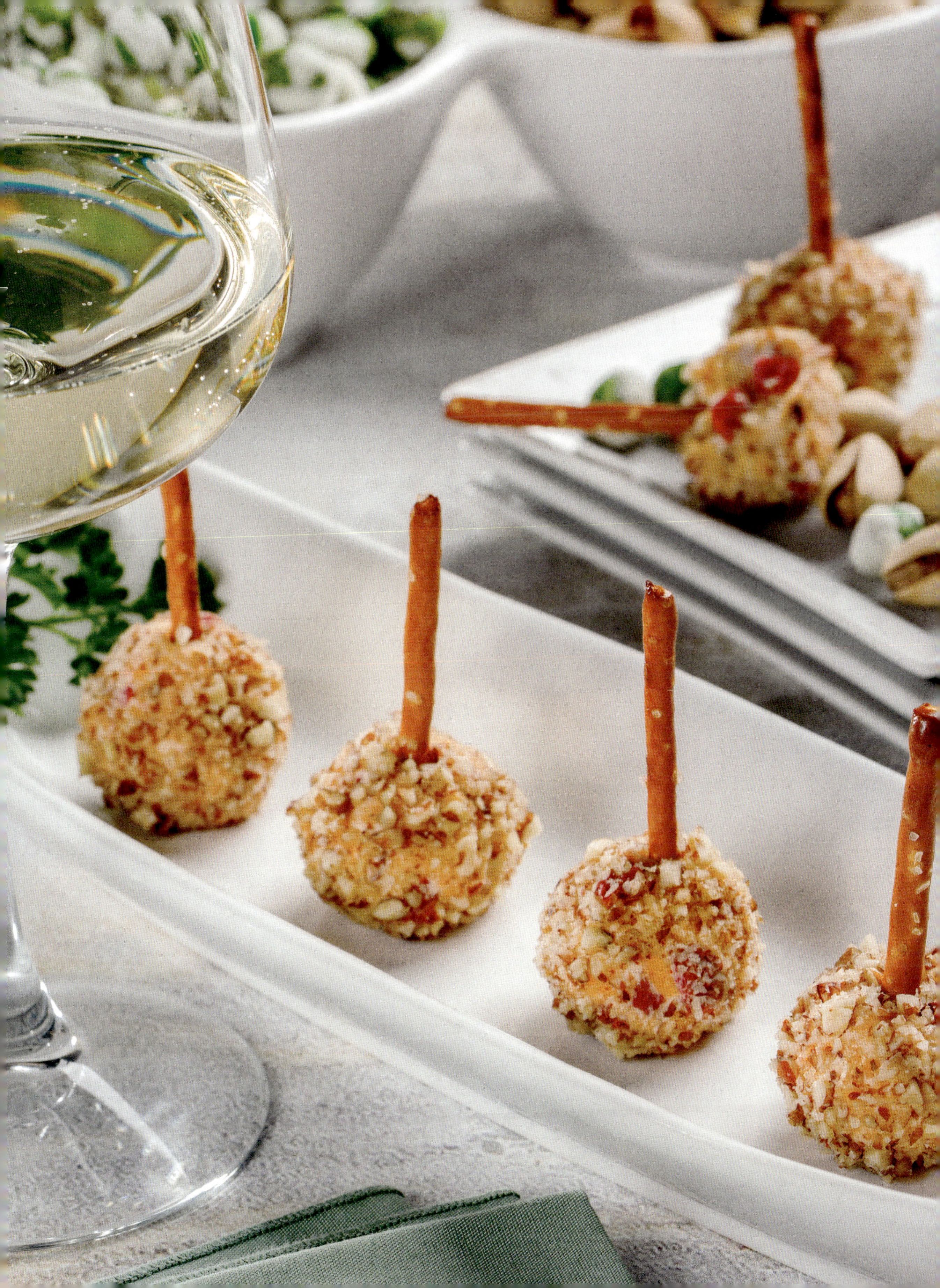

GARLICKY LEMON CHICKEN WINGS

Wings are a classic party food that everyone loves, and these pack big flavor! They're marinated overnight, which helps all the yummy garlicky lemon soak in, and ensures that every bite is as good as the first. When I serve them, I like to keep some lemon wedges nearby, in case anyone wants to squeeze even more lemon over them. These also go great with a side of horseradish sauce or ranch dressing for dipping!

Serves 4 to 6

1/4 cup olive oil

5 cloves garlic, minced

1 lemon, zested and juiced

4 sprigs fresh oregano, stems removed

1 teaspoon salt

1/2 teaspoon black pepper

4 pounds frozen chicken wings, thawed and drained

- In a large bowl or 2-gallon resealable plastic bag, combine oil, garlic, lemon zest, lemon juice, oregano, salt, and pepper; mix well. Add chicken wings and toss until evenly coated. Cover and refrigerate at least 4 hours or overnight.

- Preheat oven to 400 degrees F. Coat 2 rimmed baking sheets with cooking spray. Remove wings from marinade and place on baking sheets; discard marinade. Bake 30 minutes, turn over, and bake an additional 25 minutes or until golden and crispy.

I've discovered that these are even better when they're cooked in an air fryer. If you've got one of these amazing appliances at home, give it a try! Just set your air fryer to 400 degrees and cook for 18 to 20 minutes. Give the basket a shake halfway through the cooking time, so that they brown evenly, and enjoy! MCM

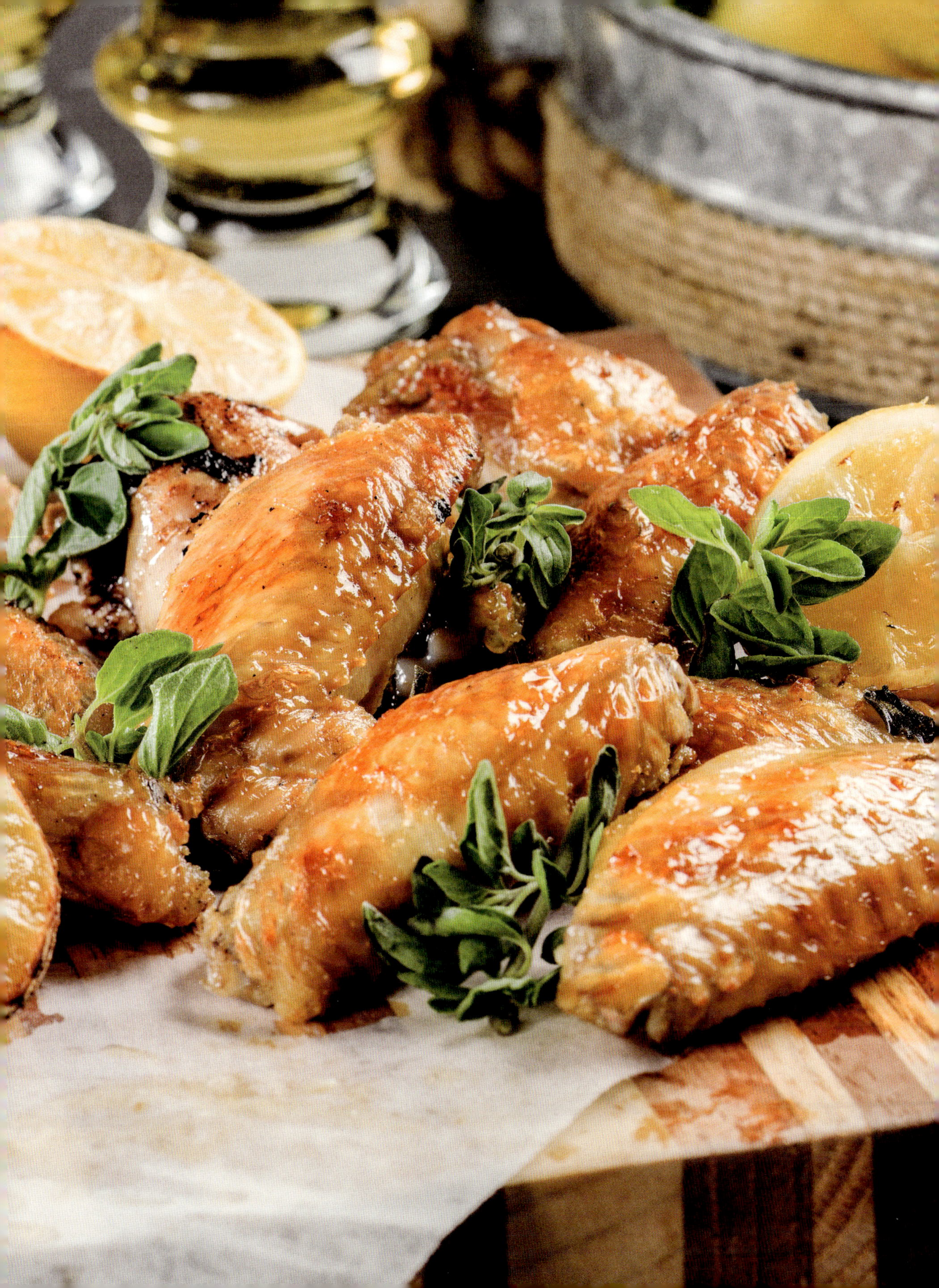

BLACK BEAN TEX-MEX HUMMUS

Have you seen how many different varieties of hummus are available in your supermarket? There's everything from roasted red pepper to dark chocolate! Despite having all of those options, I still like to make my own for special occasions — mostly because it's easy to do! I also love having the ability to create my own custom varieties. This one is inspired by Southwestern flavors and goes great with those Taco Tuesday nachos.

Makes 2 cups

2 (15-ounce) cans black beans, drained, with ¼ cup liquid reserved

3 cloves garlic, chopped

½ a chipotle pepper plus 1 tablespoon adobo sauce (from can)

3 tablespoons fresh lime juice (from 3 to 4 limes)

2 tablespoons olive oil

¼ teaspoon salt

½ cup packed fresh cilantro

- In a food processor, combine all ingredients, including the ¼ cup reserved liquid. Process until mixture is smooth and creamy, and no lumps remain, scraping down sides of bowl as needed.

- Serve immediately or cover and refrigerate until ready to serve.

Since you're making your own hummus, why not make some chips to go with it too? Just dip 6 corn tortillas quickly in water. (This helps them crisp up.) Then stack them up and cut the stack into 8 wedges. Lay the wedges on a baking sheet that you've coated with cooking spray. Spray the wedges with cooking spray, sprinkle with salt and bake 5 to 8 minutes or until crisp. MCM

LOADED POTATO BITES

I like baked potato skins as much as the next guy, but when you want to change things up, these are the way to go. They're mini baked potato cups, with the bonus that you've got your cheese and your bacon all mixed in, so they're even better. Sour cream and chives finish these off to make this a fully-loaded appetizer favorite.

Makes 24

3-½ cups frozen shredded potatoes, thawed

1 egg, beaten

½ cup all-purpose flour

¾ teaspoon salt

¼ teaspoon black pepper

1 cup shredded cheddar cheese

¼ cup crispy-cooked bacon pieces

½ cup sour cream

2 tablespoons chopped fresh chives

- Preheat oven to 400 degrees F. Coat 24 mini muffin cups with cooking spray.

- In a large bowl, combine potatoes, egg, flour, salt, and pepper; mix well. Add cheese and bacon; mix until combined. Place about a tablespoon of potato mixture into muffin cups and press down gently. (Cups should be filled to the top.)

- Bake 18 to 20 minutes or until crispy brown. Let cool slightly (about 2 minutes), then run a knife around edges and remove to a platter. Top with sour cream and chives. Serve immediately.

Feel free to use whatever bacon you've got on hand, whether it's leftover bacon from breakfast, pre-cooked and crumbled bacon from the store, or even turkey bacon (if you're watching your fat intake!). By the way, if you want to make these in advance, go ahead and bake them, then remove them from the muffin cups. When you're ready to serve them, just reheat them on a baking sheet; it takes just a few minutes. MCM

STARTERS

ROASTED EGGPLANT SPREAD

I've always considered eggplant to be one of the most under-utilized vegetables. I know they're not a favorite for many people, but I love them! This spread offers an interesting way to serve and enjoy this tasty veggie. Since it's pretty simple and not the prettiest veggie after being cooked, I like to garnish it with Kalamata olives, grape tomatoes, and a sprinkle of fresh parsley. It gives the spread a Mediterranean flair.

Serves 6 to 8

1 large eggplant, cut into 1-inch chunks

1 onion, cut into 1-inch chunks

8 cloves garlic

¼ cup plus 1 tablespoon olive oil, divided

¼ cup fresh parsley, stems removed, plus extra chopped for garnish

½ teaspoon salt

¼ teaspoon black pepper

Kalamata olives and grape tomatoes for garnish

■ Preheat oven to 400 degrees F.

■ In a large bowl, combine eggplant, onion, and garlic. Pour ¼ cup olive oil over vegetables and toss until evenly coated. Place on a rimmed baking sheet. Roast 40 minutes or until eggplant is tender, stirring halfway through roasting.

■ Place eggplant mixture, ¼ cup parsley, the salt, pepper, and remaining 1 tablespoon oil into food processor. Pulse 5 to 6 times or until thoroughly combined, but still chunky. Refrigerate 1 hour or until ready to serve. Garnish with olives, tomatoes, and chopped parsley before serving.

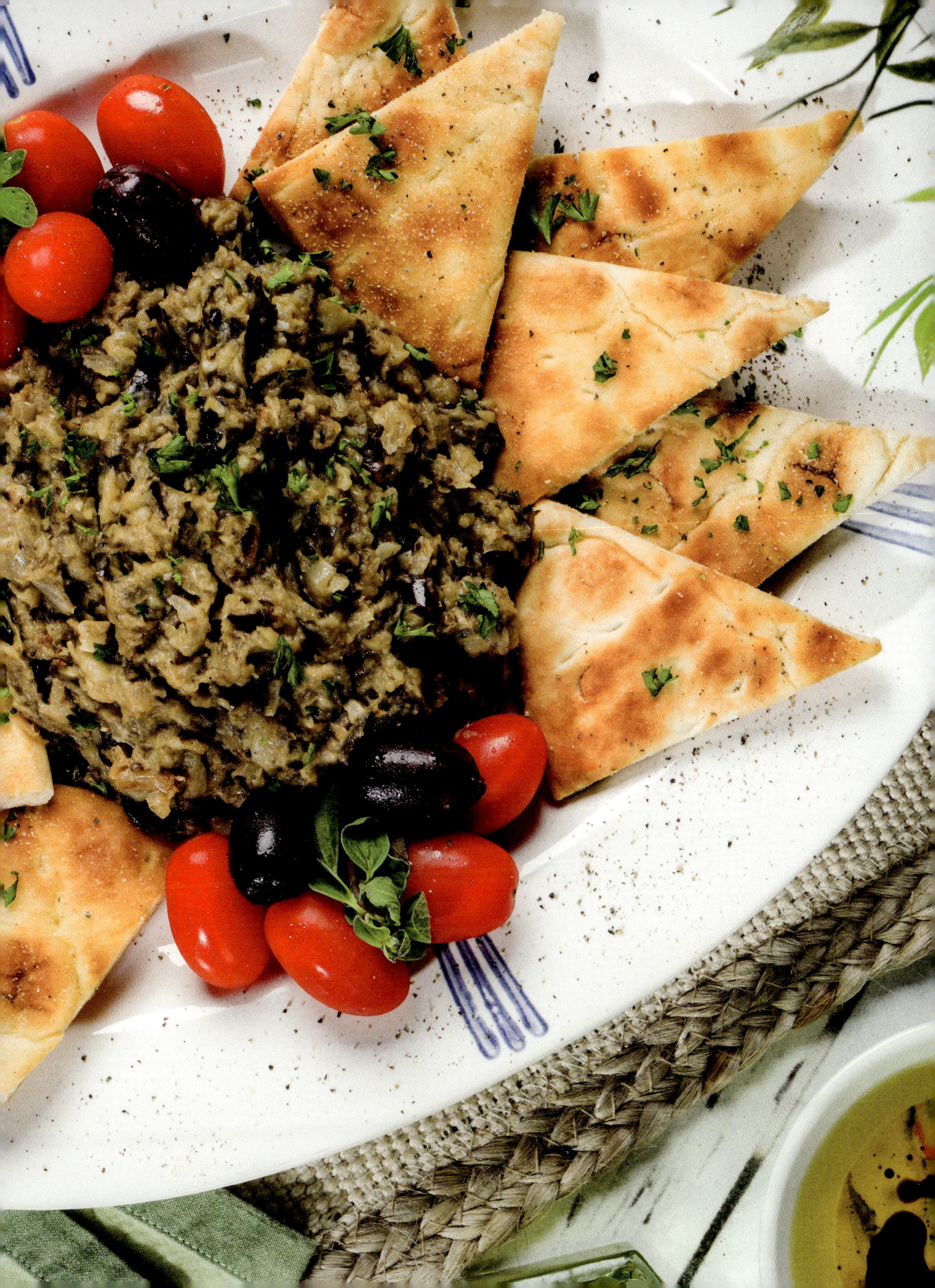

WINE & DINE GOAT CHEESE BITES

This is the appetizer you need to make when you're looking to wine and dine your friends with something extra-special. The end result may taste and look elegant, but I can assure you that this recipe is so easy, you won't even break a sweat (unless you're too close to the frying pan!). Between the creamy goat cheese, the salty crunch from the bacon and pistachios, and the sweet honey drizzle, it's hard to determine what exactly makes these so phenomenal.

Makes 15

2 slices bacon

1 (1.9-ounce) package frozen mini fillo shells

4 ounces goat cheese

2 tablespoons coarsely chopped pistachios

3 tablespoons honey

1 teaspoon balsamic vinegar

- Preheat oven to 350 degrees F.

- In a skillet over medium heat, cook bacon 6 to 8 minutes or until crisp. Drain on a paper towel-lined plate; let cool slightly then crumble.

- Place fillo shells on a baking sheet. Fill each shell evenly with bacon, goat cheese, and a sprinkle of pistachios. Bake 8 to 10 minutes or until shells are crisp.

- Meanwhile, in a small bowl, combine honey and vinegar; mix well. Right before serving, drizzle over warmed shells and serve.

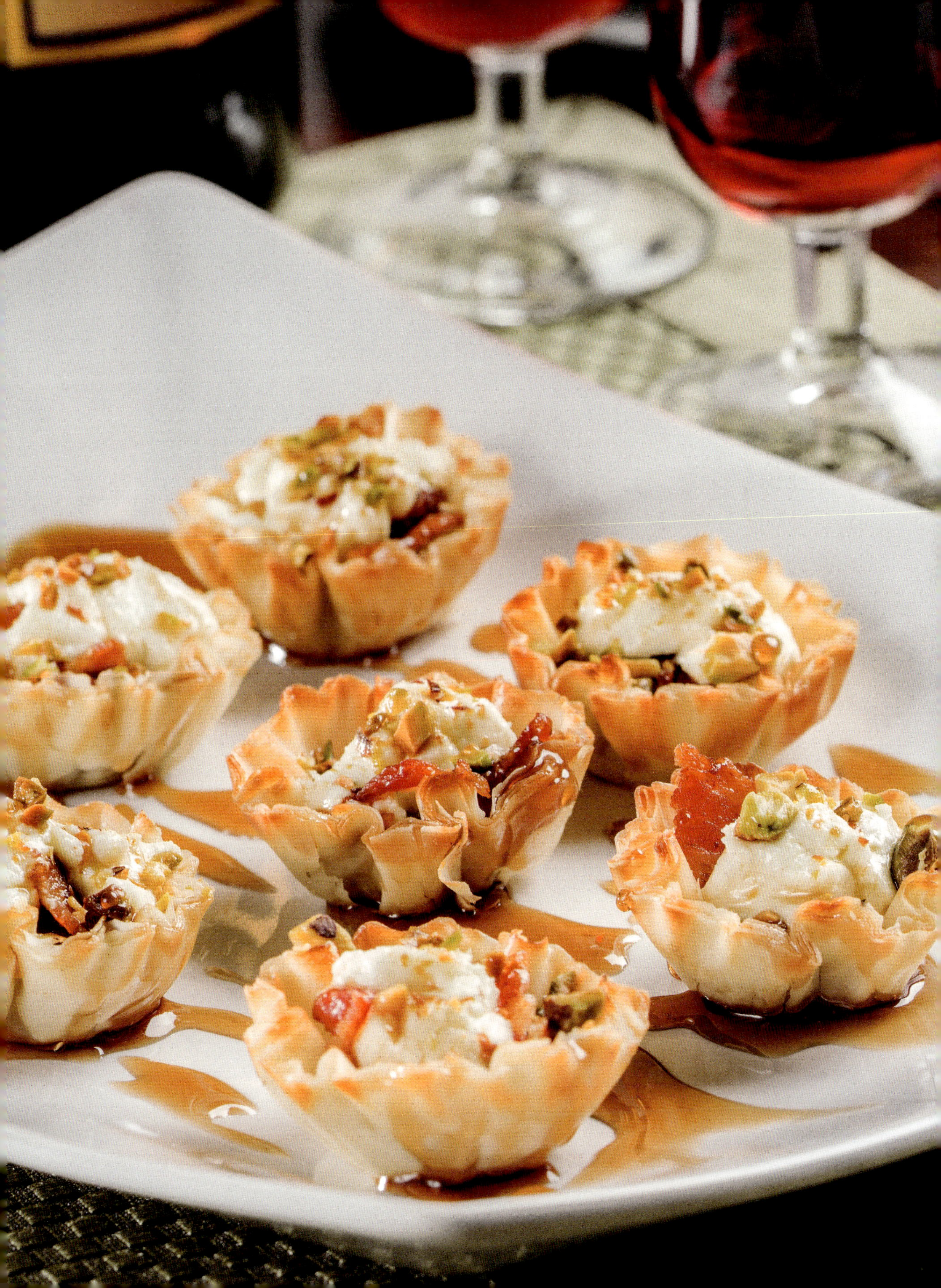

POPULAR PARTY MEATBALLS

For years, I've been making the old standby jelly and chili sauce recipe for meatballs. This sweet and tangy combo is popular at parties, and the meatballs always seem to be the first to disappear. But recently, I decided to kick things up a notch by adding in a little bit of this and a little bit of that. As it turns out, now the meatballs are better than ever.

Makes about 32

- 1-½ pounds ground beef
- 1 egg
- 2 tablespoons water
- ¼ cup bread crumbs
- 1 teaspoon salt
- ½ teaspoon onion powder
- ⅛ teaspoon black pepper
- 1 (12-ounce) jar chili sauce
- 1 cup grape jelly
- 2 tablespoons lemon juice
- 1 teaspoon dry mustard

■ Preheat oven to 350 degrees.

■ In a large bowl, combine ground beef, egg, water, bread crumbs, salt, onion powder, and pepper; mix well. Form into 1-inch meatballs and place on a rimmed baking sheet. Bake 10 minutes.

■ Meanwhile, in a soup pot, mix together chili sauce, jelly, lemon juice, and dry mustard. Bring to a boil over medium-high heat, then add meatballs. Reduce heat to low, cover, and simmer 15 to 20 minutes or until meatballs are cooked through, gently stirring occasionally.

If I can avoid a sticky situation, I will! So before placing my meatballs on the baking sheet, I always line it with either aluminum foil or a silicone baking sheet first. It makes clean-up so much easier. MCM

KEEP-IT-SIMPLE SHRIMP SCAMPI

KISS usually stands for "Keep it Simple, Stupid" but I'd never dream of saying that to you, so instead I threw on an extra "S" for "Keep-it-Simple Shrimp Scampi." This acronym will hopefully serve to remind you that you don't have to go wild with shrimp to make it taste good. Some butter, a little oil, garlic, and a few seasonings is all it takes to make this sensational shrimp appetizer.

Serves 10 to 12

2 sticks butter

3 tablespoons olive oil

10 cloves garlic, minced

1 teaspoon salt

½ teaspoon black pepper

1-½ pounds large shrimp, peeled and deveined, tails removed

2 tablespoons fresh lemon juice

2 tablespoons chopped fresh parsley

- In a large skillet over medium heat, heat butter and oil until butter is melted. Add garlic, salt, and pepper; sauté 1 to 2 minutes or until garlic is tender, but not browned.

- Stir in shrimp and cook 3 to 4 minutes, just until pink. Stir in lemon juice and parsley; mix well.

- Place shrimp in a serving bowl and serve with toothpicks.

Sometimes I serve these along with a platter of endive leaves (a great low-carb choice) or toasted baguette slices. That way, instead of having to skewer the shrimp, I leave it up to my guests to create their own tasty masterpieces by spooning the shrimp and a bit of the garlicky saucy onto an endive leaf or slice of bread. MCM

BREAD BOWL BUFFALO CHICKEN DIP

Nothing says game day like Buffalo wings with creamy blue cheese dressing and a side of celery. So I combined all of those fan-favorite flavors together and stuffed them into a hearty bread loaf to come up with the ultimate game day dip. This one is a real crowd pleaser, so be prepared to be asked for the recipe over and over again.

Serves 10 to 12

1 (1-pound) oval loaf Italian or sourdough bread, unsliced

1 (8-ounce) package cream cheese, softened

1 cup sour cream

2 cups shredded mozzarella cheese

¾ cup chopped celery

½ cup blue cheese crumbles, plus 1 tablespoon for garnish

½ cup Buffalo wing sauce

1 teaspoon garlic powder

2 cups shredded cooked chicken

- Preheat oven to 375 degrees F.
- Cut the top off the bread about ¼ of the way down and set top aside. Hollow out inside, leaving about 1 inch of bread around edges. (This will be your bread bowl.) Cut top of bread and the bread that was removed from inside into 1-inch cubes, and set aside.
- In a large bowl, combine remaining ingredients, except reserved blue cheese for garnish; mix well. Spoon mixture into bread bowl, then loosely wrap bread bowl in aluminum foil.
- Bake 45 to 50 minutes or until hot in center. Unwrap bread, garnish with reserved blue cheese, and serve with bread cubes for dipping and dunking.

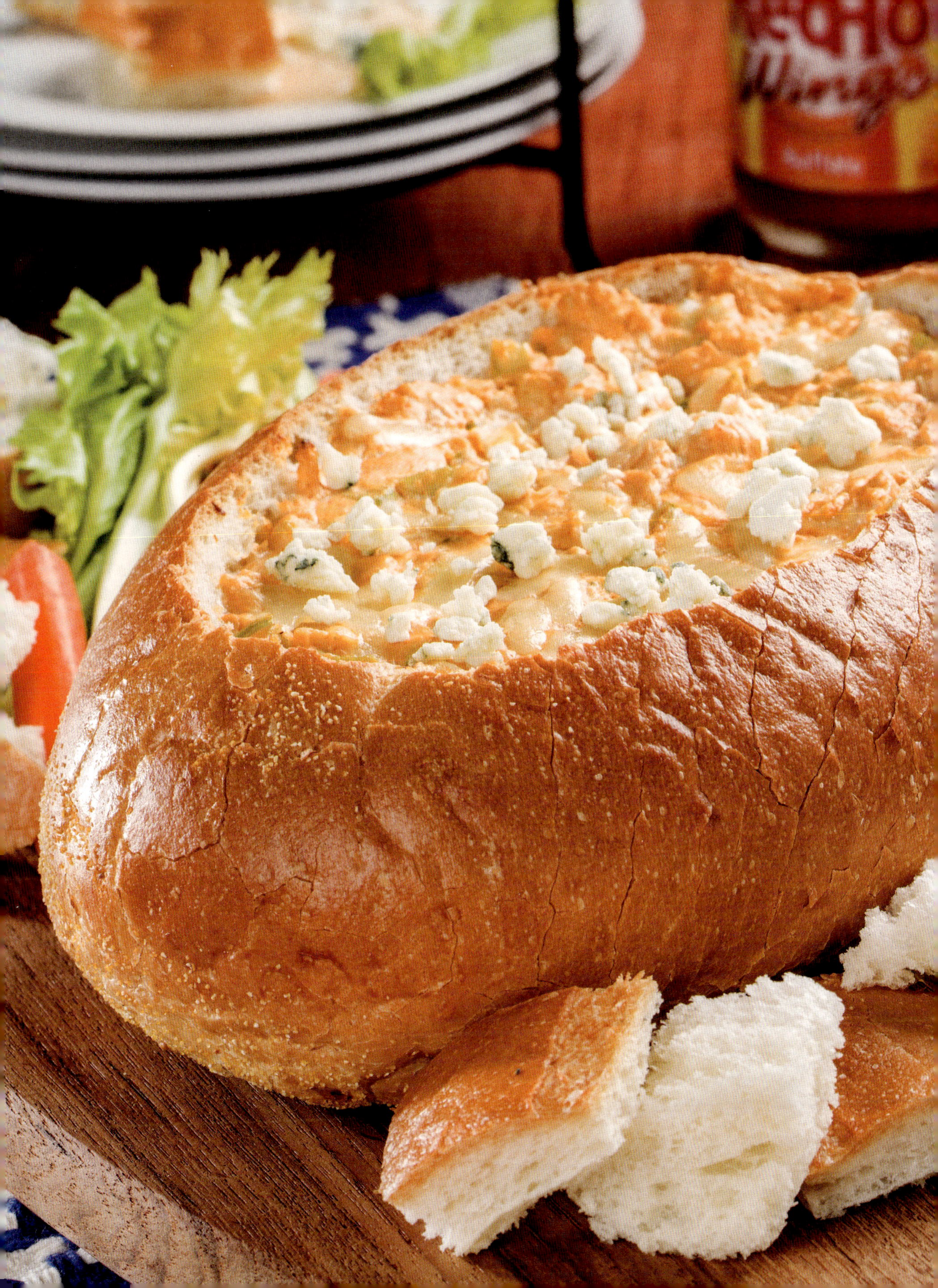

WRAPPED-UP CRANBERRY BRIE

This is one of my favorite appetizers to serve before a big holiday meal. As a cheese lover, I appreciate a dish that centers on this dairy-good ingredient. The cranberry sauce complements the Brie so well and the pecans add just the right amount of buttery crunch. My mouth is watering just thinking about all the ooey-gooey deliciousness! Make this for your next family get-together to experience what I'm talking about.

Serves 5 to 6

1 (8-ounce) can refrigerated crescent rolls

1 (8-ounce) round Brie cheese

4 tablespoons whole berry cranberry sauce, divided

2 tablespoons chopped pecans

1 egg, beaten

- Preheat oven to 350 degrees F. Coat a rimmed baking sheet with cooking spray. Unroll crescent roll dough onto a cutting board, pressing seams together.

- Slice Brie in half horizontally, and place bottom half in center of dough. Spread 3 tablespoons cranberry sauce over cut side, sprinkle with pecans, and replace top of Brie. Bring dough over top of Brie, pressing dough firmly to seal. Place seam-side down on baking sheet and brush with beaten egg.

- Bake 25 to 30 minutes or until golden. Spoon remaining tablespoon of cranberry sauce on top and serve.

CREAMY SWISS FONDUE BREAD

First there was Ooey Gooey Cheese Bread. (See my *Easy Everyday Favorites* cookbook for that recipe!) Now, I've got a new take on it to share with you, and this one is inspired by one of the biggest food trends of the 1970s — the Swiss fondue. Although this tastes just like a classic fondue, there's no dipping or fondue pot required, so there's a lot less mess. This just goes to prove that everything old, sooner or later, becomes new again.

Serves 14 to 16

1 loaf (1 pound) French bread, cut into ½-inch slices

⅓ cup mayonnaise

¼ cup dry white wine

2 tablespoons sliced scallion

2 tablespoons Dijon mustard

2 cups (8 ounces) shredded Swiss cheese

- Preheat oven to broil.
- Place bread on a baking sheet and broil until lightly toasted. (Keep an eye on it, so it doesn't burn.)
- Meanwhile, in a medium bowl, combine mayonnaise, wine, scallion, and mustard; mix well. Stir in the Swiss cheese.
- Spread cheese mixture evenly over each bread slice. Right before serving, broil for 3 to 5 minutes or until cheese is brown and bubbly. Serve immediately.

BARBECUE CHICKEN FLATBREAD

Whether you call it pizza or flatbread makes no difference to me. All I know is you're going to be saying "yum-my" after you give this recipe a try. It's my easy take on the popular barbecue chicken pizza you can find on restaurant menus everywhere. Serve it for a party, as a pre-dinner appetizer for the whole family, or as an entrée. It's great any way you slice it!

Serves 14 to 16

1 (11-ounce) package refrigerated thin crust pizza dough

1 tablespoon olive oil

Garlic powder for sprinkling

1 cup cooked shredded chicken

½ cup frozen corn, thawed

¼ cup slivered red onion

1 cup shredded mozzarella cheese

¼ cup barbecue sauce

2 tablespoons chopped fresh cilantro

- Preheat oven to 425 degrees F. Coat a 10- x 15-inch rimmed baking sheet with cooking spray.

- Unroll pizza dough and press into baking sheet; brush with oil and sprinkle lightly with garlic powder. Bake 8 minutes, then remove from oven.

- Evenly top crust with chicken, corn, onion, and mozzarella cheese. Bake 6 to 8 minutes or until heated through and cheese is melted. Drizzle with barbecue sauce, sprinkle with cilantro, and serve.

This recipe uses some supermarket shortcuts, which I'm all for. A packaged pizza crust, frozen corn, and you can even buy a rotisserie chicken to shred. Oh, and here's a tip -- the best way to drizzle barbecue sauce is with an inexpensive plastic squeeze bottle, which you can also find in the supermarket. MCM

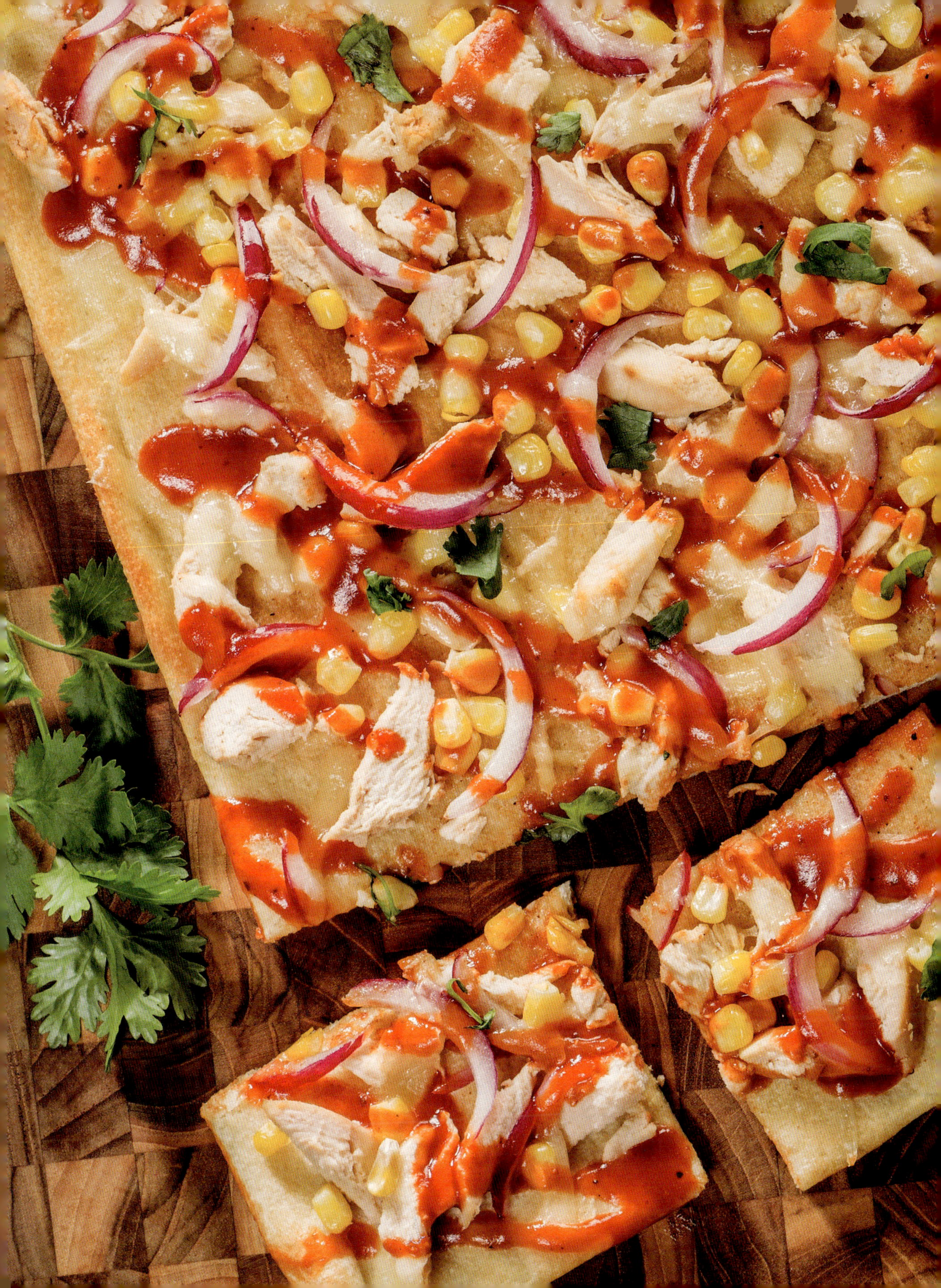

MUNCH MADNESS SNACK MIX

I hope you're ready for plenty of munching, because this snack mix is irresistibly good. It features a flavor-packed medley of spices and a crunchy combination of crackers, nuts, and pretzels. Let everything sit together for several hours so that the seasonings really absorb into the crackers. It may not be a super-quick snack mix, but it's well worth the wait!

Makes 8 cups

1 (1-ounce) packet dry ranch dressing mix

½ teaspoon garlic powder

½ teaspoon onion powder

¼ teaspoon black pepper

¼ teaspoon cayenne pepper

½ cup vegetable oil

2 cups cheese crackers (like Cheez-Its®)

2 cups oyster crackers

1 cup cashew nuts

3 cups mini pretzels

■ In a 2-gallon resealable plastic bag, combine dressing mix, garlic powder, onion powder, black pepper, and cayenne pepper; mix well. Add oil and mix well.

■ Place remaining ingredients in bag, seal, and turn bag over several times until mixture is evenly coated. Allow to sit about 1 hour before turning again. Let bag sit for at least 4 hours. Store snack mixture in bag or an airtight container until ready to serve.

If you want to serve this for a fancier occasion, break out the champagne flutes and fill them with this! That way you can hand everyone their own flute to munch out of. And since you probably don't serve champagne all that often, it's a good reason to pull out those fancy glasses and use them. MCM

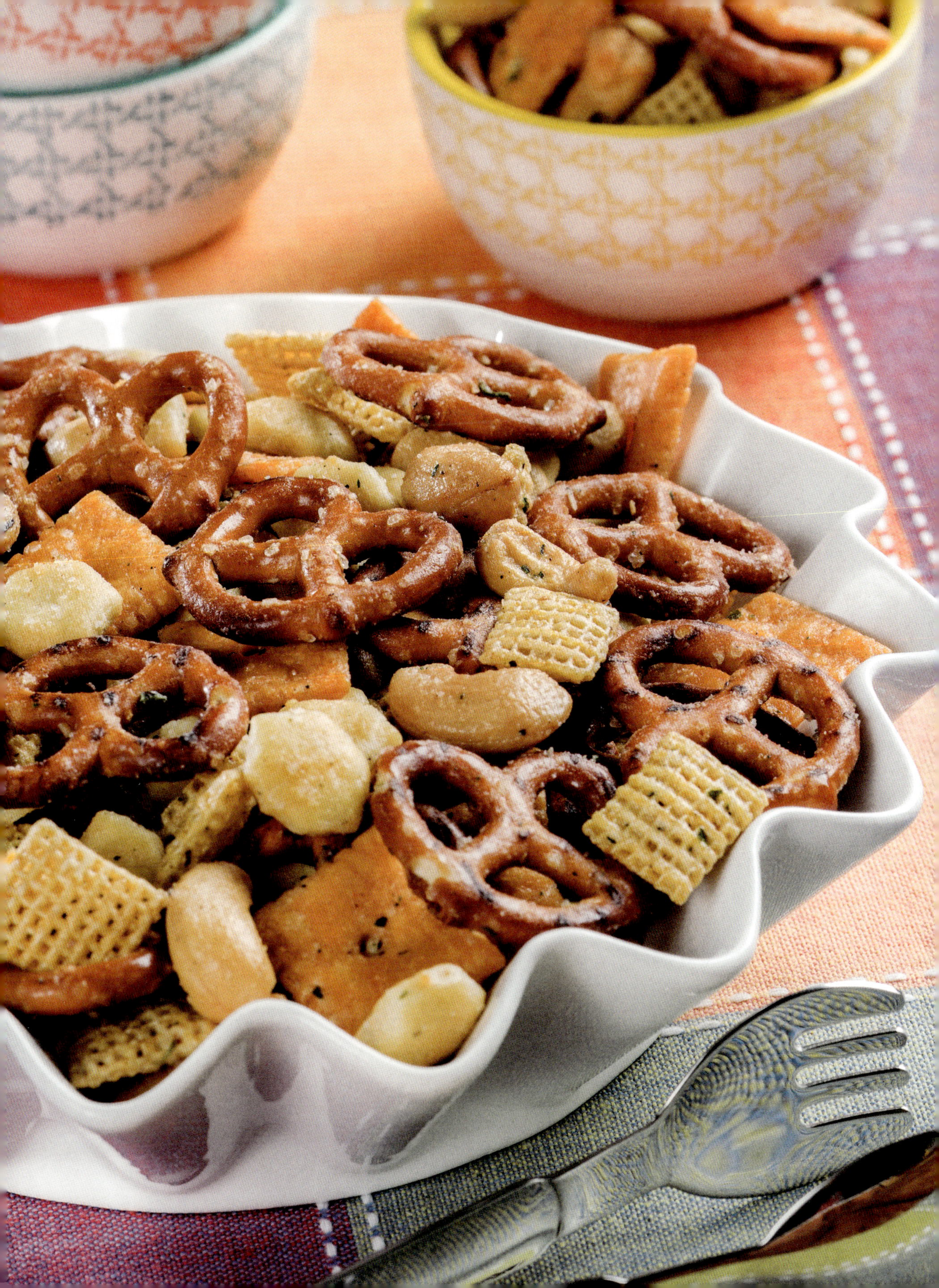

"*Who else loves dunking crusty bread into soup as much as I do? By the way, if you need to cut onions for your soup, check out these funky glasses I found they help prevent me from crying while chopping onions. Sorry, I don't sell these!*"

SOUP & SALAD

Unstuffed Cabbage Soup 56

Any Night Soup 58

Fan-Favorite Mushroom Soup 59

Roasted "Carroflower" Soup 60

Special Tuscan Tortellini Soup 62

Beefed-Up Cantina Soup 63

Asian Chicken Noodle Soup 64

Slow Cooker Split Pea Soup 66

All-In Game Day Chili 67

Hearty Harvest Salad 68

Wedge Salad with Chipotle Ranch Dressing 70

Italian Hoagie Salad 72

Wilted Bistro Salad 73

Crunchy Cabbage Salad with Peanut Dressing 74

Kinda Quiche-y Salad 76

Fruity Chicken Friendship Salad 78

Chopped Greek Salad 79

Shrimp Scampi Salad with Goat Cheese 80

UNSTUFFED CABBAGE SOUP

When you're craving stuffed cabbage, but don't want to go through all the work of cooking ... and rolling ... and cooking again, this soup is your best bet. It's old-fashioned goodness made shortcut simple, which is perfect if you're juggling a busy schedule. Enjoy this with a thick slice of your favorite hearty bread, so you can soak up all the goodness!

Serves 6 to 8

2 tablespoons vegetable oil

1 pound top round beef, cut into 1-½ inch chunks

½ head cabbage, coarsely chopped

4 cups beef broth

1 (28-ounce) can crushed tomatoes

3 tablespoons tomato paste

1 tablespoon lemon juice

½ cup packed brown sugar

½ teaspoon salt

■ In a soup pot over high heat, heat oil until hot; brown beef on all sides.

■ Add remaining ingredients, bring to a boil, then reduce heat to low and simmer 1-½ to 1-¾ hours or until beef is tender and soup is thickened.

It seems that every nationality makes stuffed cabbage a bit differently; some like it sweeter, others more tart. Go ahead and add more or less of the sugar and lemon juice until you get it just the way you like it. MCM

SOUP & SALAD

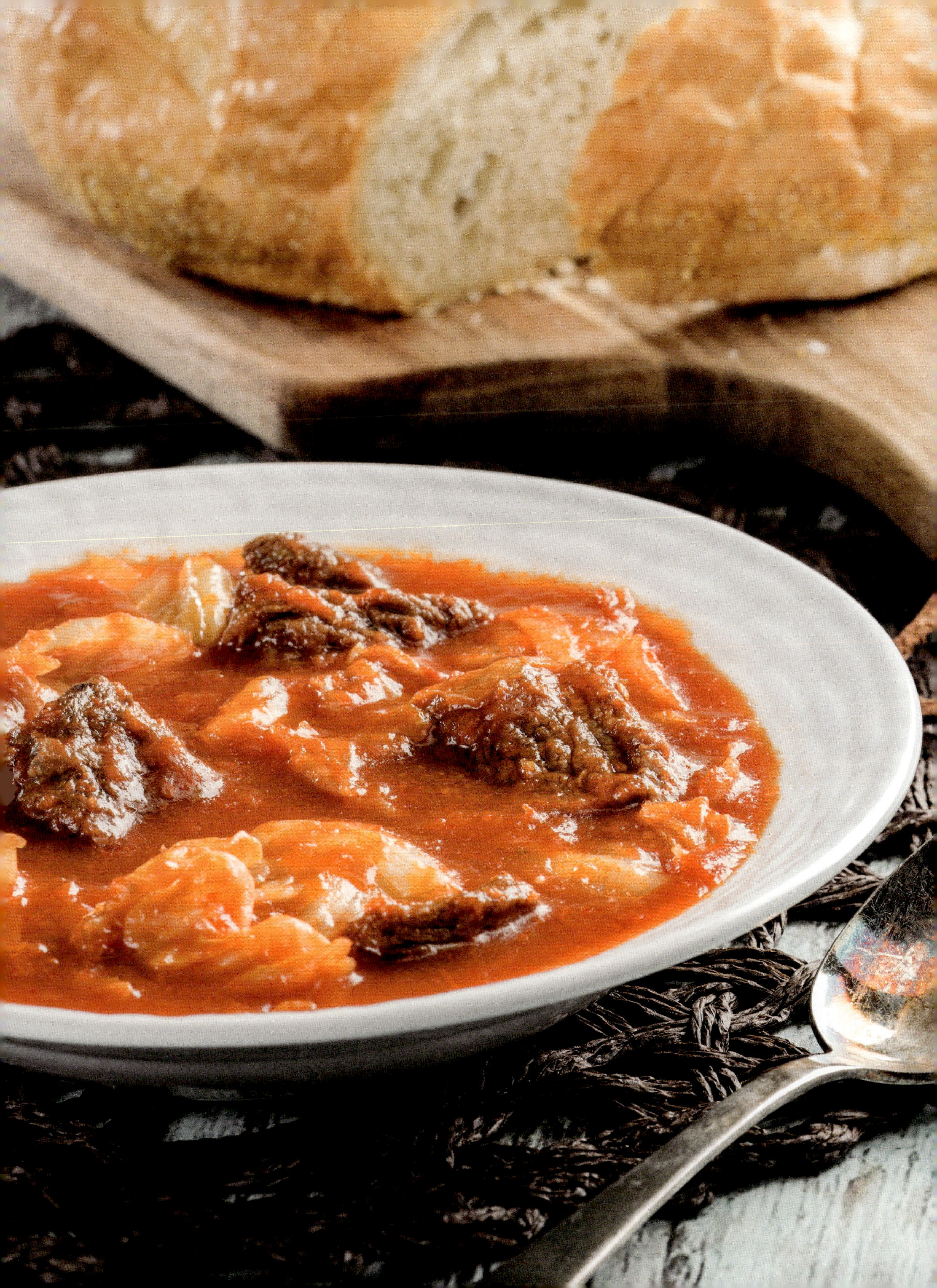

ANY NIGHT SOUP

If you're wondering where this soup got its name from, well, it's pretty self-explanatory. This started out as my go-to soup when it was cold and yucky outside and I wanted something hot and hearty, but didn't have a whole lot on hand. Since the ingredients are pretty basic, you could throw this one on the stove any night of the week and have dinner ready in under 30 minutes.

Serves 4 to 5

- 2 tablespoons olive oil
- 1 onion, finely chopped
- 1 carrot, cut in half lengthwise, and thinly sliced
- 1 stalk celery, chopped
- 4 cups chicken broth
- 2 (15.8-ounce) cans cannellini beans, undrained
- 1 pound kielbasa sausage, thinly sliced
- ¾ teaspoon garlic powder
- ½ teaspoon Italian seasoning
- ¼ teaspoon black pepper

- In a soup pot over medium-high heat, heat oil until hot. Sauté onion, carrot, and celery 6 to 8 minutes or until tender.

- Add remaining ingredients and bring to a boil. Reduce heat to low, and simmer 20 minutes.

You can clean out your veggie drawer with this soup. So if you have scallions (rather than onions), use those! No chicken broth in sight, but have a carton of beef broth? Make the switch! This is your soup, your way. MCM

SOUP & SALAD

FAN-FAVORITE MUSHROOM SOUP

You may know by now that I'm allergic to mushrooms. I can cook with them, I just can't eat them. Now this might lead you to wondering why I've included a mushroom soup in my cookbook. Well, I just know that a lot of you guys do love mushrooms, and since I love making you happy ... it's worth it. A big "thank you" to all the taste-testers who gave me feedback and helped me tweak things until we got it just right.

Serves 4 to 5

½ stick butter

1 pound fresh mushrooms, sliced

1 small onion, chopped

½ teaspoon salt

⅛ teaspoon black pepper

5 tablespoons all-purpose flour

4 cups chicken broth

1 cup half-and-half

¼ teaspoon browning and seasoning sauce (like Gravy Master® or Kitchen Bouquet®)

- In a soup pot over medium heat, melt butter. Add mushrooms, onion, salt, and pepper; sauté until tender.

- Add flour and cook 2 to 3 minutes, stirring constantly. Gradually add broth and bring to a boil, then reduce heat to low and simmer 10 minutes, stirring occasionally.

- Slowly stir in half-and-half and browning sauce and simmer 5 additional minutes or until thickened. Serve immediately.

This is a super creamy soup; however, if you want to lighten it up a bit, you can use milk rather than half-and-half. It won't be as rich-tasting, but it's still better than any canned mushroom soup you'll ever have. MCM

SOUP & SALAD

ROASTED "CARROFLOWER" SOUP

I bet you saw this and immediately asked yourself, "What the heck is a 'carroflower'?" Don't worry, I'm not asking you to go and find some mythical new veggie. It's just a fun wordplay on "carrot" and "cauliflower," the two main veggies in this heartwarming soup. The mild-tasting and versatile cauliflower pairs perfectly with the sweetness of the carrots. It's a delicious combo that always brightens my day!

Serves 6 to 8

2 tablespoons olive oil

2 sprigs fresh thyme, stems removed

1 teaspoon salt

½ teaspoon black pepper

4 large carrots, cut into chunks

1 head cauliflower, cut into florets

½ onion, cut into chunks

2 cups water, divided

4 cups vegetable or chicken broth

1 cup half-and-half

- Preheat oven to 400 degrees F.

- In a large bowl, combine oil, thyme, salt, and pepper; mix well. Add carrots, cauliflower, and onion; toss until evenly coated. Place vegetables on a baking sheet in a single layer. Roast 35 to 40 minutes or until vegetables begin to brown, then about halfway through, flip them so that they roast evenly.

- Place half the vegetables and 1 cup water into a blender. (If you have a bigger blender and you think it can handle more, go for it. Just don't get too crazy or you'll make a mess.) Process until smooth; pour mixture into a soup pot. Repeat with remaining vegetables and 1 cup water. Add broth to soup pot and heat over medium heat until hot. Slowly stir in half-and-half and heat until hot.

A great serving option would be to dig out those teacups & saucers that you never use, and serve the soup right out of them. No spoons necessary...just sip away! MCM

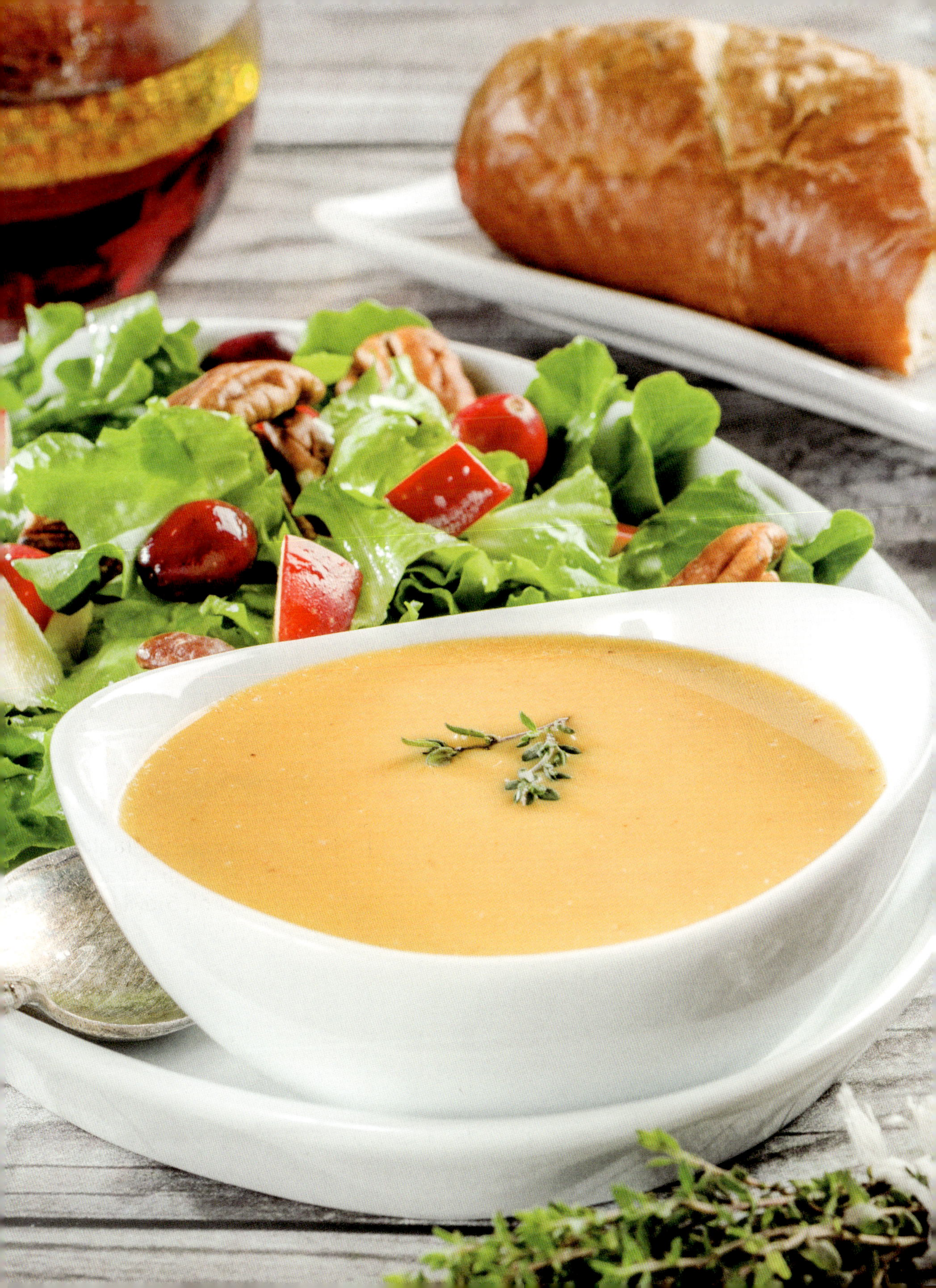

SPECIAL TUSCAN TORTELLINI SOUP

I ate a lot of tortellini soup growing up, and you can bet it was served for every special occasion. To this day, my mom still makes it for my birthday and Christmas. Over the years, I've tweaked it here and there, and now I'm excited to share it with you. When you make it, it'll almost be like we're spending my birthday together! (By the way, I love ice cream birthday cake…)

Serves 6 to 8

2 tablespoons olive oil

1 onion, chopped

2 (14-½-ounce) cans diced tomatoes, undrained

2 tablespoons balsamic vinegar

2 cloves garlic, chopped

¼ teaspoon dried oregano

¼ teaspoon salt

¼ teaspoon black pepper

4 cups water

3 (10-½-ounce) cans condensed chicken broth

1 (19-ounce) package frozen or refrigerated cheese tortellini

3 cups fresh spinach

- In a soup pot over medium-high heat, heat oil until hot.

- Sauté onion until tender, then add tomatoes with their liquid, vinegar, garlic, oregano, salt, and pepper; cook 5 to 7 minutes or until heated through.

- Stir in water and broth and bring to a boil. Add tortellini and spinach and cook 6 to 8 minutes or until tortellini are tender. Serve immediately.

If you're making this a day or so before serving it, I suggest adding the tortellini right before you heat it up. If you do it beforehand, the tortellini will most likely suck up all the broth and you'll end up with a stew. MCM

BEEFED-UP CANTINA SOUP

The good news is, you can throw together this Southwestern-inspired soup in a flash. The bad news is, you're probably going to make it disappear in a flash too. (Yeah, it's that good!) Supermarket shortcuts cut out all the work, so you can enjoy this on the busiest of days. By the way, the best part of this hearty, beefy soup is the cheesy-crunchy topping.

Serves 4 to 6

- 4 cups beef broth
- 1 (16-ounce) package frozen cocktail-sized meatballs
- 2 cups frozen corn
- 1 cup salsa
- 1 teaspoon ground cumin
- ½ cup shredded cheddar cheese
- 1 cup coarsely crushed tortilla chips

■ In a large soup pot over medium-high heat, combine broth, meatballs, corn, salsa, and cumin; bring to a boil.

■ Reduce heat to medium-low and simmer 7 to 8 minutes.

■ After dishing up each bowl, evenly sprinkle with shredded cheddar cheese and tortilla chips, then "deeg in." (That's how my grandmother would say it with her French accent.)

Change up the flavor (and the heat) by making this soup with different kinds of salsa. And if you really want to add a kick, slice up a jalapeño and let it simmer with the broth or top each bowl with them. That's one way to wake up your taste buds! MCM

SOUP & SALAD

ASIAN CHICKEN NOODLE SOUP

Although I enjoy the convenience of ordering takeout from time to time, I also love trying to recreate some of my favorite Asian flavors at home. This noodle soup is a family favorite. If I'm making it just for them, I include mushrooms. But if I'm joining in and slurping up spoonfuls, then I leave them out (allergies!) and substitute with water chestnuts. They add a tasty crunch!

Serves 6 to 8

8 cups chicken broth

1-½ tablespoons soy sauce

½ pound boneless, skinless chicken breast, cut into ½-inch chunks

2 cups sliced mushrooms

1 carrot, shredded

2 (3-ounce) packages ramen noodle soup, seasoning packets removed (see note)

½ cup shelled edamame

1 scallion, sliced

½ teaspoon ground ginger

- In a soup pot over medium-high heat, combine chicken broth, soy sauce, chicken chunks, mushrooms, and carrot; bring to a boil.

- Add noodles, edamame, scallion, and ginger, and continue boiling 3 to 4 minutes or until noodles are soft, stirring occasionally.

Wondering what to do with the seasoning packets from the noodles? You can use them in another recipe or just toss them out -- they're mostly sodium anyway! MCM

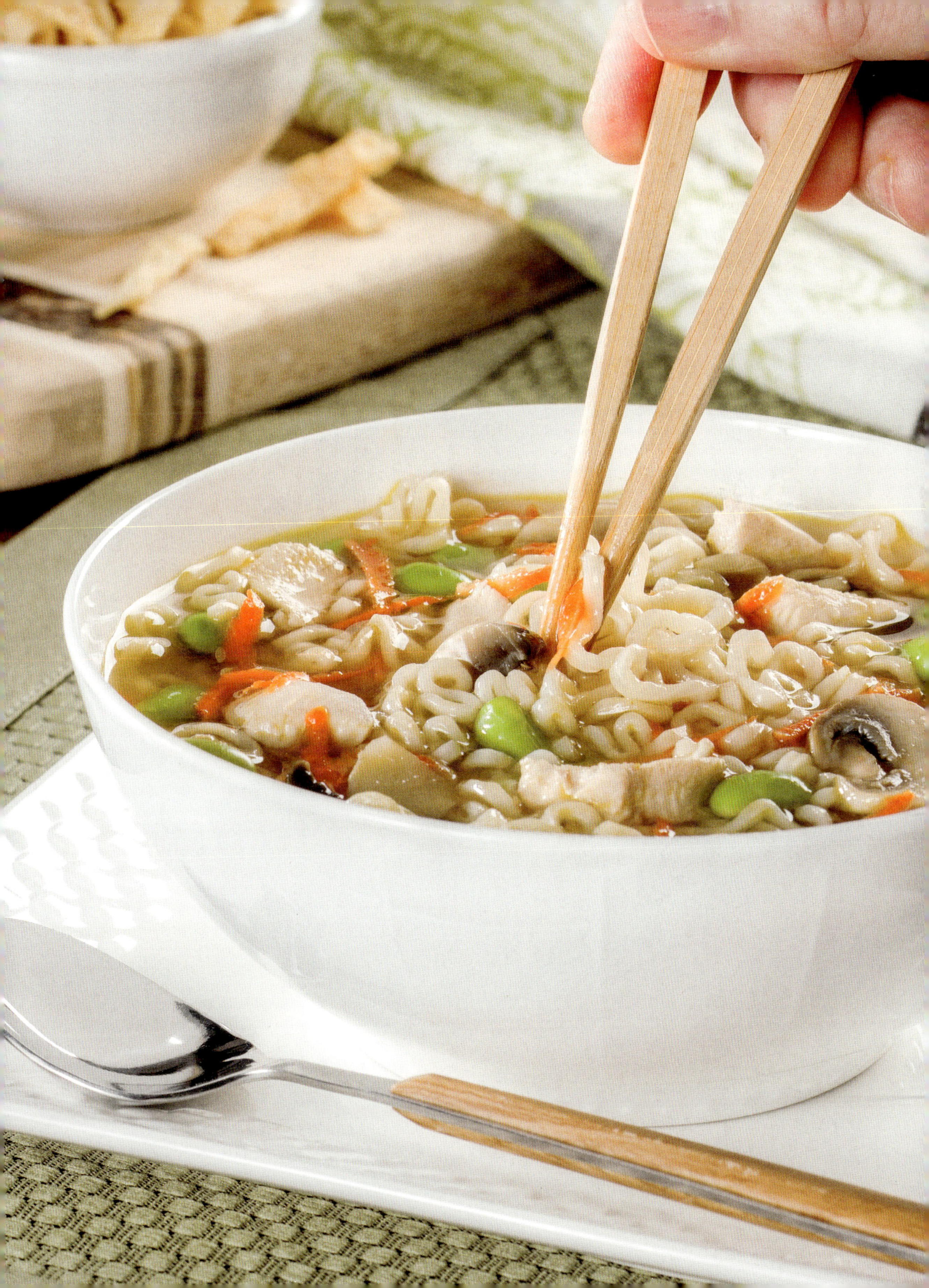

SLOW COOKER SPLIT PEA SOUP

Everyone knows that split pea soup tastes even better the next day. By cooking this in your slow cooker, you'll get the same consistency as if you let it sit overnight. That's because cooking this soup low and slow allows the peas to really soak up the flavor of the ham. Mmm ... just writing about it is making me crave a bowl right now!

Serves 7 to 8

1 (16-ounce) package dried split peas

1 pound cooked ham, diced (see note)

8 cups chicken broth

4 potatoes, peeled and diced

4 carrots, diced

¼ teaspoon cayenne pepper

½ teaspoon salt

½ teaspoon black pepper

1 bay leaf

- Place all ingredients in a 5- to 6-quart slow cooker.
- Cover and cook on HIGH 6 hours or on LOW 10 hours or until peas are tender and soup is thick. Remove and discard bay leaf. Serve immediately.

Anytime I serve ham and there is some left over, I make this hearty soup. But that doesn't mean you have to wait for leftovers to make it; some thick-cut deli ham works too! MCM

ALL-IN GAME DAY CHILI

If you're going to serve chili on game day, then you've got to go all in – I'm talking sausage and beef, beans and veggies, and plenty of spices to make things really flavorful. You can serve this in bowls with your favorite toppings or spoon it over a platter of tortilla chips; either way, you can't go wrong. This chili is so good, you might want to make it a game day staple!

Serves 7 to 8

- 1 pound bulk ground Italian sausage
- 1 pound ground beef chuck
- 2 (28-ounce) cans diced tomatoes, undrained
- 2 (15-ounce) cans red kidney beans, drained
- 1 yellow onion, chopped
- 1 green bell pepper, chopped
- ½ cup beer (see note)
- 3 tablespoons chili powder
- 1 tablespoon minced garlic
- 2 teaspoons ground cumin
- 2 teaspoons hot pepper sauce
- 1 teaspoon black pepper

- ■ In a soup pot over medium-high heat, sauté sausage and ground beef 8 to 10 minutes or until browned, breaking apart with a spoon. Drain excess liquid.
- ■ Add remaining ingredients. Stir to combine, then cover and simmer over low heat at least 1 hour, stirring occasionally.

I'm not about to tell you what kind of beer you should be using, especially with all the different kinds available! Use whatever you've got in the fridge or maybe experiment with something new. As for me, I usually go with a darker beer for this recipe, since I think it adds a richer and deeper flavor. MCM

SOUP & SALAD

HEARTY HARVEST SALAD

I've noticed that a lot of us tend to eat tons of salad in the late spring and summertime, when the weather makes us want to stay as far away from our ovens as possible, but then we forget all about salads in the later parts of the year. With all the yummy veggies that are in season during the fall, why aren't we making more salads that incorporate them? This hearty harvest salad is my answer to this dilemma. You're welcome.

Serves 4 to 6

⅓ cup water

¾ pound fresh Brussels sprouts, cut in half

½ pound cubed fresh butternut squash

2 tablespoons vegetable oil

½ teaspoon salt

¼ teaspoon black pepper

6 cups chopped kale

½ apple, thinly sliced

2 tablespoons dried cranberries

2 tablespoons sunflower seeds

Poppy seed dressing for drizzling

- In a large skillet over medium-high heat, bring water, Brussels sprouts, and squash to a boil. Cook 5 to 6 minutes or until water evaporates. Add oil, salt, and pepper to skillet and sauté 4 to 5 minutes or until vegetables begin to brown and are fork-tender, stirring occasionally.

- Place kale on a serving platter. Top with sautéed vegetables, apple slices, cranberries, and sunflower seeds. Drizzle with dressing and serve.

Since I like my veggies browned and crispy, sometimes I cook the Brussels sprouts and squash a bit longer. I also like to assemble the salad in a deep bowl, so I can toss everything with the dressing before plating it. (This helps ensure that the dressing is distributed evenly.) Once I've got it plated, I "dress it up" even more with an extra drizzle! MCM

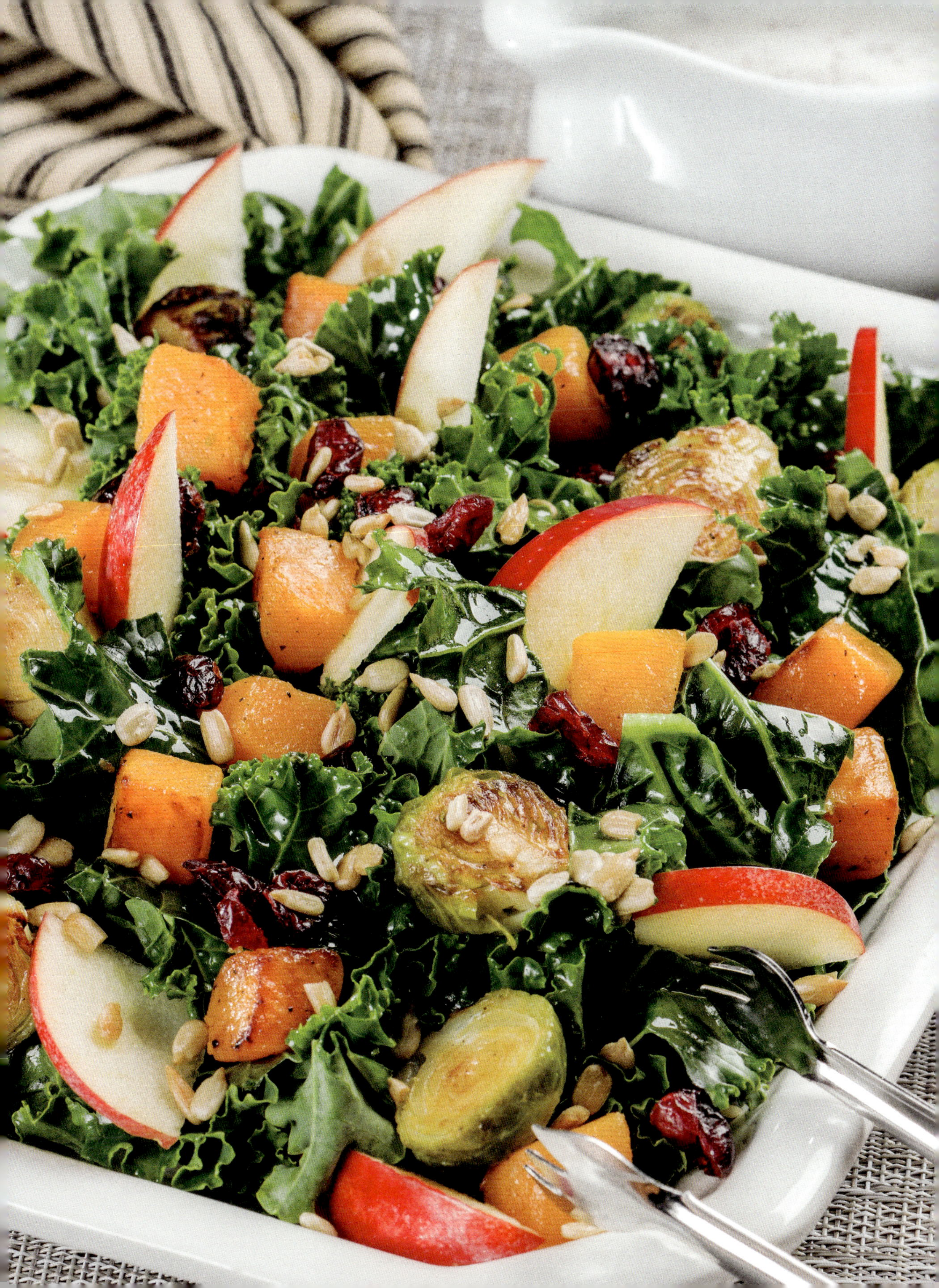

WEDGE SALAD WITH CHIPOTLE RANCH DRESSING

I used to order a salad like this from a restaurant around the corner from my house. I loved how simple, yet flavorful, it was and the presentation was always so impressive! One day, I finally decided to make it at home and the results were amazing. So of course, I had to share it with you. (P.S. This is a great dinner party salad!)

Serves 6

½ cup sour cream

½ cup mayonnaise

1 chipotle pepper packed in adobo sauce, plus 1 teaspoon adobo sauce

1-½ teaspoons lime juice

½ teaspoon smoked paprika

½ teaspoon garlic powder

½ teaspoon salt

¼ teaspoon black pepper

½ cup lightly packed cilantro

8 ounces chorizo sausage, casing removed

1 head iceberg lettuce, cut into 6 wedges

4 Roma tomatoes, sliced

1 avocado, cut into ½-inch chunks

■ In a food processor or blender combine sour cream, mayonnaise, chipotle pepper and adobo sauce, lime juice, paprika, garlic powder, salt, pepper, and cilantro. Process until smooth. Refrigerate until ready to use.

■ In a medium skillet over medium heat, cook chorizo sausage 5 to 6 minutes or until cooked through, stirring gently to crumble.

■ Place a wedge of lettuce on each serving plate and evenly arrange with tomato, avocado, and chorizo sausage. Drizzle with dressing and serve.

I love a really crunchy wedge. If you do too, then I recommend soaking the whole head of lettuce in a bowl of ice water for about 30 minutes. Make sure you drain it really well before cutting it into wedges and assembling your salad! MCM

SOUP & SALAD

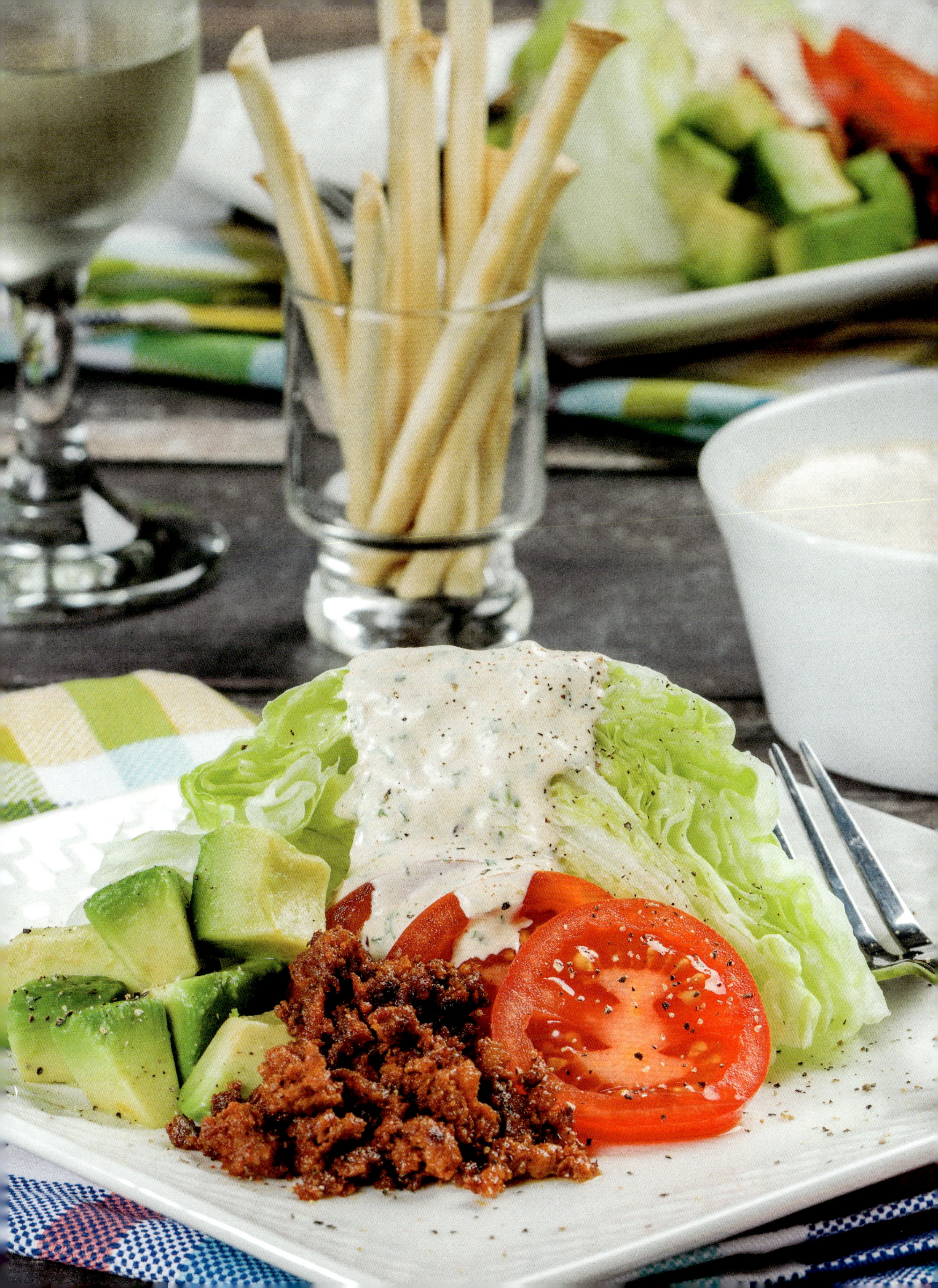

ITALIAN HOAGIE SALAD

Living in Philly, you get to know a thing or two about Italian hoagies. (Did you know that the term "hoagie" actually originated in Philadelphia?) This recipe was inspired by the famous sandwiches of the city I currently call home. It's got all the same ingredients, just chopped up into bite-sized pieces and served inside a crusty, hollowed-out bread loaf. Give it a try and fall in love with the hoagie in a whole new way.

Serves 4

½ head iceberg lettuce, coarsely chopped

1 tomato, chopped

½ cup chopped artichoke hearts, drained

⅓ cup chopped roasted red peppers, drained

¼ cup sliced pepperoncini, drained

1 (2.25-ounce) can sliced black olives

2 (½-inch-thick) slices genoa salami, diced

5 (1-ounce) slices provolone cheese, diced

½ cup vinaigrette dressing

1 (1-pound) French bread, cut in half horizontally and hollowed out (saving bread that was removed for another use)

- In a large bowl, combine all ingredients except bread; toss until evenly coated.

- Spoon salad mixture into bottom half of bread and replace top. Evenly slice into 4 pieces and serve.

If you're planning on making this ahead, it's okay to mix everything together. Just don't spoon the salad into the bread until just before you're ready to serve it or the bread will get all soggy. MCM

WILTED BISTRO SALAD

A "wilted" salad? It's not what you think! If you've ever cooked with fresh spinach, then you know exactly what I mean. The minute you start to heat it up, it reduces to half (or less!) of its size. It's like a magic trick. Anyway, this salad is full of flavor and simply delicious. I especially love the crunchy, buttery pine nuts and the salty, crispy bacon. What a combo!

Serves 4 to 5

- 2 tablespoons olive oil
- 1 (10-ounce) package fresh spinach
- 3 cloves garlic, minced
- 1/4 teaspoon salt
- 1/4 teaspoon black pepper
- 1/2 cup chopped oil-packed sun-dried tomatoes
- 2 tablespoons pine nuts, toasted
- 4 slices crispy cooked bacon, crumbled

■ In a large skillet or soup pot over medium heat, heat oil until hot. Add spinach, garlic, salt, and pepper, and cook 30 to 45 seconds or just until spinach begins to wilt, stirring occasionally.

■ Remove skillet from heat and toss spinach with sun-dried tomatoes and pine nuts; top with bacon and serve immediately.

CRUNCHY CABBAGE SALAD WITH PEANUT DRESSING

As someone who loves crunchy textures, this salad is everything. It not only features crisp veggies, like raw bell peppers and carrots, but it also gets a bonus crunch from the cashews. And to make things even better, everything gets tossed in my homemade spicy peanut dressing, which is ridiculously addictive. Make this whenever you're craving Asian flavors or really just anytime ... because it's good.

Serves 4 to 6

5 cups finely shredded Napa cabbage or bok choy

1 red bell pepper, chopped

1 cucumber, peeled and chopped

1 cup cooked, shelled edamame

½ cup shredded carrots

½ cup coarsely chopped roasted cashew nuts

SPICY PEANUT DRESSING

½ cup creamy peanut butter

3 tablespoons soy sauce

3 tablespoons warm water

2 tablespoons sesame oil

2 tablespoons honey

1 tablespoon lime juice

½ teaspoon crushed red pepper

- In a large serving bowl, combine cabbage, bell pepper, cucumber, edamame, carrots, and cashews.

- To make Spicy Peanut Dressing, in a medium bowl, whisk peanut butter, soy sauce, warm water, sesame oil, honey, lime juice, and crushed red pepper until combined. Then either drizzle dressing over the salad and toss it or serve it on the side and let everyone add their own.

Turn this into a hearty, main dish salad by adding your favorite protein. I recommend shrimp or grilled chicken. MCM

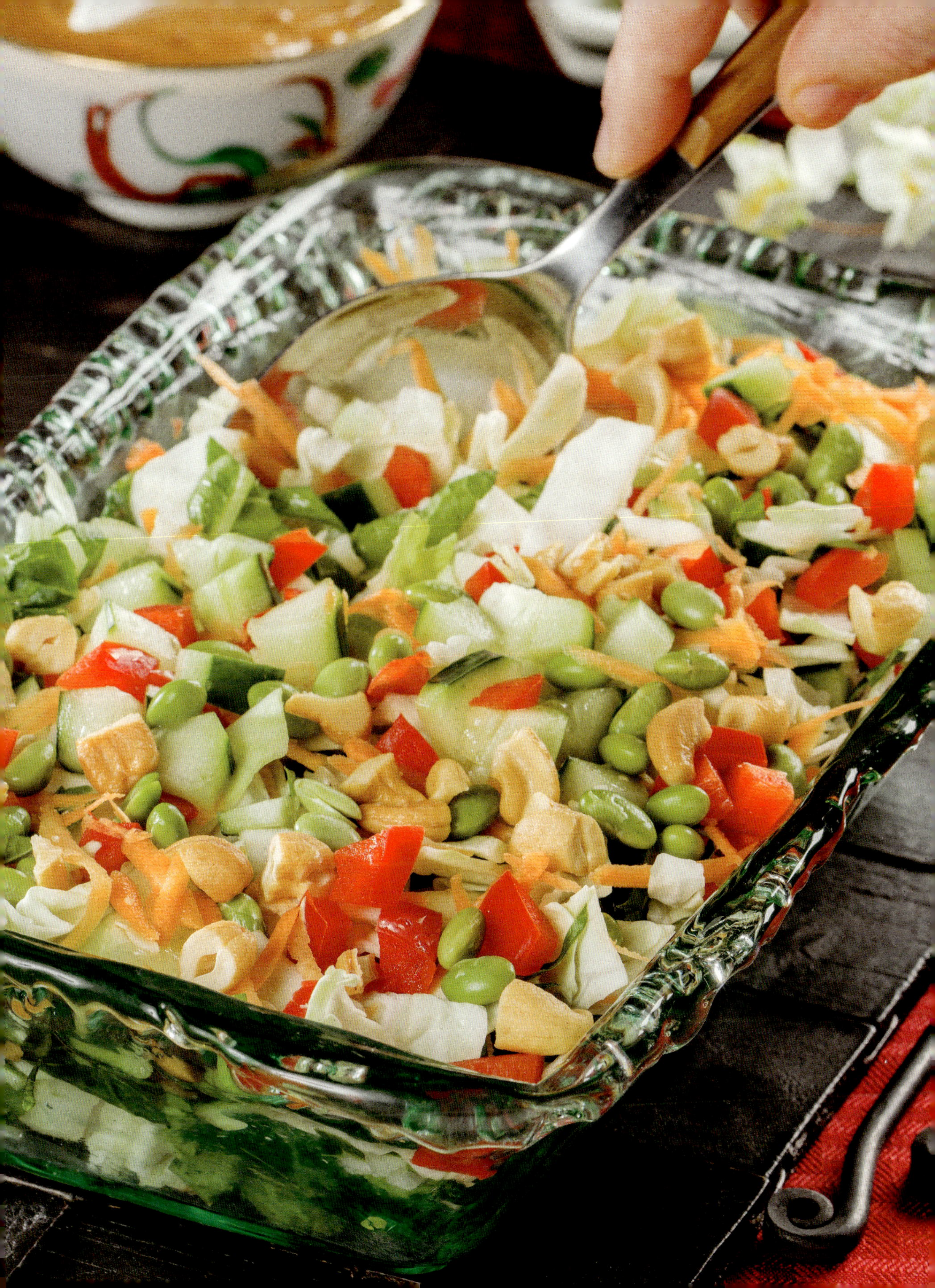

KINDA QUICHE-Y SALAD

Ever heard of a Quiche Lorraine? It's a savory, creamy, egg, Swiss cheese, and bacon mixture that's baked in a pie crust. This salad is my kitschy (or quiche-y!) spin on that tasty brunch favorite. It's super simple to make and looks great on the dining table. (Everyone is going to have something to say about it!) Most importantly, it tastes phenomenal.

Serves 4 to 6

1 refrigerated rolled pie crust (from a 14.1-ounce box)

Garlic powder for sprinkling

1 medium head romaine lettuce, cut into bite-sized pieces

1 cup shredded Swiss cheese, plus 1 tablespoon reserved for garnish

6 strips crispy cooked bacon, crumbled, with 1 tablespoon reserved for garnish

¾ cup buttermilk salad dressing

- Preheat oven to 450 degrees F.
- Press pie crust into a 9-inch deep-dish pie plate, flute edges, and prick bottom and sides of crust with fork. Lightly sprinkle with garlic powder. Bake 10 to 12 minutes or until golden. Let cool.
- In a large bowl, combine lettuce, 1 cup cheese, 6 strips crumbled bacon, and buttermilk dressing; toss until evenly coated. Spoon lettuce mixture into pie crust, sprinkle with reserved bacon and cheese; serve immediately.

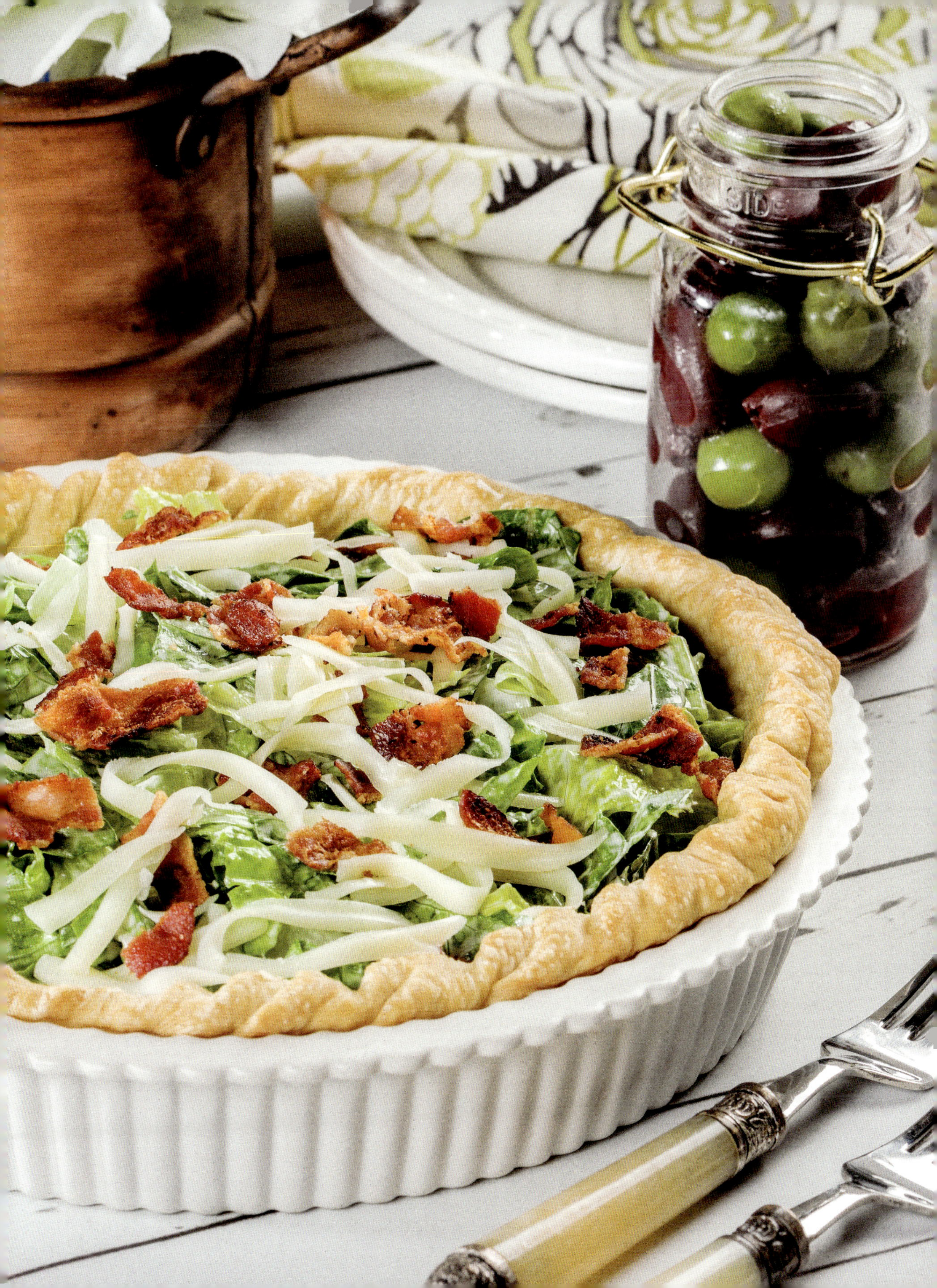

FRUITY CHICKEN FRIENDSHIP SALAD

Did you know that pineapples are a symbol of hospitality and friendship? If you're going to host a potluck or have a few friends over, then wouldn't it be great to incorporate a pineapple somehow? I've got you covered. This salad is served out of a pineapple half and features an amazing mashup of fresh fruit and hearty chicken in tangy yogurt. Trust me, it's a great one.

Serves 3 to 4

1 fresh pineapple

1 cup red seedless grapes, sliced in half

1 cup green seedless grapes, sliced in half

½ cup fresh blueberries

1 red apple, cored and cut into ½ inch chunks

2 cups cooked chicken chunks

3 stalks celery, chopped

1 cup walnuts, coarsely chopped

1-½ cups vanilla yogurt

- Cut off and discard top of pineapple. Cut pineapple in half. Hollow out half of pineapple, cutting fruit into ½-inch chunks, and setting the shell aside. (Save other half for another use.)

- In a large bowl, combine all ingredients including pineapple chunks; mix gently until well combined and everything is evenly coated.

- Spoon mixture into hollowed-out pineapple shell and serve.

To change things up, sometimes I use Greek yogurt, which gives the salad a thicker consistency and adds some extra protein. Also, when you chop up the walnuts, make sure you don't chop them too finely or they'll make the yogurt mixture taste gritty. MCM

CHOPPED GREEK SALAD

You can't go wrong with a simple Greek salad, a glass of your favorite wine, and warm pita bread. Sometimes I serve this before a big Mediterranean-inspired dinner, and sometimes this salad IS dinner. (I add some grilled chicken breast if it is!) No matter what, it always satisfies. (Although every time I serve it, it makes me want to book another trip to the Greek Isles!)

Serves 4 to 6

2 tomatoes, cut into 1-inch chunks

1 cucumber, cut into ½-inch chunks

1 red onion, cut into ½-inch chunks

½ cup pitted Kalamata olives

4 cups chopped romaine lettuce

½ cup cubed feta cheese

GREEK DRESSING

½ cup olive oil

¼ cup red wine vinegar

2 teaspoons lemon juice

1 teaspoon dried oregano

1 teaspoon garlic powder

1 teaspoon salt

■ In a medium bowl, combine tomatoes, cucumber, onion, and olives.

■ To make Greek Dressing, in a small bowl, whisk oil, vinegar, lemon juice, oregano, garlic powder, and salt. Pour over vegetables and toss until coated.

■ Place lettuce on a platter. Spoon vegetable mixture over lettuce, top with cheese, and serve.

SOUP & SALAD

SHRIMP SCAMPI SALAD WITH GOAT CHEESE

I have to admit it, I absolutely love goat cheese. I add it to my cheese boards, float crumbles of it on my tomato soup, and sprinkle it over my salads. It has a very distinctive and tart flavor that's good on just about anything, including this salad. Serve this with a side of toasted multigrain bread and enjoy every flavorful bite!

Serves 4 to 6

- 2 tablespoons butter
- 12 ounces medium raw shrimp, peeled and deveined
- 2 cloves garlic, minced
- ¼ teaspoon salt
- ¼ teaspoon black pepper
- 8 ounces mixed greens
- 1 cup cherry tomatoes, cut in half
- ¾ cup frozen corn, thawed
- 4 ounces crumbled goat cheese
- Vinaigrette for drizzling

■ In a large skillet over medium heat, melt butter; sauté shrimp, garlic, salt, and pepper 3 to 5 minutes or until pink, turning occasionally.

■ In a large bowl, combine mixed greens, tomatoes, corn, cooked shrimp, and goat cheese. Drizzle with vinaigrette and toss until evenly coated. Serve immediately.

For a fun way to serve salads at a party or special occasion, fill shot or cordial glasses with a few different varieties of dressings and let every choose their favorite. How fun is that? MCM

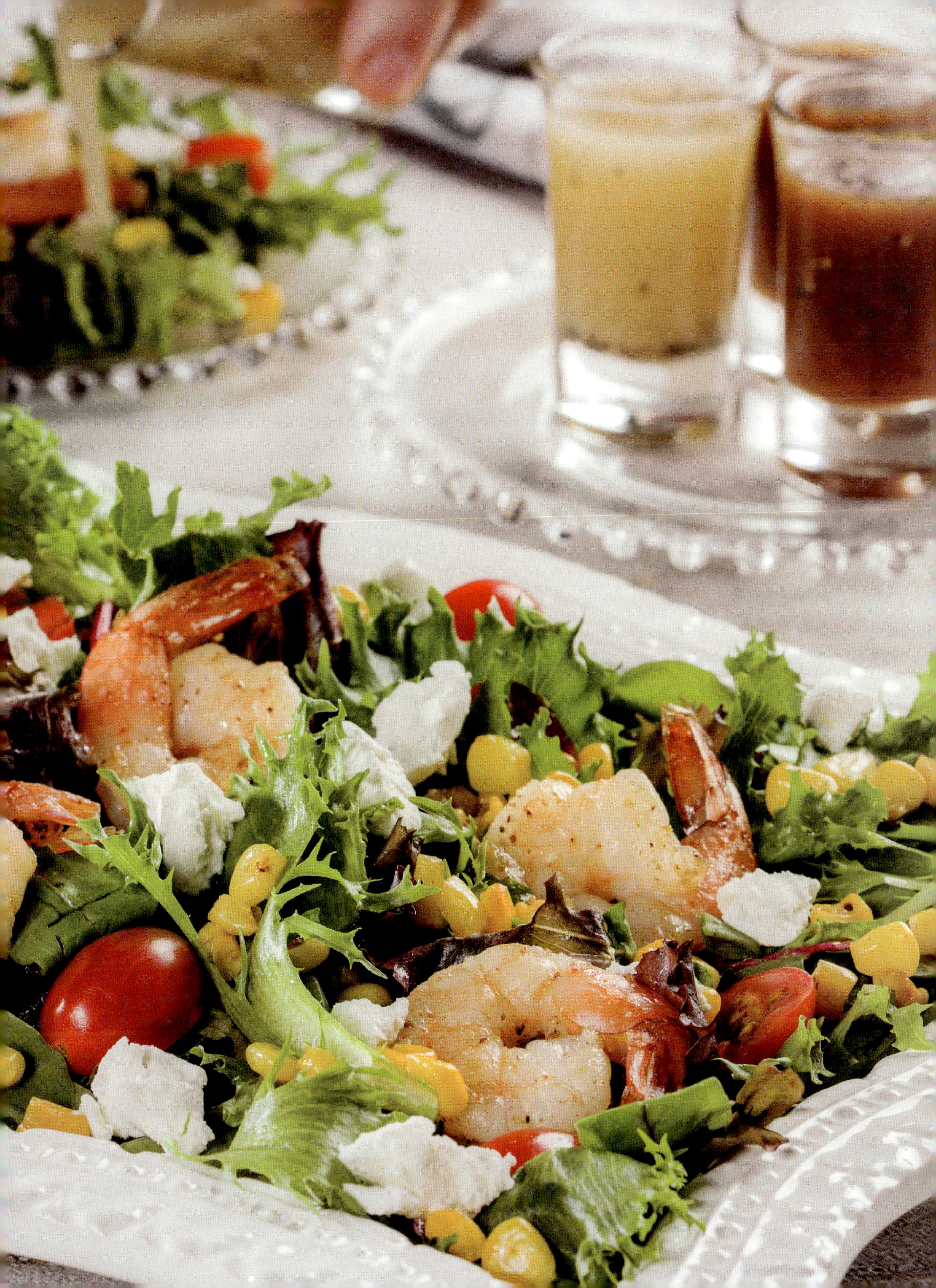

> "I'm a big fan of creative tablescapes. Not only do they make everything we eat look extra special, but they give your guests something to talk about too!"

CHICKEN & TURKEY

Cranberry-Herb Glazed Chicken 84

Spatchcocked Greek Chicken 86

Slow Cooker Italian Chicken 88

Crispy-Crunchy Fried Chicken 89

Really Classy Chicken 90

Soda Fountain Grilled Chicken 92

Quick & Hearty Spanish Paella 93

Two-in-One Stuffed Peppers 94

Honey Butter Chicken Tenders 96

Tex-Mex Chicken Burritos 97

Artichoke Dip Company Chicken 98

Maple-Pecan Chicken Breasts 100

Creamy Pesto Chicken Rolls 101

Chicken Caesar Salad Pizza 102

Cheesy Chicken Tortilla Bake 104

BBQ Chicken Party Ring 105

Semi-Homemade Chicken & Dumplings 106

Turkey Cordon Bleu 108

10-Minute Turkey Tacos 110

CRANBERRY-HERB GLAZED CHICKEN

I don't know about you, but I don't think cranberries get the recognition they deserve. Sure, a lot of people serve them on Thanksgiving, but how often do you enjoy these tart berries outside of the holiday? Hopefully, this flavor-packed recipe will get you excited about eating more cranberries. The mouthwatering glaze features a hint of citrus, plenty of fresh rosemary and garlic, and a balance of cranberry tartness with sugary sweetness.

Serves 4 to 5

1 tablespoon olive oil

1- to 1-½-pounds skin-on, bone-in chicken thighs

Salt for sprinkling

Black pepper for sprinkling

2 tablespoons butter

1-½ cups fresh or frozen cranberries

⅓ cup balsamic vinegar

2 tablespoons brown sugar

2 cloves garlic, minced

3 sprigs fresh rosemary

Zest of 1 orange

- Preheat oven to 350 degrees F.

- In a large skillet over medium-high heat, heat oil until hot. Evenly sprinkle both sides of chicken with salt and pepper. Place chicken in skillet and cook 2 to 3 minutes per side or until golden and skin is crispy. Place chicken in a 9- x 13-inch baking dish, skin-side up.

- In the same skillet over medium heat, melt butter. Add cranberries, vinegar, brown sugar, garlic, rosemary, and orange zest. Simmer 4 to 5 minutes or until mixture begins to thicken and cranberries start to soften. Pour mixture over chicken.

- Bake 50 to 55 minutes or until chicken is no longer pink in center.

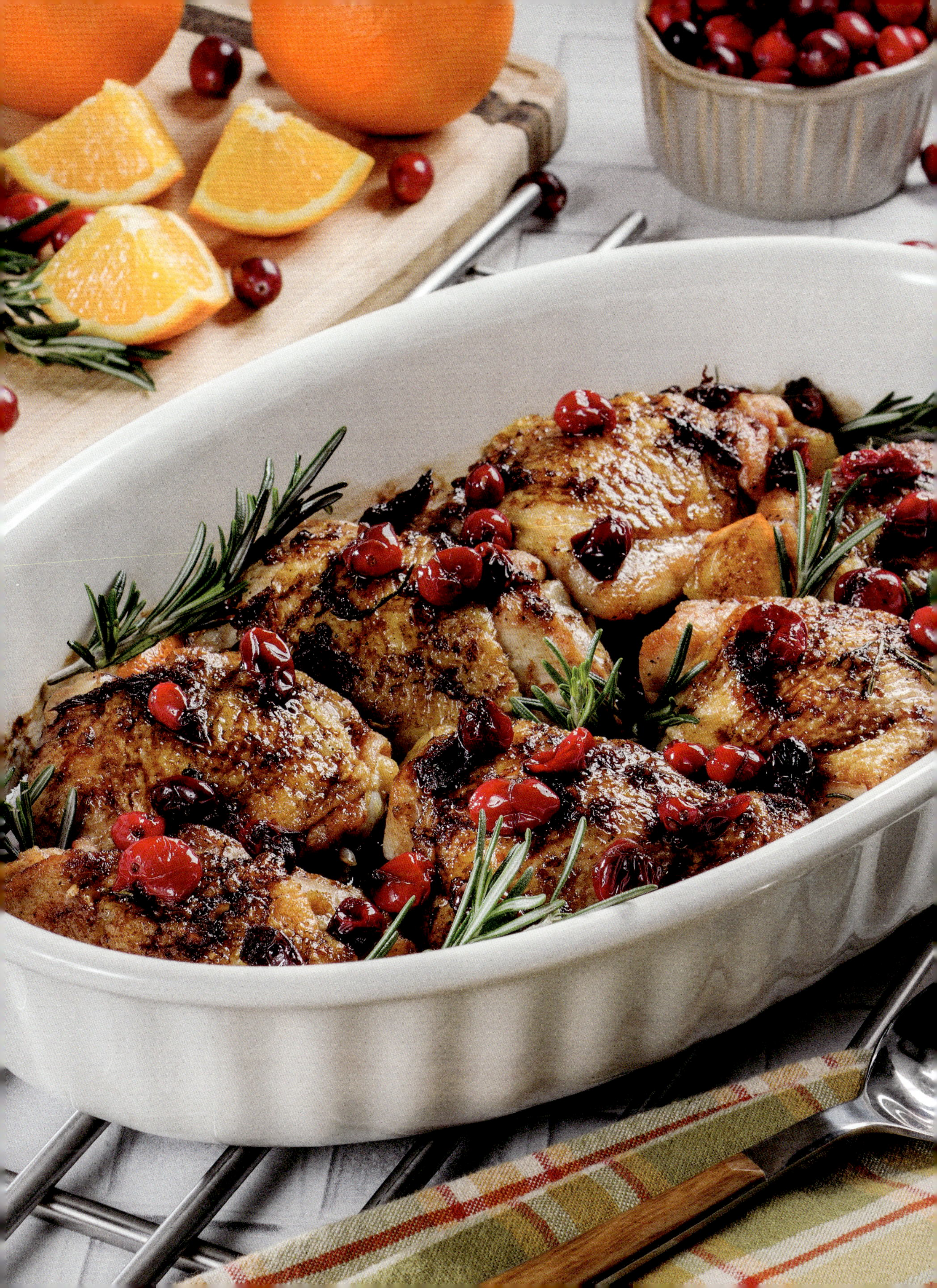

SPATCHCOCKED GREEK CHICKEN

Oh no, my chicken's been spatchcocked! Sounds dreadful, yet there's nothing to be alarmed about. When you spatchcock a chicken, all it means you're doing is cutting a whole chicken down the back bone, so that you can cook it flat (as shown). This helps the chicken cook faster and more evenly. It also results in more crispy skin, and some of the juiciest chicken you've ever tasted.

Serves 4 to 6

- 3 tablespoons olive oil
- ½ teaspoon garlic powder
- ½ teaspoon onion powder
- ¾ teaspoon salt
- ¼ teaspoon black pepper
- 2 sprigs fresh oregano, stems removed
- 1 (3-½- to 4-pound) whole chicken
- 1 lemon, cut in half
- 2 tablespoons sliced black olives
- ¼ cup crumbled feta cheese

- Preheat oven to 400 degrees F. Place a roasting rack on a rimmed baking sheet and coat with cooking spray.

- In a small bowl, combine oil, garlic and onion powders, salt, pepper, and oregano; mix well.

- Place chicken breast-side down on a cutting board. With a pair of poultry shears or a sharp knife, cut along both sides of the back bone, and remove the back bone. Flip chicken so that it's breast-side up, and press firmly down in chicken's center to crack the breast bone. (This will allow chicken to lay completely flat.) Transfer chicken, breast-side up, to a roasting rack.

- Brush half of oil mixture evenly over entire surface of chicken. Squeeze half of lemon over chicken. Place both halves of lemon on roasting rack.

- Roast chicken 40 minutes, then brush with remaining oil mixture and continue roasting 15 to 20 minutes or until no longer pink in center. Top with olives and feta cheese, and drizzle with juice from remaining roasted lemon half.

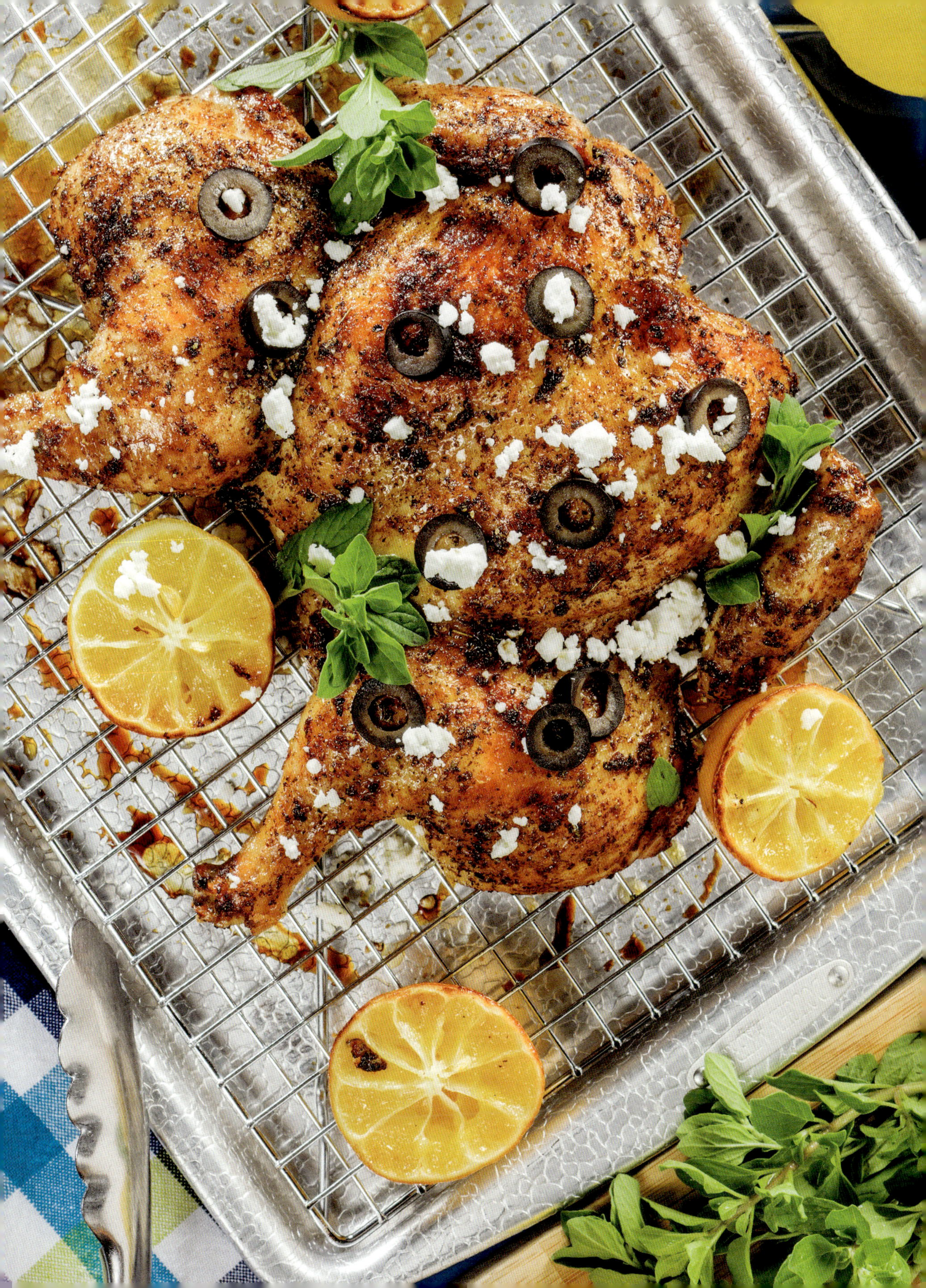

SLOW COOKER ITALIAN CHICKEN

My father was born in Italy, so naturally, I grew up eating a lot of, well, lets just say… everything Italian. It wasn't all just pasta and pizza. Sometimes, we ate Italian antipasto salads or big bowls of veggie-filled soups with crusty bread for dipping. Other times, we ate saucy dishes, just like this one. This Italian-style chicken is one my dad would've loved. I think of him and smile whenever I make it.

Serves 4 to 5

4 tablespoons olive oil, divided

1 (3-½-pound) chicken, cut into 8 pieces

1-½ cups sliced baby bella mushrooms

1 onion, diced

2 cloves garlic, minced

1 cup chicken broth

1 (6-ounce) can tomato paste

⅓ cup dry red wine

2 teaspoons sugar

1 teaspoon oregano

½ teaspoon salt

¼ teaspoon black pepper

2 tablespoons slivered fresh basil

- In a skillet over medium heat, heat 2 tablespoons oil until hot. Brown half the chicken pieces on each side 3 to 5 minutes, turning once. Remove, add remaining oil, and brown remaining chicken; set aside.

- Place mushrooms, onion, and garlic in a 6-quart or larger slow cooker and top with chicken pieces. In a bowl, combine broth, tomato paste, wine, sugar, oregano, salt, and pepper. Pour over chicken.

- Cover and cook on LOW 7 to 8 hours or on HIGH 3 to 4 hours, or until chicken is cooked through and no pink remains. Top with basil and serve.

If you're allergic to mushrooms (like I am) or if you just don't like them, go ahead and substitute with artichoke hearts instead. MCM

CRISPY-CRUNCHY FRIED CHICKEN

If you're not getting a loud crunch every time you bite into your fried chicken, then it's time to retire that recipe and give this one a try. My fried chicken is extra crispy on the outside, yet juicy and tender on the inside. It's the kind of dish that keeps people hushed around the dinner table. They'll be so busy enjoying their chicken, they don't have time to talk!

Serve 4 to 5

1 (3-½ to 4-pound) chicken, cut into 8 pieces

2 cups self-rising flour

2 teaspoons garlic powder

1 teaspoon paprika

2 teaspoons salt

1 teaspoon black pepper

3 eggs

1 tablespoon hot sauce

2 tablespoons water

2 cups vegetable oil

- Place chicken in a large bowl of ice water; let sit 30 minutes. (This will make your chicken nice and crispy after it's cooked.)

- In another large bowl, combine flour, garlic powder, paprika, salt, and pepper; mix well. In a third large bowl, mix eggs, hot sauce, and water. Remove chicken from ice water, shaking off any excess water. Dip in flour mixture, then in egg mixture, then back in flour mixture, coating completely each time.

- In a large deep skillet over medium-low heat, heat oil until hot, but not smoking. Fry chicken in batches, 10 to 12 minutes per side, or until golden and no pink remains. Drain on a paper towel-lined platter. Serve immediately.

There's nothing like fried chicken straight out of the skillet, but if you want to make this ahead of time, you definitely can. Just reheat your chicken on a rimmed baking sheet right before it's time to eat, for about 20 to 30 minutes in a 325 degree oven. Then it's ready to "DEEG-IN!". MCM

CHICKEN & TURKEY

REALLY CLASSY CHICKEN

I love to make this whenever I get the "mid-week blahs." You know what I'm talking about, right? It's that feeling you get when you're kind of bored with everything you've been eating and you're craving something new and exciting. This chicken dish always brightens my day. The combination of flavors might sound a bit odd, but they totally work together. Plus, it's "classy" enough to serve to company too!

Serves 4 to 5

¼ cup light brown sugar

¼ cup dried apricots, cut into strips

¼ cup red wine vinegar

⅓ cup olive oil

2 tablespoons capers, drained

2 tablespoons dried oregano

1 tablespoon chopped fresh parsley

1 tablespoon chopped garlic

1 teaspoon salt

½ teaspoon black pepper

1 (3- to 3-½-pound) chicken, cut into 8 pieces

- In a large resealable plastic bag, combine all ingredients except chicken; mix well.
- Add chicken to bag, seal, and let marinate in refrigerator at least 4 hours or overnight, turning bag over occasionally.
- Preheat oven to 350 degrees F. Place chicken, skin side up, and marinade in a 9- x 13-inch baking dish.
- Roast uncovered 55 to 60 minutes or until no pink remains, basting occasionally with pan juices. Serve topped with roasted apricots and flavor-packed pan juices.

I love how a dish comes to life whenever you add a splash of vinegar or citrus to it. Although this recipe calls for red wine vinegar, you can have some fun experimenting with other types of vinegar, like apple cider or rice vinegar. MCM

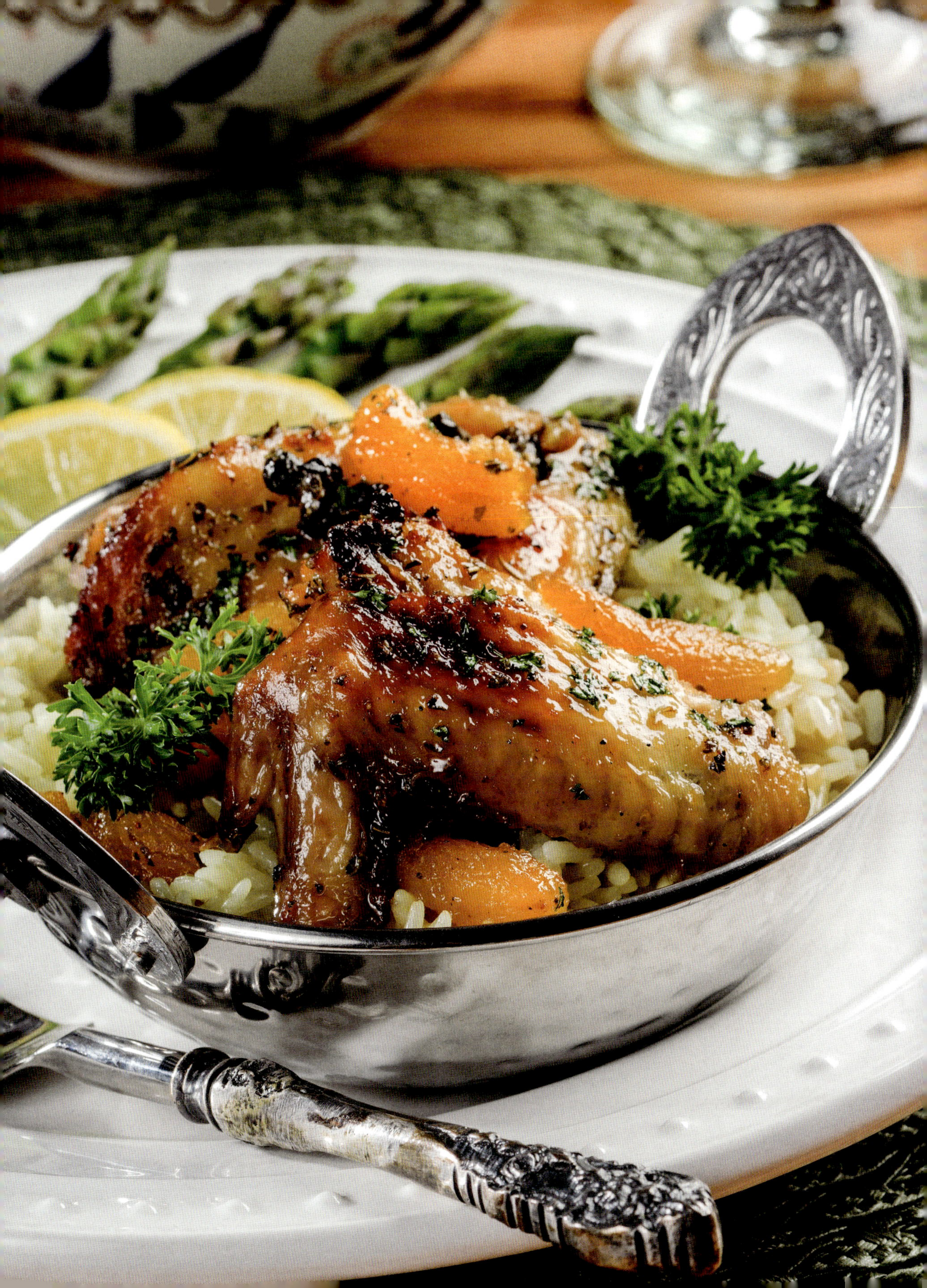

SODA FOUNTAIN GRILLED CHICKEN

This chicken dish is inspired by the soda fountains of the 50s. I don't know about you, but one of the first things that come to mind when I think of an old-time soda fountain is a root beer float. It's the retro blend between ice cream and a thirst quencher. Here, rather than pairing root beer with ice cream and a cherry, I've combined it with ketchup, Worcestershire, sugar, and some spices creating a sauce that will knock your socks off. It's fantastic!

Serves 4 to 5

- 1 (3-½- to 4-pound) chicken, cut into 8 pieces
- ¼ teaspoon salt
- ¼ teaspoon black pepper
- 1 cup root beer
- 1 cup ketchup
- ¼ cup fresh lemon juice
- 3 tablespoons Worcestershire sauce
- 3 tablespoons light brown sugar
- ½ teaspoon ground ginger
- ½ teaspoon onion powder
- ½ teaspoon garlic powder

■ Preheat oven to 350 degrees F. Coat a 9- x 13-inch baking dish with cooking spray. Place chicken pieces in baking dish; season with salt and pepper.

■ Roast 45 to 50 minutes or until no pink remains in chicken and juices run clear.

■ In a medium saucepan, combine remaining ingredients; mix well and bring to a boil over medium heat, stirring occasionally. Reduce heat to medium-low and simmer 20 minutes or until sauce is reduced by half. (Be patient—as it thickens, the flavors will intensify.)

■ Preheat grill to medium heat. Brush chicken with sauce and grill 5 minutes per side, basting frequently with sauce. Serve remaining sauce with chicken.

Good news -- you can make this recipe even if you don't have an outdoor grill! After roasting the chicken, rather than finishing it on the grill, you can pull out the electric indoor grill and cook it on that or pop it back into the oven and continue to roast it until the sauce begins to caramelize. MCM

QUICK & HEARTY SPANISH PAELLA

I've been very fortunate to have traveled to Spain, where the people are as wonderful as the food is amazing. One of my favorite dishes is called "paella." It's a big rice dish that's full of chicken, sausage, seafood, and veggies. Traditionally, it takes a while to prepare, but I've come up with a simple and quick version that delivers a whole lot of flavor in just half the time. I can't wait to hear what you think of it!

Serve 5 to 6

- 1 (10-ounce) package yellow rice
- 1 tablespoon olive oil
- 1 pound boneless, skinless chicken thighs, cut into 1-inch chunks
- ½ pound chorizo sausage, cut into ¼-inch slices
- 1 cup chicken broth
- 1 red bell pepper, cut into ½-inch chunks
- 1 green bell pepper, cut into ½-inch chunks
- ½ cup chopped onion
- 2 cups frozen peas
- 1 pound frozen shrimp, peeled and deveined, thawed
- 1 teaspoon paprika
- 1 teaspoon kosher salt

- Cook rice according to package directions; set aside
- In a large skillet over medium-high heat, heat oil until hot. Add chicken and sausage; cook 5 to 7 minutes or until browned. Transfer to a plate and set aside.
- In the same skillet, add broth; bring to a simmer. Add bell pepper, onion, and peas. Cook 4 to 6 minutes or until heated through, stirring occasionally. Add shrimp; cook 2 to 4 minutes or until pink. Stir in paprika, salt, and cooked rice. Return chicken and sausage to skillet, reduce heat to medium, and cook until heated through. Serve immediately.

I like serving this with a glass (or two) of sangria to complete the Spanish dining experience. MCM

TWO-IN-ONE STUFFED PEPPERS

Just when you think you've had every version of chicken parmigiana and every version of stuffed peppers ... you come across a perfect mash-up of the two. This dish is going to surprise you, in a good way. Not only is it super easy (thanks to a supermarket shortcut!), but it's so flavorful and cheesy. If you regularly make stuffed peppers for your family, this is another tasty option to serve them.

Serves 6

- 6 bell peppers, any color
- 4 frozen breaded chicken tenders, heated according to package directions, and diced
- 1 cup cooked orzo
- 2 tablespoons grated Parmesan cheese
- 1-¾ cups spaghetti sauce, divided
- 2 cups shredded mozzarella cheese, divided
- 1 tablespoon chopped fresh basil
- 1 teaspoon garlic powder
- ¼ teaspoon salt
- ¼ cup water

- Preheat oven to 375 degrees F. Wash and cut stem end off peppers, then core, removing all seeds.

- In a large bowl, combine chicken, orzo, Parmesan cheese, ¾ cup spaghetti sauce, 1 cup mozzarella cheese, the basil, garlic powder, and salt; mix well. Evenly fill each pepper with chicken mixture.

- Place ½ cup spaghetti sauce and water into baking dish. Place peppers on top of sauce, then spoon remaining ½ cup sauce over peppers; cover with aluminum foil.

- Bake 45 minutes, uncover, and sprinkle evenly with remaining 1 cup mozzarella cheese. Bake 5 more minutes or until pepper is fork-tender and cheese is melted.

If your peppers are really huge or kind of small, you may need to make more or less than the 6 I suggest. You want to make sure they're filled almost to the top. If your peppers are really huge, as they often are in the middle of the summer, rather than cutting the tops off, you can cut each one in half, starting at the stem end. That way, you'll only need three peppers to feed a crowd. MCM

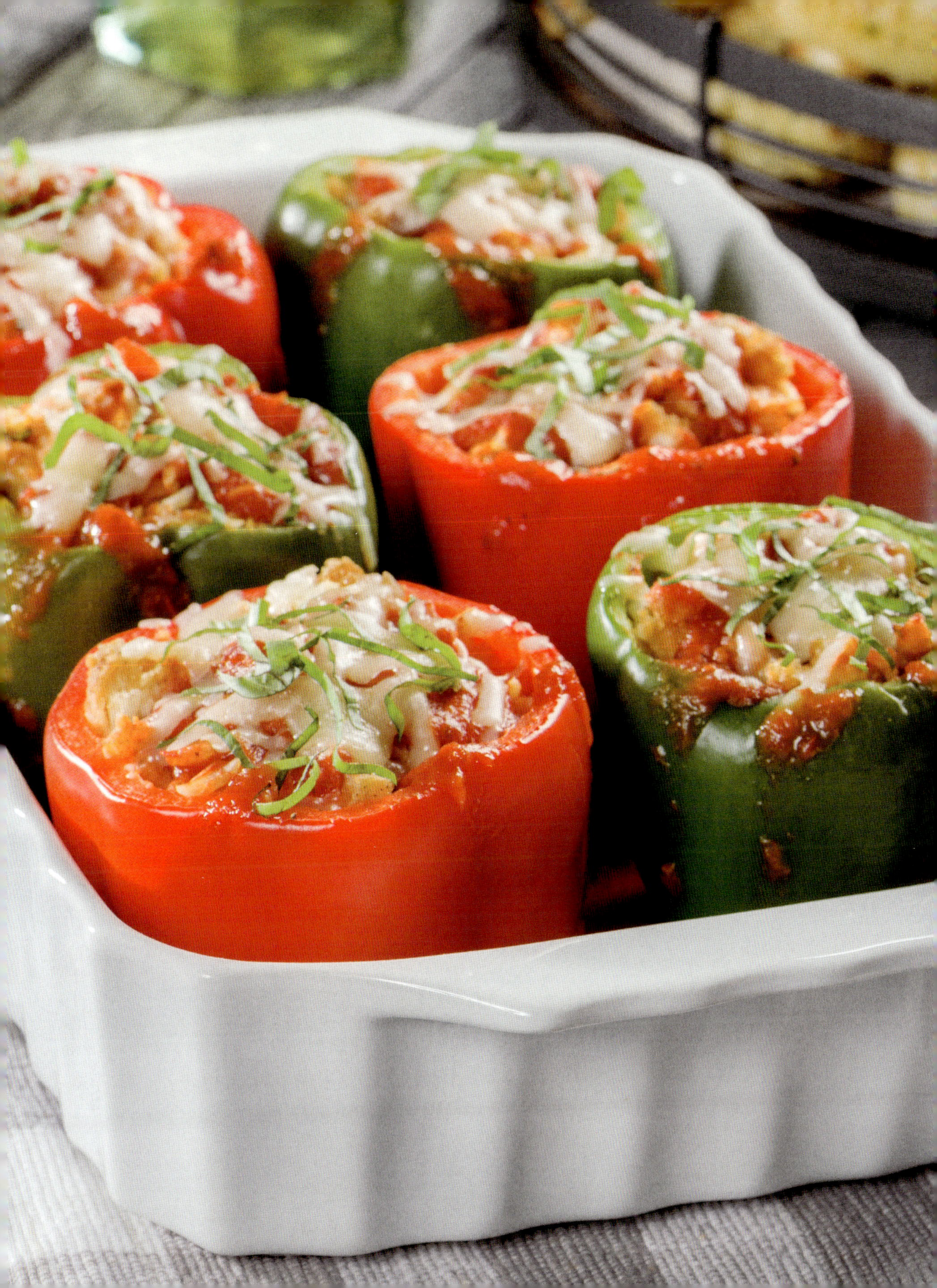

HONEY BUTTER CHICKEN TENDERS

This was one of the first recipes I made in my air fryer when I first brought it home. I wanted to test whether a traditionally fried recipe would have the same tasty results when cooked in an air fryer. The answer is yes! These chicken tenders have a wonderful crispy coating and are moist all the way through. The quick, homemade honey butter just makes them all the better.

Serves 4 to 5

3 cups corn flakes, finely crushed

2 tablespoons sugar

1 teaspoon salt

½ teaspoon ground cinnamon

½ cup milk

1 egg

1 teaspoon hot sauce

1-½ pounds chicken tenders

Cooking spray

½ cup honey

1 tablespoon butter

- In a shallow dish, combine corn flakes, sugar, salt, and cinnamon; mix well. In another shallow dish, combine milk, egg, and hot sauce; mix well.

- Dip chicken tenders into milk mixture, then roll in cereal mixture, coating completely.

- Preheat air fryer to 360 degrees F. Evenly spray air fryer basket with cooking spray. Place tenders into air fryer basket; spray lightly with cooking spray. Working in batches if necessary, air-fry 5 to 6 minutes. Turn over, spray lightly with cooking spray, and continue to cook 5 to 6 more minutes or until chicken is no longer pink in center.

- Meanwhile, in a small microwave-safe bowl, combine honey and butter; microwave 1 minute or until butter is melted and honey is warm. Serve as a dipping sauce or drizzle over chicken.

I love using honey as a natural way to sweeten things up. There are lots of different types of honey and each has its own unique flavor, so rather than sticking to your usual clover honey, why not experiment with something new? MCM

TEX-MEX CHICKEN BURRITOS

I love Mexican food so much, I typically eat it at least once a week. While I don't think I'll be giving up my favorite taco spot anytime soon, I do make an effort to make some of my favorites at home, from time to time. These burritos are easy to throw together and are great to have on hand for lunch or a quick dinner. They're loaded with all the delicious fixins' of a burrito, so you know you're going to end up feeling full and satisfied.

Serves 3

- 1 cup water
- 2 tablespoons lime juice
- 1 cup instant rice
- 2 tablespoons chopped fresh cilantro
- 1 (15-ounce) can black beans, rinsed and drained
- 2 cups diced rotisserie or pre-cooked chicken
- 1 teaspoon ground cumin
- 3 (10-inch) flour tortillas
- ½ cup salsa
- ¾ cup corn
- ½ cup shredded Colby-Jack cheese

- Preheat oven to 400 degrees F. Cut 3 (12- x 12-inch) pieces of aluminum foil.

- In a small saucepan over high heat, combine water, lime juice, and rice; bring to a boil, cover, remove from heat, and let sit 5 minutes or until water is absorbed and rice is fluffy. Stir in cilantro and black beans.

- In a medium bowl, combine chicken and cumin; mix well. Spoon rice mixture evenly down center of each tortilla. Top with chicken, salsa, corn, and cheese. Fold bottom of tortilla over mixture. Fold left side in, then right side, and roll up forming a cylinder shape. Place burritos seam-side down on foil and roll up. Place on a rimmed baking sheet.

- Bake 5 to 7 minutes or until warmed through.

If you don't want to serve these right away, keep them in the fridge for a couple of days until you're craving them. Then just bake them in a 350 degree oven for about 20 minutes or until the filling is hot. These take a little longer to reheat than when you first make them because you're starting with cold filling. MCM

ARTICHOKE DIP COMPANY CHICKEN

You've got company coming over and I've got the perfect dish for you to make. Oh yeah, you're going to impress everyone with a chicken dinner that only requires six ingredients and 30 minutes of your time, but they don't have to know that! This creamy chicken looks like something you'd order from a 5-star restaurant. I like to pair it with some blistered tomatoes, couscous, and a bright green veggie to complete the meal.

Serves 4

- 1 (14-ounce) can artichoke hearts in water, drained and chopped
- ¾ cup mayonnaise
- ½ cup grated Parmesan cheese
- 1 teaspoon garlic powder
- ½ teaspoon paprika
- 4 boneless, skinless chicken breasts, pounded slightly

- Preheat oven to 375 degrees F. Coat a 9- x 13-inch baking dish with cooking spray.
- In a medium bowl, combine artichokes, mayonnaise, Parmesan cheese, garlic powder, and paprika. Place chicken in baking dish and spread artichoke mixture over top.
- Bake 25 to 30 minutes or until no pink remains in chicken and juices run clear.

This is one recipe where I think it really makes a difference whether you use freshly grated Parmesan cheese versus the stuff you get in the can. The fresh Parmesan just adds a richer taste, which makes it all the more company-perfect. MCM

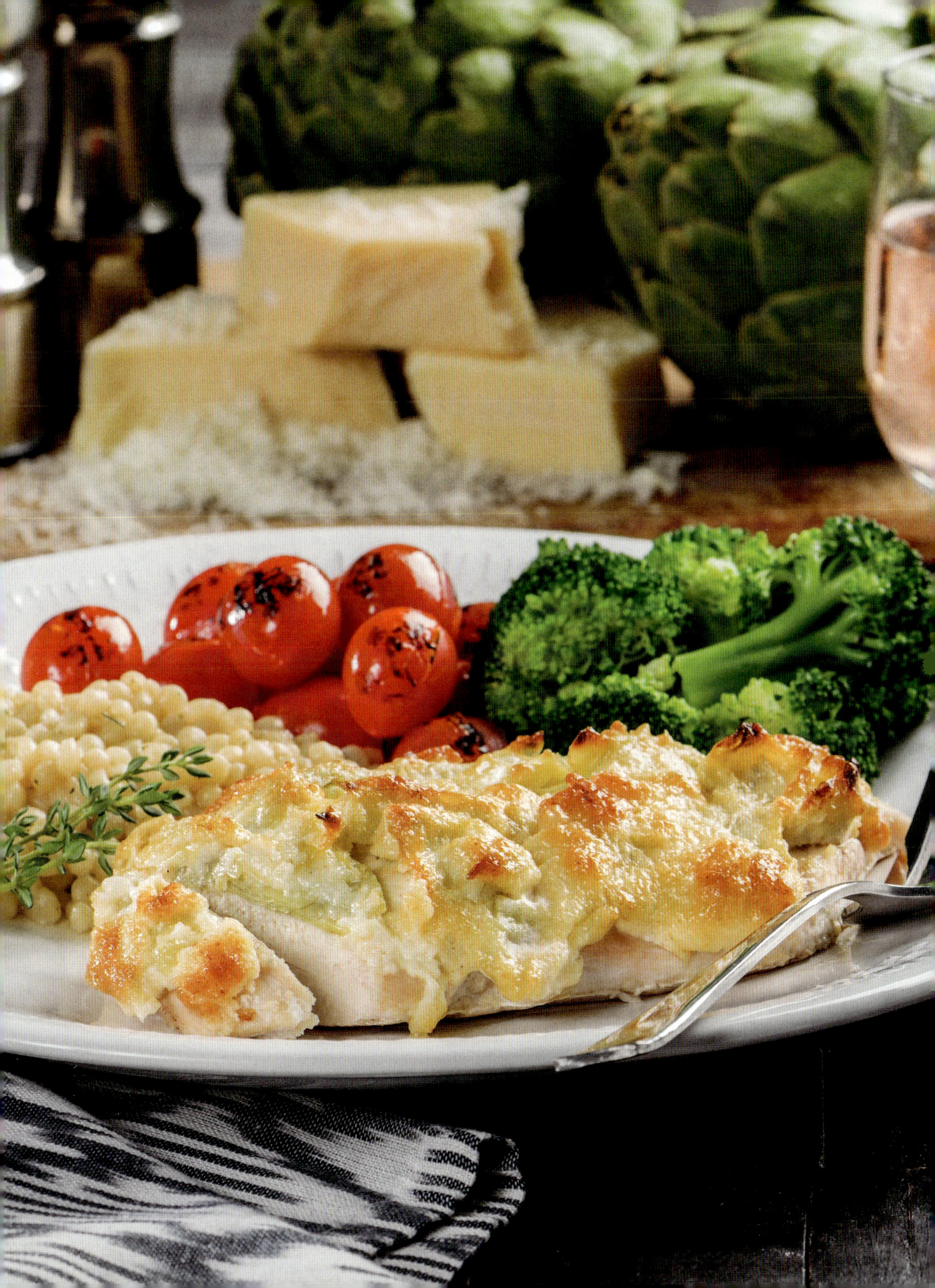

MAPLE-PECAN CHICKEN BREASTS

I think it's time for you to "fall" in love with a new recipe! Here, I paired two classic autumn flavors (maple syrup and pecans) to come up with a chicken dish that's a little unusual, but 100% tasty. (Seriously, don't knock it until you try it!) There's a little kick from the cayenne, a buttery crunch from the pecans and the bread crumbs, and an oomph from the syrupy bourbon mayo.

Serves 4

- 1/3 cup maple syrup
- 2 tablespoons mayonnaise
- 1 tablespoon bourbon (optional)
- 3/4 cup panko bread crumbs
- 1/2 cup finely chopped pecans
- 1 tablespoon sugar
- 1/8 teaspoon cayenne pepper
- 4 boneless, skinless chicken breasts
- 1/2 teaspoon salt
- Cooking spray

- Preheat oven to 375 degrees F. Coat a 9- x 13-inch baking sheet with cooking spray.

- In a shallow dish, combine syrup, mayonnaise, and bourbon, if desired; mix well. In another shallow dish, combine bread crumbs, pecans, sugar, and cayenne pepper; mix well.

- Lightly sprinkle chicken with salt and dip into syrup mixture; then place in pecan mixture, pressing coating onto chicken until coated completely. Place on baking sheet and lightly spray coating with cooking spray. (This will help coating crisp up while it cooks.)

- Roast 18 to 20 minutes or until coating is golden and chicken is no longer pink in center.

You don't have to use the bourbon, but it does add another dimension of flavor. And if you don't have bourbon at home, many liquor stores sell the miniature bottles (like the ones sold by airlines), which is all you'll need. MCM

CREAMY PESTO CHICKEN ROLLS

If you follow me on social media or watch me on QVC, then you know I like to go all out when I entertain. I love setting a nice table and making sure that everything is perfect. These chicken rolls are a great way for me to show off my presentation skills. When they're rolled up just right, each one contains a creamy pesto surprise. Add some greens to the plate and maybe a bright veggie or two to make this meal really stand out.

Serves 4

- 4 boneless, skinless chicken breasts, pounded to ½-inch thickness
- ½ teaspoon salt
- ½ teaspoon black pepper
- 3 ounces cream cheese, softened
- ¼ cup prepared pesto sauce
- ½ cup chopped roasted red peppers, drained
- ¾ cup crushed corn flakes
- 3 tablespoons grated Parmesan cheese
- ½ teaspoon paprika

- Preheat oven to 400 degrees F. Coat a 9- x 13-inch baking dish with cooking spray.
- Sprinkle chicken evenly with salt and pepper.
- In a medium bowl, combine cream cheese, pesto, and red peppers; mix well. Spread cheese mixture over chicken, roll up jellyroll-style, and secure with wooden toothpicks.
- In a shallow dish, combine corn flakes, Parmesan cheese, and paprika. Place chicken rolls in corn flake mixture, coating completely, and place seam-side down in baking dish.
- Roast 25 to 30 minutes or until no pink remains and juices run clear. Remove toothpicks and serve.

Before you start pounding at the chicken, I suggest covering it with some plastic wrap. This will help you keep your kitchen clean (rather than having it splattered with raw chicken juice). MCM

CHICKEN CAESAR SALAD PIZZA

If you thought my recipe for Two-in-One Stuffed Peppers (page 94) was the only mash-up recipe I was going to share, you're in for a surprise. Here's another one that helps me satisfy my cravings for pizza and salad in a whole new way. I love the idea of getting to eat salad with my hands! If you already love a classic chicken Caesar salad, you're going to love this one too.

Serves 3 to 4

1 boneless, skinless chicken breast, pounded to ¼-ich thickness

¼ teaspoon salt

1 tablespoon olive oil

1 (13.8-ounce) can refrigerated pizza crust dough

¼ cup plus 2 tablespoons Caesar dressing, divided

1 cup shredded mozzarella cheese

2 cups shredded romaine lettuce

2 tablespoons shaved Parmesan cheese

Coarse black pepper for sprinkling

- Preheat oven to 425 degrees F. Coat a 10- x 15- inch baking sheet with cooking spray.

- Sprinkle chicken evenly with salt. In a large skillet over medium-high heat, heat oil until hot. Cook chicken 3 to 4 minutes per side or until no longer pink in center. Cut chicken across the grain into thin slices.

- Unroll pizza dough on baking sheet; using your fingers, press dough to edges of baking sheet. Bake 8 minutes.

- Remove dough from oven and spread ¼ cup Caesar dressing evenly over top. Top evenly with mozzarella. Bake 8 to 10 minutes or until crust is light golden.

- Meanwhile, in a medium bowl, toss lettuce with remaining 2 tablespoons Caesar dressing. Top pizza evenly with lettuce, chicken, and Parmesan cheese, sprinkle with black pepper, cut into 8 slices, and serve.

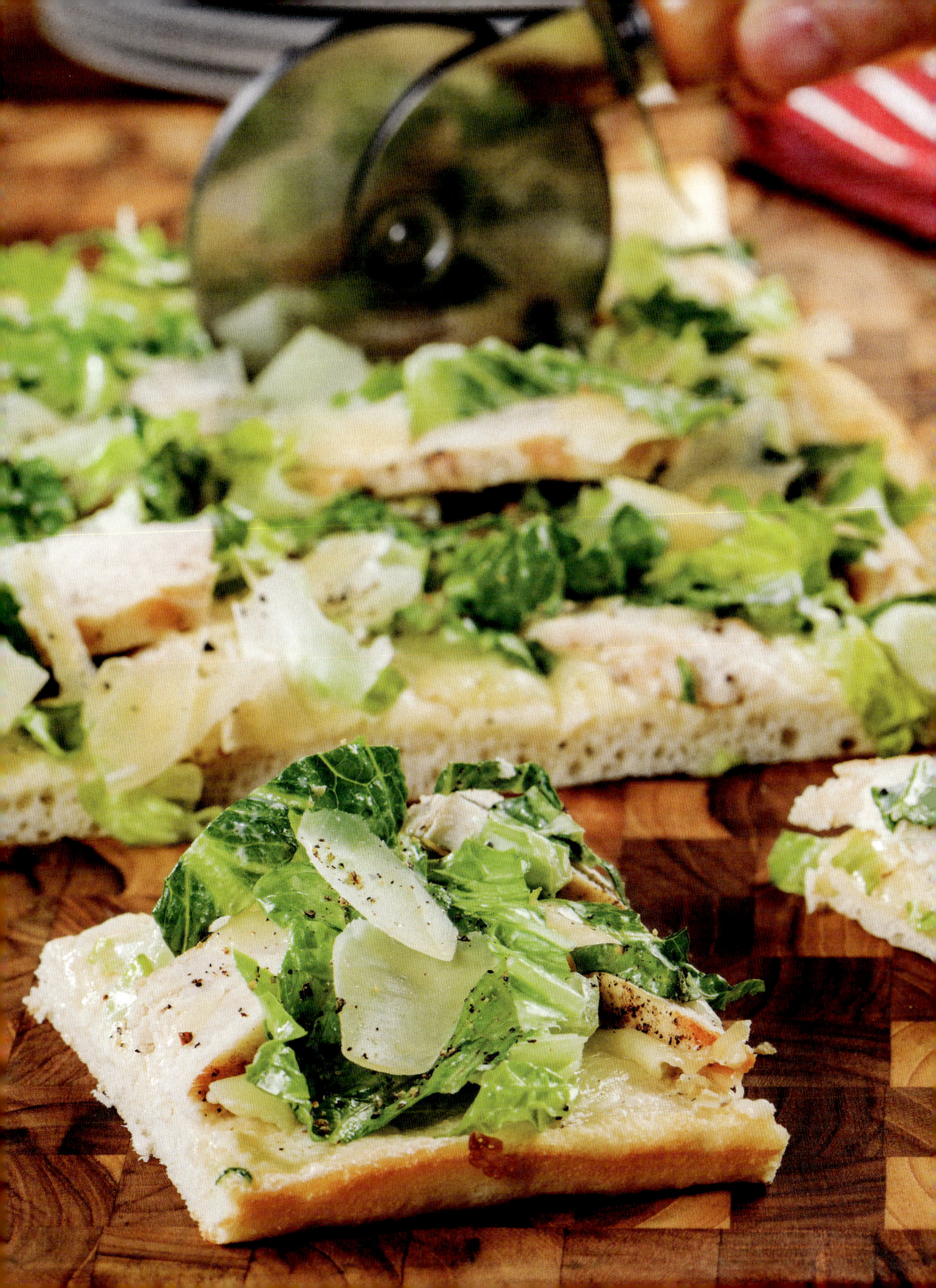

CHEESY CHICKEN TORTILLA BAKE

It's hard to go wrong with a good ol' comforting casserole. They're great for busy weeknights and for feeding big families on a budget. This one is done Mexican-style and features plenty of chicken, cheese, tortilla strips, and corn in a creamy mixture. Every bite is full of creamy, cheesy goodness. The whole family is going to enjoy digging in!

Serves 4 to 6

1 (14.5-ounce) can diced tomatoes, undrained

1 (10-½-ounce) can cream of chicken soup

1 cup frozen corn, thawed

1 (2.25-ounce) can sliced black olives, drained

2 teaspoons ground cumin

2 teaspoons chili powder

½ teaspoon salt

12 corn tortillas, cut into ½-inch strips

4 cups shredded cooked chicken

1 cup sliced scallions

2 cups (8 ounces) shredded Mexican cheese blend

- Preheat oven to 350 degrees F. Coat a 9- x 13-inch baking dish with cooking spray.

- In a large bowl, combine tomatoes, soup, corn, black olives, cumin, chili powder, and salt.

- Line bottom of baking dish with half the tortilla strips. Sprinkle half the chicken over the tortilla strips. Top with half the soup mixture, half the scallions, and half the cheese. Repeat layers (it's kind of like making a lasagna!).

- Bake 30 to 35 minutes or until bubbly and hot.

Save yourself even more time by buying a supermarket rotisserie chicken and pulling the meat off of it. It's one of my favorite supermarket shortcuts! MCM

BBQ CHICKEN PARTY RING

I love bread, so anything stuffed in bread is definitely a favorite too. While I usually make single-serve items like empanadas, meat pies, and calzones, I wanted to try my hand at a family-style recipe that's all wrapped up. I'll admit I'm pleased with the results! This is a great tear-and-share recipe that's good for family dinner night and game night with friends.

Serves 4 to 6

- ¾ cup frozen corn, thawed
- ¾ cup barbecue sauce
- ½ cup chopped red onion
- 2 cups shredded cooked chicken
- 1 cup shredded cheddar cheese
- 2 (8-ounce) cans refrigerated crescent rolls

- Preheat oven to 375 degrees F.
- In a large skillet over medium heat, heat corn, barbecue sauce, and onion 3 minutes; stir in chicken and cheese and heat an additional 1 to 2 minutes or until hot.
- Unroll and separate crescent rolls into triangles. On an ungreased large baking sheet or pizza pan, arrange triangles in a ring so short sides of triangles form a 5-inch circle in center. (The dough will overlap and the dough ring should look like a sun.) Spoon chicken mixture in center of each triangle. Bring points of triangles over chicken mixture, tucking ends under in the center.
- Bake 20 to 22 minutes or until golden brown. Let cool 5 minutes before cutting into 12 pieces.

Since you know I'm always encouraging you to add your own personal touch to these recipes, feel free to use a Mexican cheese blend rather than cheddar, toss in some sliced jalapenos to give it a kick, or swap out the red onions with scallions. It's your masterpiece!

MCM

CHICKEN & TURKEY

SEMI-HOMEMADE CHICKEN & DUMPLINGS

This isn't your grandma's half-day-in-the-kitchen-making-chicken-and-dumplings recipe. This is your quick, to the point, get-that-deliciousness-in-my-mouth-right-now version. It's so easy, I don't even wait around till it's cold out to eat it. I make it any time I'm craving a soul-soothing dish. All you need are some basic supermarket shortcuts. Before you know it, you'll be settling in to a bowl of comfort too.

Serves 4 to 6

1 (12-ounce) package frozen mixed vegetables

2 cups diced cooked chicken

2 (12-ounce) jars chicken gravy

1 teaspoon onion powder

½ teaspoon thyme leaf

½ teaspoon black pepper

1 (16.3-ounce) can refrigerated buttermilk biscuits (8 biscuits)

- In a large bowl, combine all ingredients except biscuits. Pour into a deep skillet and over medium heat, cook 3 to 5 minutes or until heated through.

- Top with biscuits, cover, and cook on medium heat 18 to 20 minutes or until hot and bubbly and biscuits are steamed.

So you know, the biscuit dumplings in this recipe are steamed, rather than crusty, like some other chicken and biscuit recipes. MCM

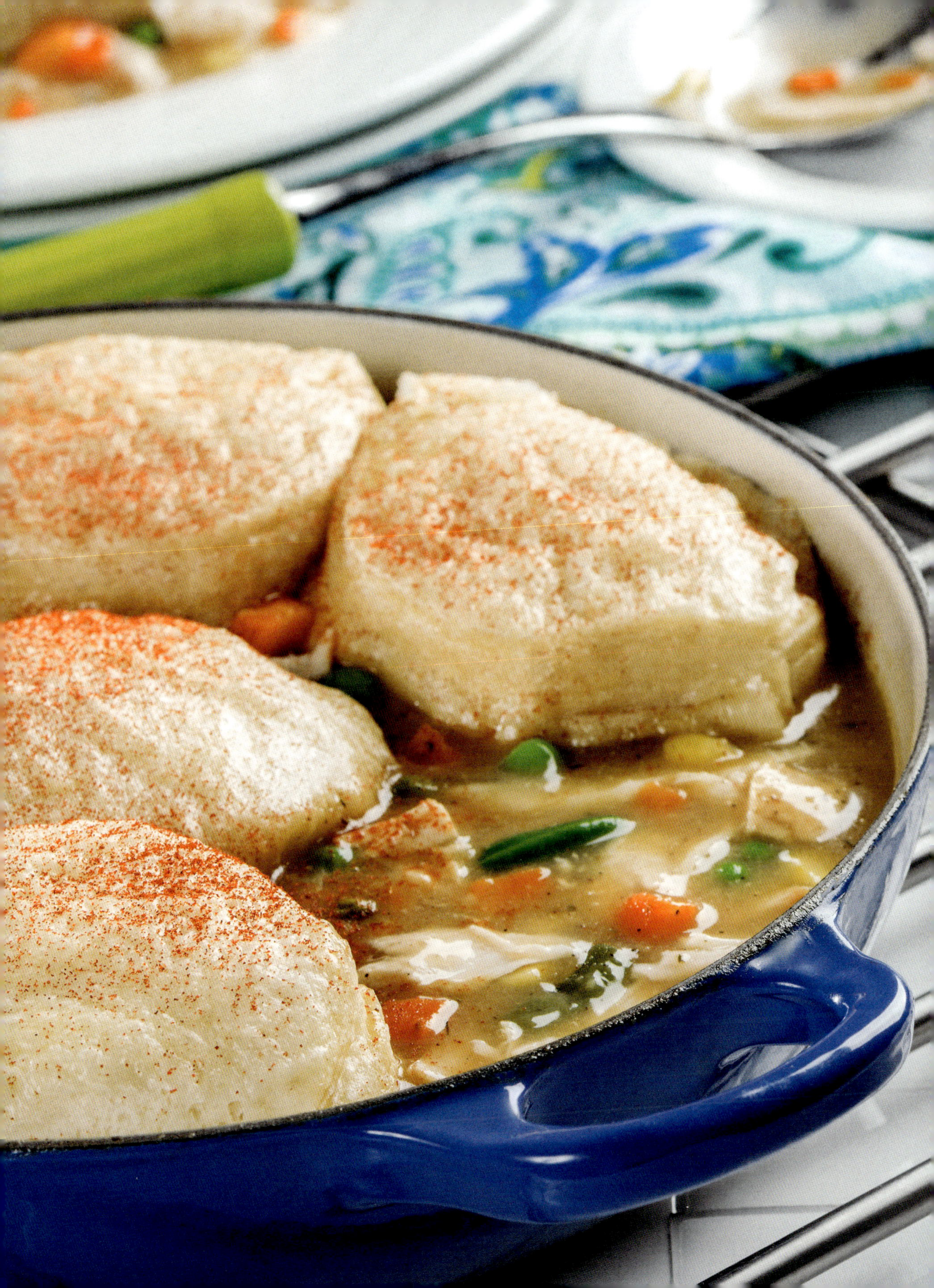

TURKEY CORDON BLEU

I don't know why more people aren't using turkey to make their cordon bleu. Turkey cutlets are a tasty alternative that are just as great when rolled up with ham and cheese. The spaghetti sauce on the side is a nod to my Italian heritage. (We love a good spaghetti sauce with just about anything!) Get your dip on and enjoy!

Serves 4

- 4 boneless, skinless turkey cutlets, pounded to ¼-inch thickness (1-½ to 2 pounds total)
- ½ teaspoon salt
- ¼ teaspoon black pepper
- ¼ pound deli ham, thinly sliced
- ¼ pound provolone cheese, thinly sliced
- ¼ teaspoon garlic powder
- 1 tablespoon olive oil
- 1 (24-ounce) jar spaghetti sauce, warmed

- ■ Preheat oven to 350 degrees F. Coat a rimmed baking sheet with cooking spray.

- ■ Sprinkle turkey cutlets evenly with salt and pepper. Top each cutlet with even amounts of ham, provolone, and garlic powder. Roll up jellyroll-style and secure with wooden toothpicks.

- ■ In a large skillet over medium-high heat, heat oil. Add rollups to skillet and brown on all sides. Place on baking sheet, seam-side down. Roast 10 to 15 minutes or until turkey is no longer pink in center.

- ■ Right before serving, remove toothpicks, cut into slices, and serve with spaghetti sauce.

Adding a garnish of fresh basil gives your chicken a fancier look and adds an extra touch of flavor. If you're not growing some fresh herbs on your window sill or in your garden, what are you waiting for? It's really easy and worth the kitchen rewards! MCM

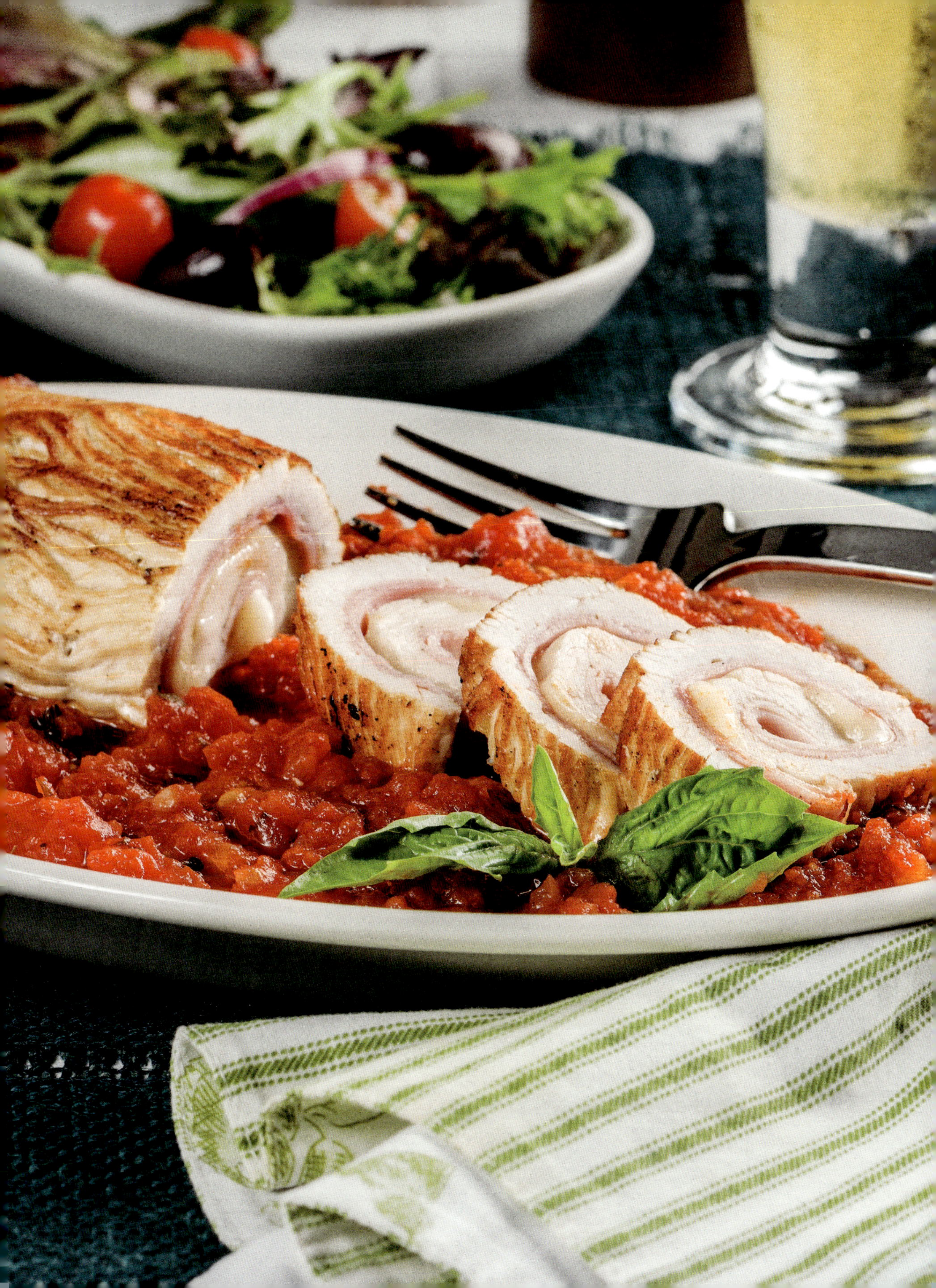

10-MINUTE TURKEY TACOS

Whip up some tacos worthy of a Taco Tuesday celebration with this super-quick recipe. This recipe will cure your cravings without cutting into your nightly relaxation time or weekly grocery budget. You can let everyone build their own tacos by setting out the meat and all the toppings in bowls. That way, everyone's cravings are satisfied just as they see fit.

Serves 4

- 1 tablespoon vegetable oil
- 1 pound ground turkey
- 1 (1-ounce) package taco seasoning mix
- ½ cup water
- 1 cup black beans, rinsed and drained
- 8 (6-inch) flour tortillas
- 1 cup shredded lettuce
- 1 cup salsa
- 1 cup shredded cheddar cheese
- ½ cup sour cream

- In a large skillet over medium heat, heat oil until hot. Sauté turkey 5 to 7 minutes or until browned, stirring occasionally to break apart. Stir in taco seasoning mix, water, and black beans, and heat until hot.

- Top flour tortillas with turkey mixture. Serve with bowls of lettuce, salsa, cheese, and sour cream so everyone can make their own.

When you're looking in the meat case, you'll find both fresh ground turkey and fresh ground turkey breast. The turkey breast is leaner and not as moist, but healthier. Try both and see which one you like better! MCM

CHICKEN & TURKEY

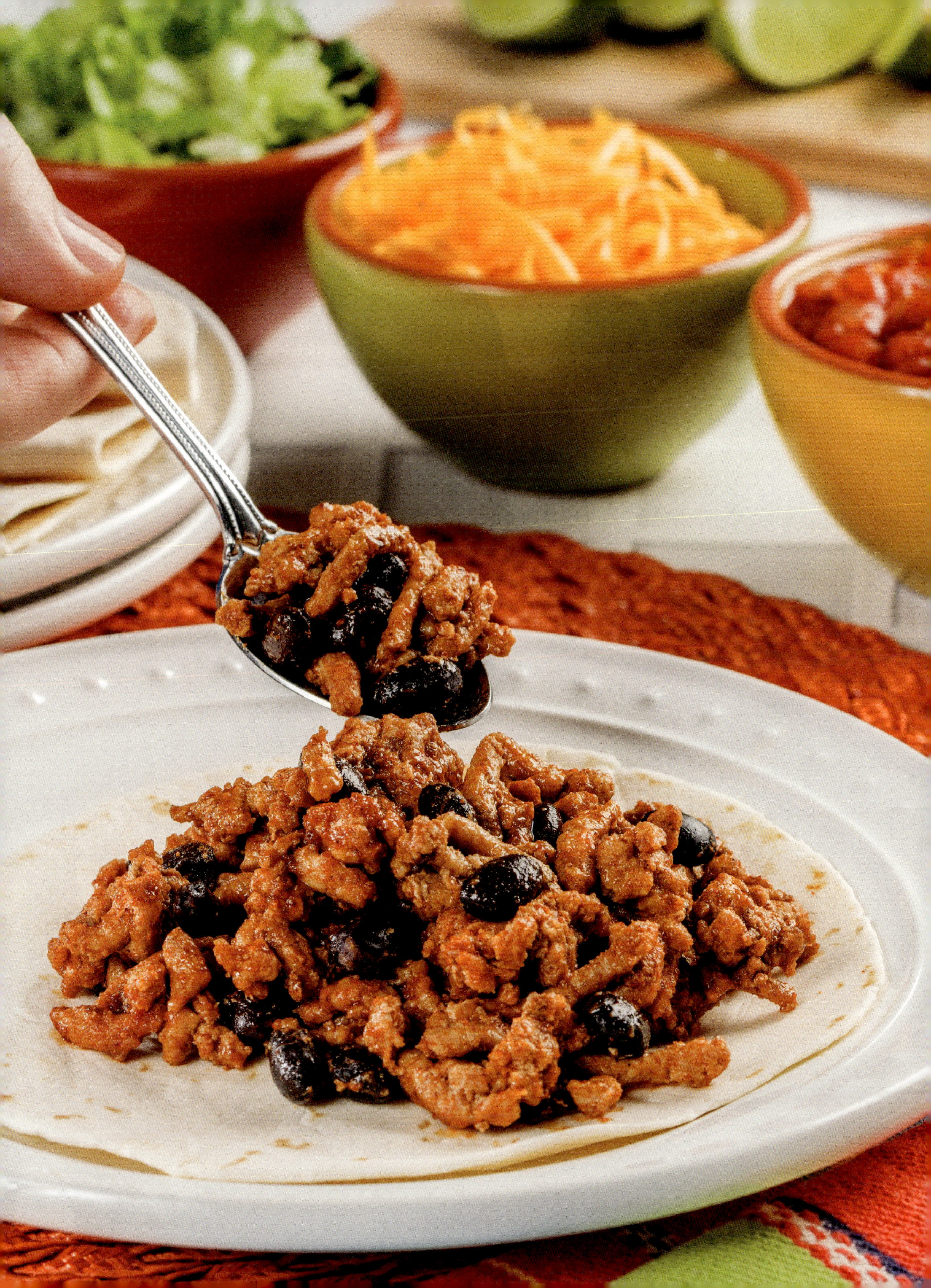

"When I entertain, I usually start my day at the farmer's market. Once that's out of the way, the cooking begins. Whether I serve a simple steak on the grill or whip up a big feast, I always want to make sure everything is just right."

BEEF & PORK

Yabba Dabba T-Bone Steak 114

Irish-American Corned Beef & Cabbage 116

The Better Brisket Dinner 118

Skillet Steak & Potato Wedges 119

All-in-One Meatball Bake 120

Really Sloppy, Sloppy Joes 122

Cheesy BBQ Meatloaf 123

Corn Chip Taco Pie 124

My Go-To Burgers 126

Irish Pub Beef Stew 127

Real Deal Texas Chili 128

Korean Beef Bulgogi 130

Old World Sausage 'n' Cabbage 131

Parmesan-Crusted Pork Milanese 132

"Spaghetti" & Pork Chunks 134

Saucy Balsamic Pork Chops 136

Sticky Fingers Spareribs 137

Pork Tenderloin with Creamy Mustard Sauce 138

YABBA DABBA T-BONE STEAK

T-bone steaks remind me of a certain modern Stone Age family. If you know what I'm talking about, then sorry to tell ya, but we're getting old! If you don't, a quick Google search of "Flintstones T-Bone" should clear things up for you. While Fred would've loved to eat this dinosaur-sized steak on his own, I think one is perfect for sharing. Wait till you taste how flavorful and tender it is – you'll both be saying, "yabba dabba yum!"

Serves 2

1 (1-½ pound) bone-in T-bone steak

Kosher salt for sprinkling

Freshly ground black pepper for sprinkling

1 tablespoon vegetable oil

GARLIC DIJON BUTTER

½ stick butter, softened

2 teaspoons Dijon mustard

2 cloves garlic, minced

1 teaspoon chopped fresh parsley

- About 30 minutes before cooking, remove steak from refrigerator. (This will help it cook more evenly.) Preheat oven to 450 degrees F.

- Sprinkle steak evenly on both sides with salt and pepper. In a large, oven-proof grill pan or skillet over medium-high heat, heat oil until hot. Add steak and cook 4 minutes on each side or until both sides are seared. Place pan in oven. Roast 6 to 8 minutes for medium-rare or to desired doneness.

- Meanwhile, to make the Garlic Dijon Butter, in a small bowl, combine butter, Dijon mustard, garlic, and parsley; mix well and set aside.

- Place steak on a platter or cutting board and top with a dollop of Garlic Dijon Butter. Allow to melt slightly, then enjoy.

If it's a beautiful day out, you can definitely cook this on your outdoor grill without finishing it off in the oven. The time will vary based on how hot your grill is. Since your outdoor grill is hotter than your grill pan, I suggest testing it a bit before the time suggested above. MCM

BEEF & PORK

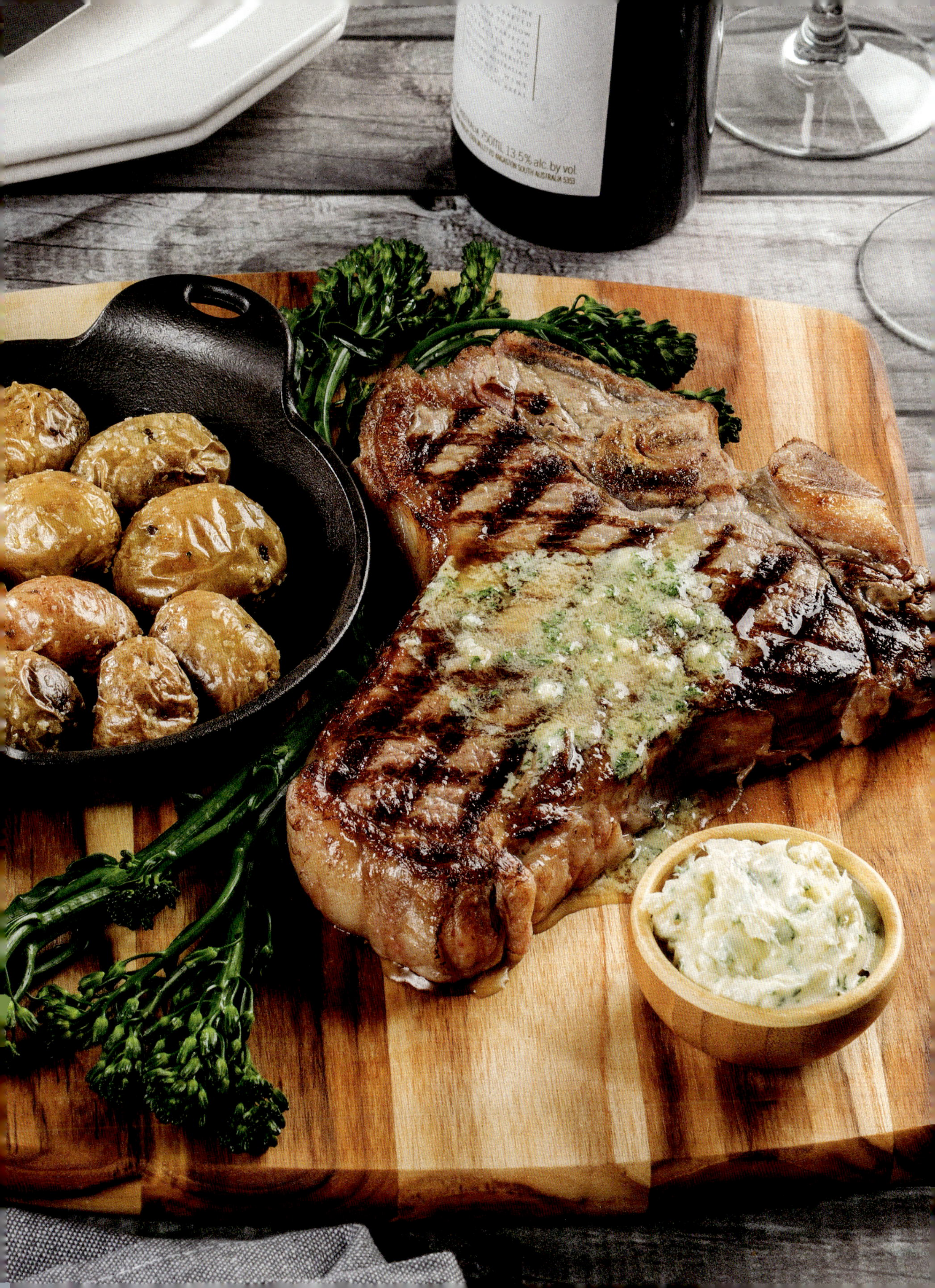
750mL 13.5% alc by vol.

IRISH-AMERICAN CORNED BEEF & CABBAGE

The first time my Irish brother-in-law had corned beef and cabbage was when I made it for him. Like most people, I thought corned beef and cabbage was the ultimate Irish dish. But in Ireland, they don't typically eat corned beef and cabbage on St. Patrick's Day (or any other day); it's more of an Irish-American tradition. (In Ireland, it's more common to have bacon and cabbage.) Nevertheless, my brother-in-law loved this and I'm sure you will too!

Serves 5 to 6

1 (3- to 3-½-pound) corned beef brisket with pickling spices

1 (12-ounce) bottle beer

4 cups water

4 potatoes, peeled and cut into quarters

4 carrots, cut into 2-inch chunks

1 green cabbage, cut into 2-inch wedges

- In a large Dutch oven over medium-high heat, add corned beef (along with pickling spices), beer, and water; mix well and bring to a boil. Reduce heat to low, cover, and simmer 1-½ hours or until beef is almost fork-tender.

- Add potatoes, carrots, and cabbage and continue cooking, covered, 25 to 30 minutes or until vegetables and corned beef are fork-tender.

- Place corned beef on a cutting board and slice across the grain. (You want to make sure you cut across the grain, otherwise it'll be stringy and tough.) Serve with vegetables.

Don't be surprised if the corned beef shrinks during cooking; that's what it's supposed to do! MCM

BEEF & PORK

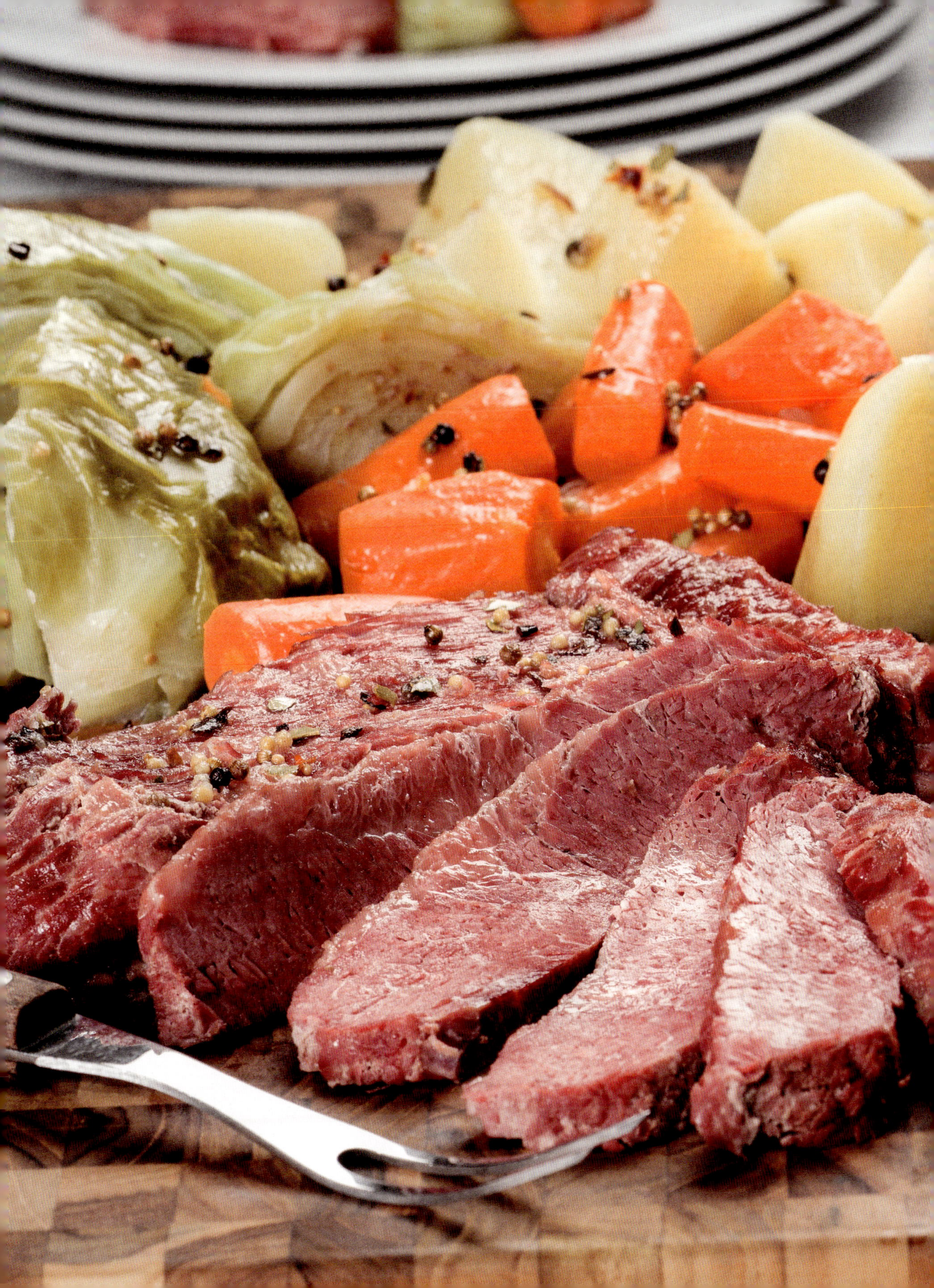

THE BETTER BRISKET DINNER

Cooking brisket low and slow in a slow cooker ensures that you're going to end up with a fall-apart, melts-in-your-mouth kind of meal. I almost feel guilty when I get compliments on it, since the slow cooker does all the work. However, I do like to take credit for my "secret ingredient." Oh yeah, that cup of coffee in the sauce is what makes this "The Better Brisket Dinner."

Serves 4 to 6

1 pound new potatoes (about 12)

1 onion, cut into 1-inch chunks

1 pound carrots, cut into 2-inch chunks

1 (3-pound) beef brisket, trimmed

1 teaspoon salt

¾ teaspoon black pepper

1 (15-ounce) can tomato sauce

1 cup black coffee

½ cup light brown sugar

¼ cup Worcestershire sauce

- In a 6-quart or larger slow cooker, add potatoes, onion, and carrots. Sprinkle beef with salt and pepper and place over vegetables.

- In a medium bowl, combine tomato sauce, coffee, brown sugar, and Worcestershire sauce; mix well. Pour over beef and vegetables.

- Cover and cook on LOW 8 to 9 hours or until beef is fork-tender. Slice beef across the grain; serve with vegetables and sauce.

Don't see a 3-pound brisket in your supermarket's meat case? Just ask the butcher if they can cut and trim one for you.   MCM

SKILLET STEAK & POTATO WEDGES

This is one of those recipes that I never get tired of serving or eating. It's fast, filling, and never fails. When I have a little more time on my hands, I start with my own oven-roasted potatoes, but I love how the refrigerated wedges make things so quick and easy. Whether you serve it for lunch or dinner, you can't go wrong. (Hey, fry up an egg and you might even get away with serving it as an extra-hearty breakfast!)

Serves 3 to 4

- 3 tablespoons vegetable oil, divided
- 1 (20-ounce) package refrigerated potato wedges
- 1 red bell pepper, cut into ½-inch chunks
- ½ cup chopped onion
- ½ teaspoon salt
- ¼ teaspoon black pepper
- 1 (1-¼ pound) top sirloin steak
- 1 teaspoon Montreal steak seasoning

- In a large skillet over medium-high heat, heat 2 tablespoons oil until hot. Add potato wedges, bell pepper, onion, salt, and black pepper, and sauté, covered, 10 to 12 minutes or until potatoes begin to brown, stirring occasionally.

- Meanwhile, evenly sprinkle steak with steak seasoning. In another skillet over medium-high heat, heat remaining 1 tablespoon oil until hot. Cook steak 5 minutes per side or to desired doneness. (I like mine medium rare.) Let steak rest 5 minutes before slicing across the grain, into strips. Serve over potatoes.

I always suggest letting cooked steak or roast rest for about 5 to 10 minutes after taking it off the heat. This helps ensure that the juices stay in the meat once it's cut.

MCM

BEEF & PORK

ALL-IN-ONE MEATBALL BAKE

This isn't your traditional meatball bake, but once you give it a try, I have a feeling it'll become a regular on your weeknight dinner menu. From the chunks of crowd-favorite Texas toast to the smothered-in-cheesy-goodness meatballs, it's hard to decide which part of this dish makes it so spectacular. The best I can do is to let you figure it out for yourself. Happy eating!

Serves 8 to 10

- 8 slices frozen Texas toast
- 2 cups ricotta cheese
- 1 (1-ounce) packet ranch dressing and seasoning mix
- 2 cups shredded mozzarella cheese, divided
- 1 (14-ounce) package frozen meatballs
- 1 (24-ounce) jar spaghetti sauce

- Preheat oven to 400 degrees F. Place Texas toast on a baking sheet; bake 8 minutes or until golden and crispy. Coat a 9- x 13-inch baking dish with cooking spray.

- Meanwhile, in a medium bowl, combine ricotta cheese with ranch dressing and seasoning mix; set aside.

- Cut bread into 1-inch pieces, then arrange in baking dish, packing tightly to fit. Sprinkle with 1 cup mozzarella cheese. Spoon dollops of ricotta cheese mixture evenly over bread. Arrange meatballs over bread, then pour spaghetti sauce over top. Bake 30 to 35 minutes or until meatballs are heated through.

- Top with remaining 1 cup mozzarella cheese and bake 4 to 5 additional minutes or until cheese is melted and everything is heated through.

If you're old-school Italian and you have some homemade sauce in the freezer, pull it out for this recipe. My grandmother always froze her sauce in pint-sized plastic containers and labeled them with masking tape. MCM

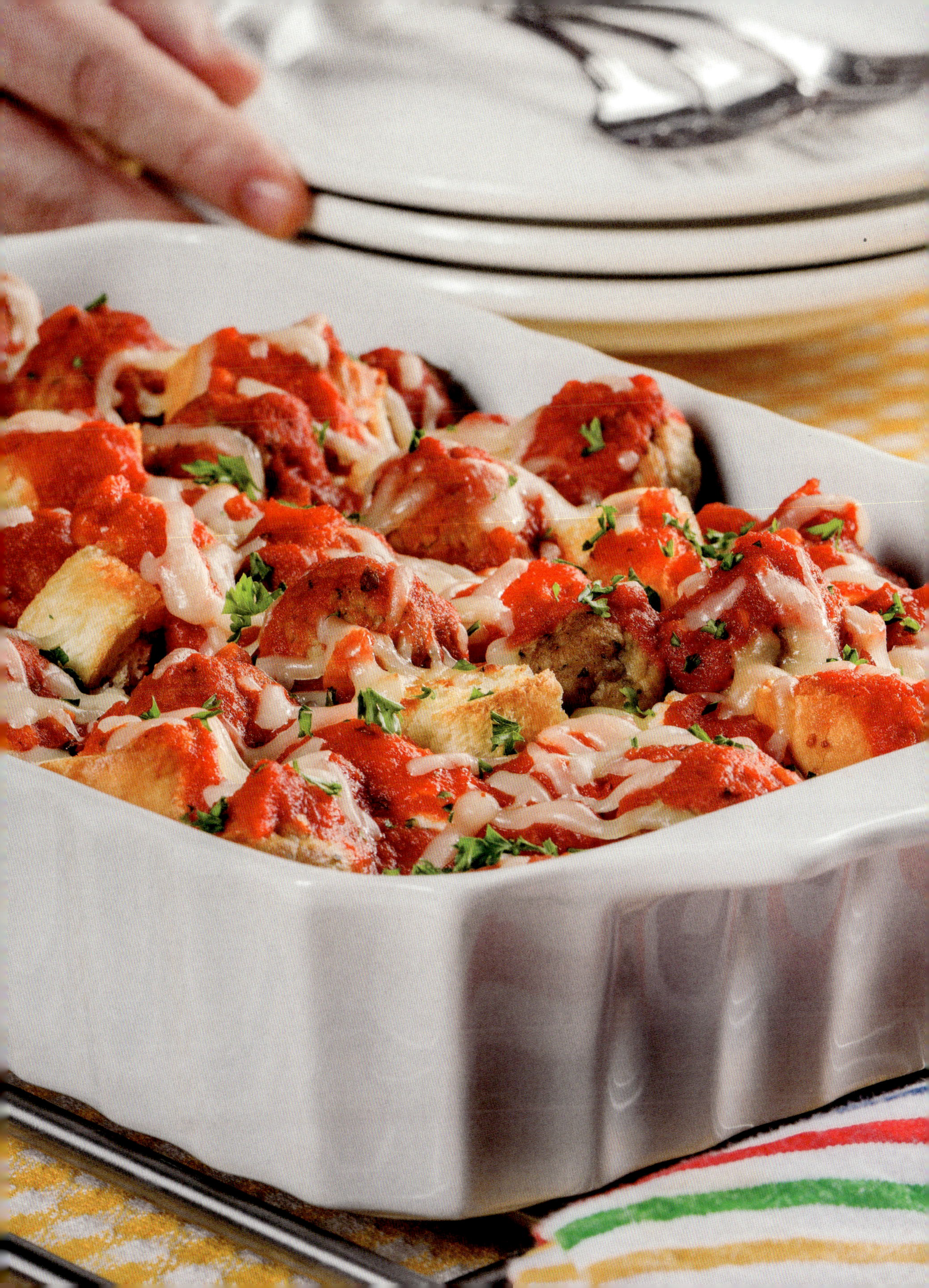

REALLY SLOPPY, SLOPPY JOES

Sloppy Joes aren't called sloppy for nothing – these babies are deliciously messy. If you're hoping to remain spot-free, I suggest you tuck a paper towel into your shirt collar before taking that first bite. If you don't mind a little sauce dripping down your chin (and maybe a little spillage on your lap) … I can almost guarantee you're going to get it. Oh, and in case you couldn't guess, this one is really popular with kids!

Makes 6

- 2 to 2-½ pounds ground beef
- 1 onion, chopped
- 1 green bell pepper, chopped
- 2 (15-ounce) cans tomato sauce
- 2 tablespoons brown sugar
- ½ teaspoon garlic powder
- ½ teaspoon salt
- ¼ teaspoon black pepper
- 6 sandwich rolls or hamburger buns, split, buttered, and toasted

■ In a large skillet over medium-high heat, brown ground beef, onion, and bell pepper 7 to 9 minutes or until no pink remains in beef; drain excess liquid.

■ Add remaining ingredients except sandwich rolls; mix well. Reduce heat to low and simmer 8 to 10 minutes or until heated through, stirring occasionally. Spoon mixture onto rolls and serve.

If you're a cheese lover (like I am!), sprinkle these with some shredded cheese right before serving. The hot mixture will melt the cheese in no time. MCM

CHEESY BBQ MEATLOAF

I'm positive that meatloaves are never going out of style. They're a family favorite that can be made just about any way you want. In my *Easy Everyday Favorites* cookbook, I shared a recipe for a more traditional meatloaf, but this time around I wanted to give you a meatloaf with a bit of a twist. By subbing ketchup with barbecue sauce and adding in lots of cheese, along with a crunchy onion topping, I've given my traditional meatloaf a tasty makeover!

Serves 6 to 8

2 pounds lean ground beef

3 slices white bread, torn into ½-inch pieces

2 eggs

¼ cup prepared yellow mustard

1 teaspoon salt

1/8 teaspoon black pepper

2-¼ cups (9 ounces) shredded sharp cheddar cheese, divided

1 cup barbecue sauce

¼ cup French fried onions

- Preheat oven to 400 degrees F. Coat a 9- x 13-inch baking dish with cooking spray.

- In a medium bowl, combine ground beef, bread, eggs, mustard, salt, and pepper. Using your hands, mix until well blended. (You can use plastic gloves if it makes you feel more comfortable.)

- Place mixture on a 12- x 16-inch piece of wax paper and pat it out, creating a 10- x 12-inch rectangle, about ½-inch thick. Sprinkle 2 cups cheese evenly over ground beef mixture. Roll it up, jellyroll-style, starting from the short end. Make sure to lift the wax paper, removing it as you roll up. Seal seam by pinching together, and place seam-side down in baking dish.

- Pour barbecue sauce over the top and roast 55 to 60 minutes. Meanwhile, in a small bowl, mix remaining ¼ cup cheese with French fried onions. Sprinkle over meatloaf and cook 5 more minutes or until no pink remains in beef and juices run clear.

- Remove from oven and allow to stand 10 minutes. Then, slice and serve.

BEEF & PORK

CORN CHIP TACO PIE

Is it even possible to get tired of finding new ways to enjoy tacos? I mean, really, sometimes I wonder if there's a little extra magic sprinkled into that taco seasoning... Anyway, I've got another taco-inspired dish for you to fall in love with. It's crunchy, it's beefy, and boy, does it deliver! I kept things simple with just some cheese, salsa, and sour cream, but you can really customize this to include all of your favorites – beans, black olives, tomatoes, you name it!

Serves 5 to 6

1 to 1-¼ pounds ground beef

½ cup chopped onion

1 (1-ounce) packet taco seasoning mix

¼ cup water

1 (8-ounce) can refrigerated crescent dinner rolls

3 cups coarsely crushed corn chips, divided

1 cup shredded cheddar cheese

Salsa for topping

Sour cream for topping

- Heat oven to 375 degrees F. In a large skillet over high heat, brown ground beef and onion 5 to 6 minutes or until no pink remains in beef, stirring frequently; drain excess liquid. Stir in taco seasoning and water; cook 3 minutes or until heated through.

- Meanwhile, separate crescent dough into 8 triangles. In an ungreased 9-inch deep-dish pie plate, arrange triangles with the points facing the center, pressing seams together to create a crust. Sprinkle half of the corn chips over crust. Top with a layer of beef mixture, cheese, and remaining half of corn chips.

- Bake 20 to 25 minutes or until crust is golden brown. Cut in wedges. Top with salsa and sour cream.

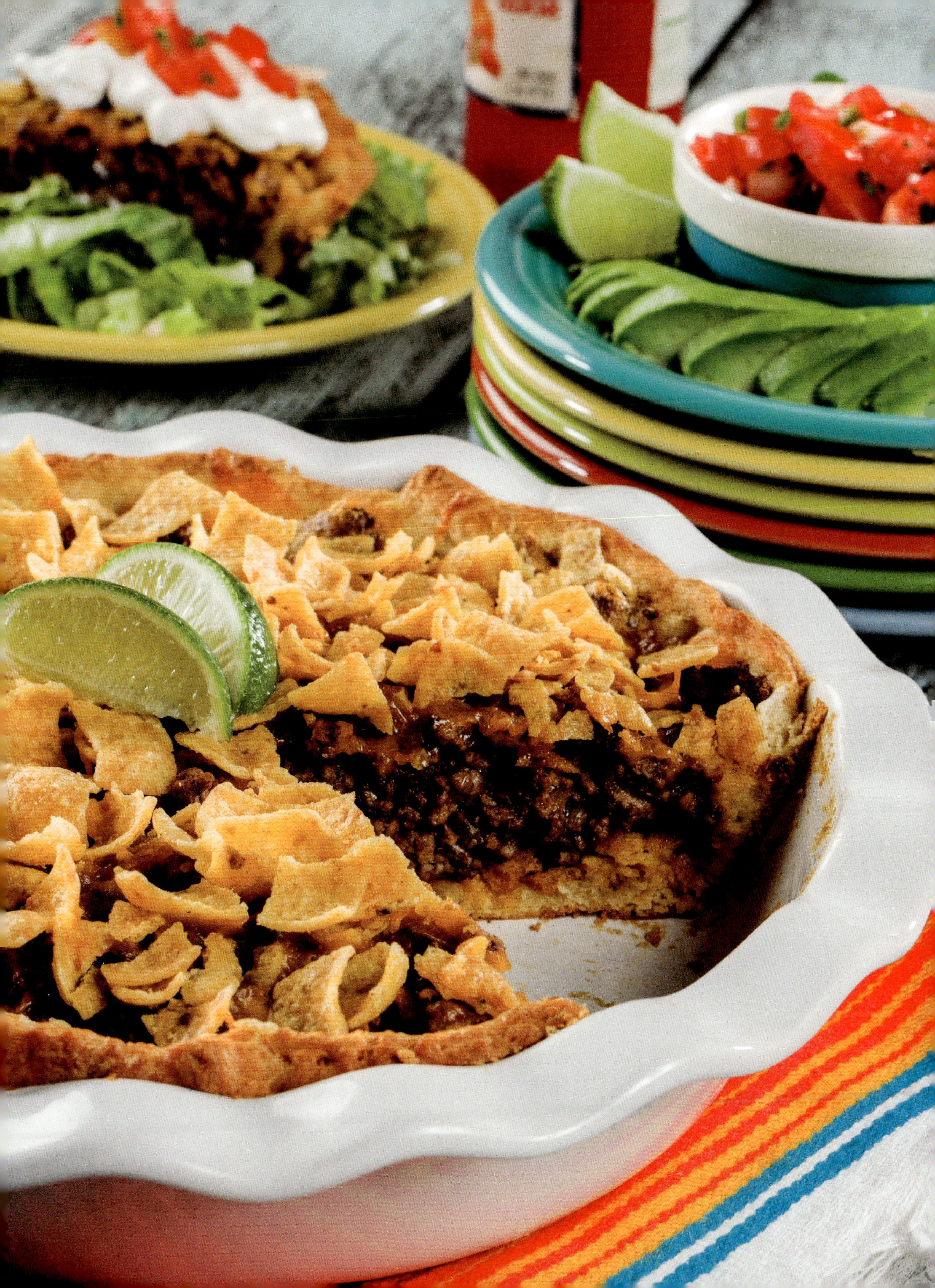

MY GO-TO BURGERS

I'm a big believer that you only need a handful of good "go-to" recipes. These burgers are definitely at the top of my list. There's just something great about having a little bit of bacon and cheese in every bite, combined with some basic, but winning spices. These juicy burgers have never let me down.

Makes 6

2 pounds ground chuck

4 ounces Monterey Jack cheese, diced

¼ cup real bacon bits

2 teaspoons Worcestershire sauce

¼ cup water

½ teaspoon garlic powder

½ teaspoon salt

½ teaspoon black pepper

6 hamburger buns, split

- In a large bowl, combine ground chuck, cheese, bacon bits, Worcestershire sauce, water, garlic powder, salt, and pepper; mix just until combined. Shape mixture into 6 equal-sized patties. With your thumb, make an indentation in the center of each burger. (This will help prevent your burger from puffing up while it cooks.)

- Heat a large skillet or grill pan over medium-high heat and cook patties 4 to 5 minutes per side, or until no longer pink. (You can also cook these on your outdoor grill.) Place in buns and serve.

Sure, you could make these with ground beef rather than ground chuck, if that's what you have on-hand (or if that's what's on sale!), but using ground chuck makes a big difference. Ground chuck is a fattier cut that'll help make your burgers extra juicy and even more flavorful. MCM

IRISH PUB BEEF STEW

If you've ever had the opportunity to enjoy a beef stew in an Irish pub, then I don't have to tell you just how good and hearty it is. However, if you're new to Irish beef stew, then you should know, it's incomparable to any other kind of stew you've had before. This stew's unique flavor profile comes from the beer, which not only tenderizes the meat as it cooks, but also adds layers of rich and nutty flavors to the gravy. It's so tasty!

Serves 5 to 6

- 3 slices uncooked bacon, chopped
- 1 tablespoon vegetable oil
- 2 pounds beef stew meat
- 1 (12-ounce) bottle Guiness® beer (see note)
- 3 cups beef stock
- 2 cloves garlic, minced
- ½ teaspoon salt
- ½ teaspoon black pepper
- 4 carrots, cut into 1-inch chunks
- 4 stalks celery, sliced into ½-inch chunks
- 1 onion, peeled and cut into half moons
- 2 tablespoons all-purpose flour
- ⅓ cup water

■ In a heavy soup pot over high heat, cook bacon until crisp. Add in oil and meat, and stir. Continue cooking 8 to 10 minutes or until meat is browned.

■ Stir in beer, beef stock, garlic, salt, and pepper; reduce heat to low and simmer, covered, 30 minutes. Add carrots, celery, and onion; stir well and cook 1 hour or until meat is tender.

■ In a small bowl, combine flour and water, then stir into stew. Cook 1 to 2 minutes or until sauce is thickened. Ladle into bowls and enjoy.

I like using a traditional dark Irish beer, like Guinness, but if you don't have any, you can use whatever beer you have on hand. You can also use non-alcoholic varieties, if you prefer. MCM

REAL DEAL TEXAS CHILI

Ah, at last we've come to the great chili debate – beans or no beans? While most of the country is in favor of tossing in some hearty legumes, Texans are pretty adamant about remaining bean-less. For them, it's all about the beef, the heat, and the all-around flavors. Serve it over a bed of plain rice or alongside some tortilla chips or crusty bread. No matter what you choose, you're in for a hearty-good time.

Serves 5 to 6

¼ cup vegetable oil

3 pounds beef brisket, well-trimmed and cut into 1-inch cubes

1 onion, chopped

4 cloves garlic, minced

3 tablespoons chili powder

1 tablespoon ground cumin

1 teaspoon salt

2 teaspoons hot pepper sauce

3 cups beef broth

3 cups water

1 (4-ounce) can chopped green chilies, undrained

- In a heavy soup pot over medium-high heat, heat oil until hot; add beef and sear 5 minutes. Add onion and garlic, and sauté 5 minutes or until beef is browned on all sides, stirring frequently.

- Stir in chili powder, cumin, salt, and hot sauce; cook 1 minute. Add beef broth, water, and chilies with their liquid, and bring to a boil, stirring occasionally. Reduce heat to low, cover, and simmer 45 minutes, then remove cover and simmer an additional 45 to 50 minutes or until beef is fork-tender.

Everyone has a different threshold for heat, so be sure to use as little or as much hot pepper sauce as you like. (As-is, this chili is flavorful, without being overpoweringly spicy.) If you do want to kick things up a bit, add in some chopped jalapeño peppers when you uncover it. MCM

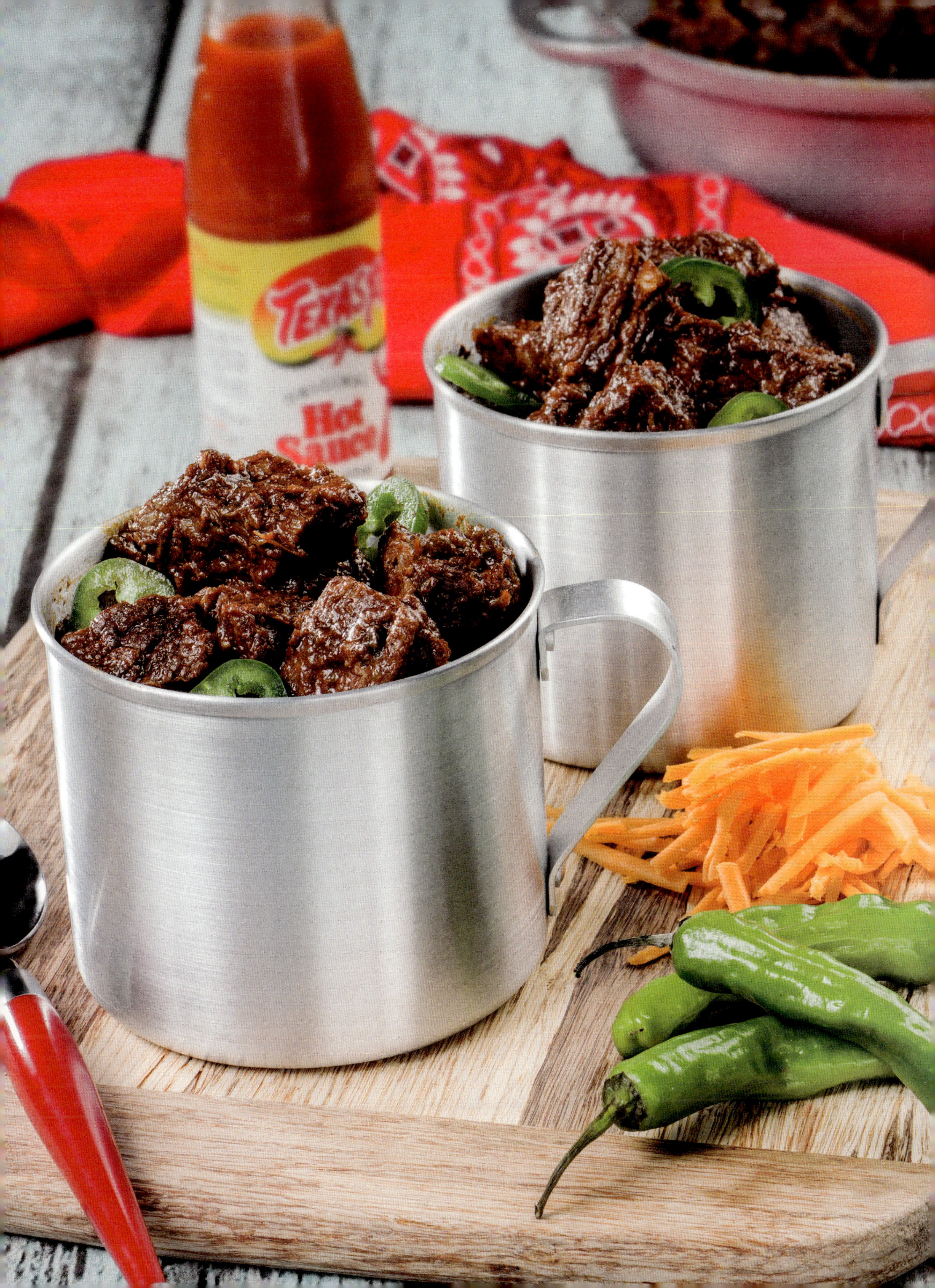
Hot Sauce

KOREAN BEEF BULGOGI

I pride myself on being willing to try new dishes from faraway places. So when I heard that the 2018 Winter Olympics were taking place in Korea, I started searching for Korean dishes I could make at home. "Bulgogi" is a stir-fried beef dish that's both sweet and savory, as well as really, really tasty. Now I have my own easy way of cooking up this international favorite.

Serves 3 to 4

1/3 cup soy sauce

2 tablespoons rice wine vinegar

1 tablespoon sesame oil

1 small red apple, grated

4 cloves garlic, minced

1 teaspoon minced fresh ginger

3 tablespoons brown sugar

1/8 teaspoon black pepper

1-1/2 pounds thinly sliced sirloin beef

1 tablespoon vegetable oil

1 cup thinly sliced onion

1 carrot, thinly sliced

2 scallions, sliced

1 teaspoon sesame seeds (optional)

- In a large resealable plastic bag, combine soy sauce, rice wine vinegar, sesame oil, apple, garlic, ginger, brown sugar, and pepper; mix well. Add beef, then seal and toss until beef is evenly coated. Refrigerate at least 4 hours.

- Preheat a wok or large skillet over high heat. Add vegetable oil, onion, and carrot, and sauté 5 to 7 minutes or until onion begins to brown.

- Remove beef from marinade (do not discard) and add beef to skillet. Cook 5 minutes or until beef is no longer pink, stirring occasionally. Add marinade and cook 2 minutes or until sauce has thickened. Stir in scallions and sesame seeds, if desired, then serve.

OLD WORLD SAUSAGE 'N' CABBAGE

Although it's always exciting when I come across a new recipe, some of my favorites are ones that have been passed down from generation to generation. This Old World-style recipe has Polish roots (like I do on my mother's side) that reflect the way that comfort food used to be – heartwarming and simple. Whenever I sit down to a meal like this, it always puts a smile on my face.

Serves 4 to 6

1 (14-ounce) package kielbasa sausage, sliced about 1-inch thick

1 tablespoon vegetable oil

1 green bell pepper, cut into thin strips

1 onion, thinly sliced

6 cups coarsely chopped cabbage (about ½ a head)

½ cup chicken broth

½ teaspoon caraway seeds

½ teaspoon salt

¼ teaspoon black pepper

- Coat a large skillet with cooking spray. Over medium heat, sauté kielbasa 3 to 5 minutes or until browned. Remove to a plate.

- In the same skillet, heat oil until hot; sauté bell pepper and onion 5 minutes or until tender. Add cabbage and cook 8 minutes, stirring occasionally.

- Add sausage back into skillet, along with remaining ingredients. Reduce heat to medium-low and cook 5 minutes or until cabbage is tender. Serve immediately.

Of course you can use any smoked sausage you find in your supermarket, but if you ever have the chance to pick up some authentic Polish kielbasa from a real Polish deli, I promise you'll be in for a special treat. MCM

BEEF & PORK

PARMESAN-CRUSTED PORK MILANESE

In my experience, you can always judge a restaurant based on their Milanese, whether it's chicken, veal, or pork. If their Milanese is delicious, then I know it's a quality restaurant. While Milanese-style dishes are some of my favorites to order at restaurants, I also love making them at home. This pork variation features the yummy addition of Parmesan in the crust.

Serves 4

1 cup grated Parmesan cheese

½ cup panko bread crumbs

⅓ cup all-purpose flour

2 eggs, lightly beaten

4 boneless, center cut pork loin chops, trimmed and pounded to ¼-inch thickness

¼ teaspoon salt

¼ teaspoon black pepper

6 tablespoons olive oil

4 cups arugula

1 tomato, cut into chunks

Vinaigrette for drizzling (see note)

- In a shallow dish, combine Parmesan cheese and bread crumbs; mix well. Place flour and eggs in 2 separate shallow dishes; set aside.

- Season pork chops with salt and pepper. Evenly coat pork with flour, then egg, and finally bread crumb mixture.

- In a large skillet over medium heat, heat 3 tablespoons oil until hot. Cook pork in batches 2 to 3 minutes per side or until golden and no pink remains, adding more oil as needed.

- When ready to serve, place a cooked cutlet on a plate and top evenly with arugula and tomato. Drizzle with vinaigrette and enjoy.

To make an easy homemade vinaigrette, all you have to do is add these ingredients to a bowl and whisk together: 1 cup olive oil, ¼ cup white vinegar, 1 teaspoon garlic powder, 1 teaspoon onion powder, 1 teaspoon salt, and ½ teaspoon black pepper. MCM

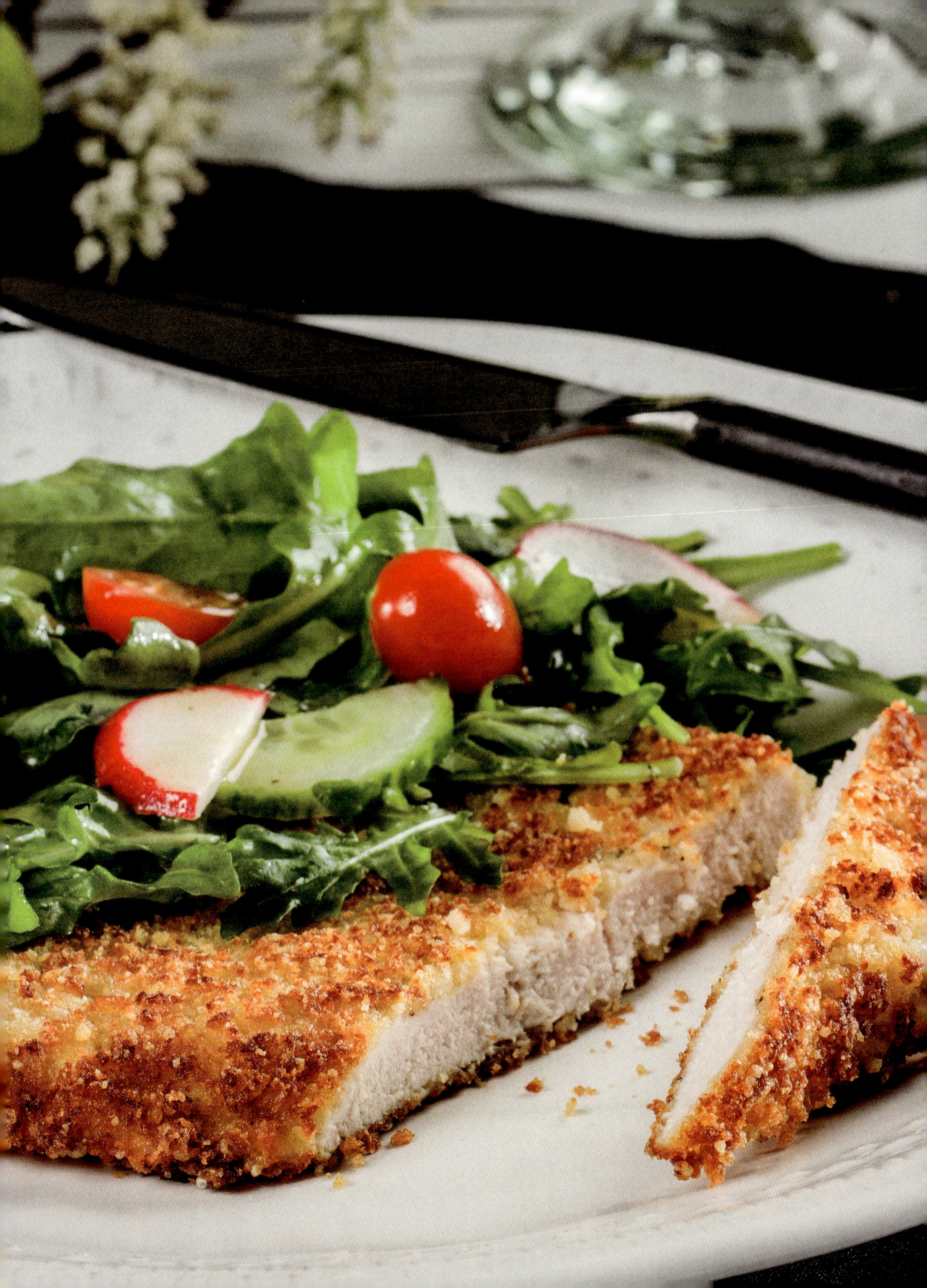

"SPAGHETTI" & PORK CHUNKS

As you might know, it isn't always easy to lose weight. So when I set out to trim down, one of the first things I cut back on was pasta. But since I love my pasta, I've found a way to get my fix in, while still reducing the number of carbs in my diet. The answer is: spaghetti squash. This pasta-like veggie, topped with flavor-packed slow cooker pork helps me stick to my goals while still treating my taste buds to a tasty meal.

Serves 6 to 8

1 (4- to 5-pound) pork butt or shoulder

1 tablespoon chili powder

1 teaspoon cumin

Salt for sprinkling

Black pepper for sprinkling

½ cup taco sauce

1 onion, diced

2 cloves garlic, crushed

1 spaghetti squash

- Evenly sprinkle pork with chili powder, cumin, salt, and pepper, and place in a 5 quart or larger slow cooker. Top with taco sauce, onion, and garlic. Cook on HIGH 5 to 6 hours or LOW 7 to 8 hours, or until meat is fall-apart tender. Cut pork into 1-inch chunks.

- Meanwhile, fill a soup pot with 1-inch of water and place whole squash into pot. Bring to a boil over high heat, cover, and cook 25 to 30 minutes or until tender when pierced with a knife. Remove squash to a cutting board and allow to cool slightly.

- Carefully cut squash in half lengthwise (it will be very hot), and using a spoon, remove and discard seeds. Scrape inside of squash with a fork, shredding into noodle-like strands.

- Serve pork with pan drippings over spaghetti squash.

Want to add a little extra flavor? Sprinkle on some crumbly cotija cheese just before serving. It's a hard cheese from Mexico that tastes somewhere between feta and Parmesan. MCM

BEEF & PORK

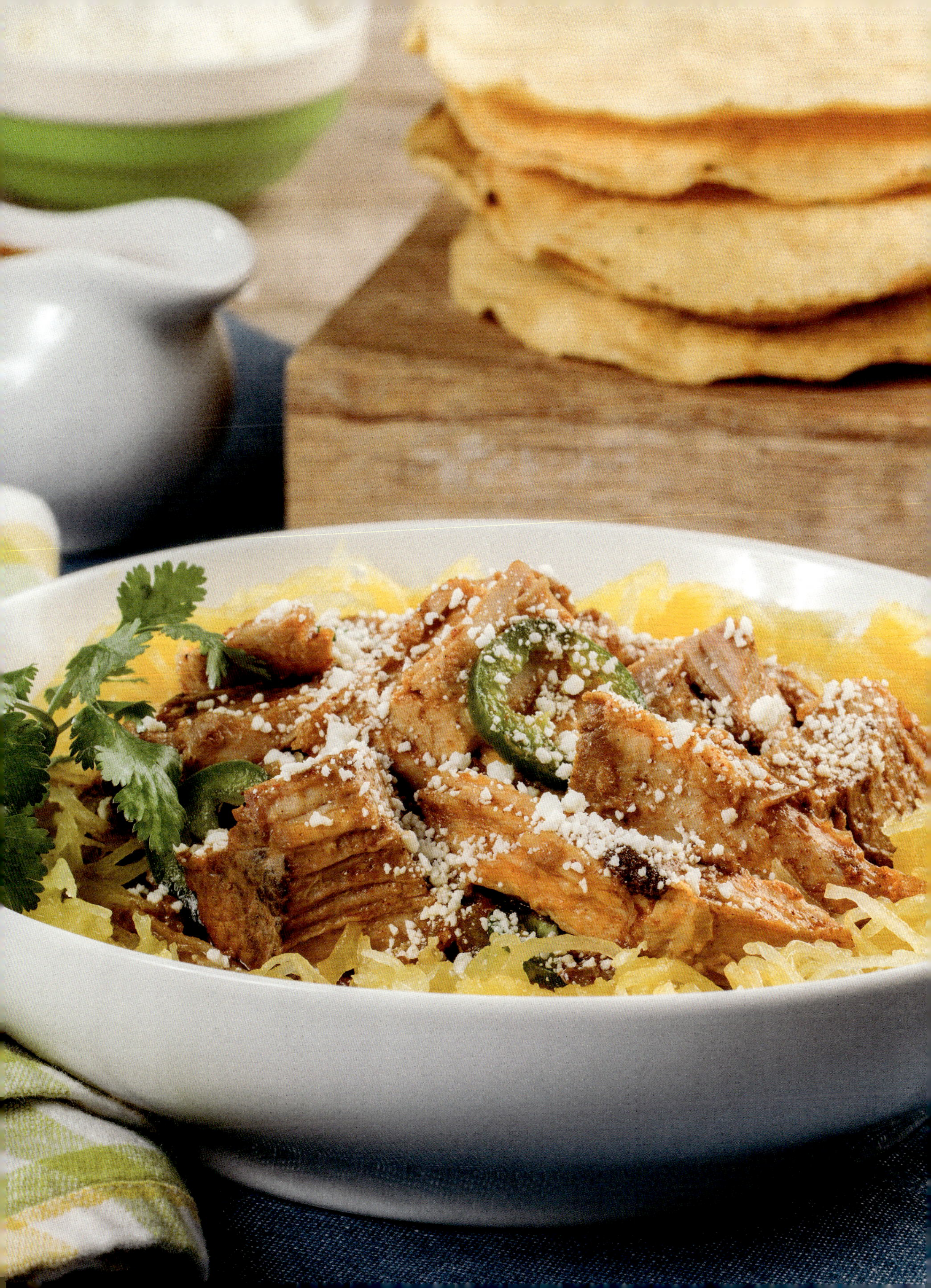

SAUCY BALSAMIC PORK CHOPS

I love it when I can whip up something tasty for dinner in under 15 minutes, especially since my QVC schedule can keep me pretty busy at times! This quick pork dish features a homemade balsamic sauce that makes it just a little more special-tasting. I like to serve these over a bed of fresh spinach, since the heat from the pork chops wilts the spinach perfectly and the balsamic makes a darn good sauce too.

Serves 4

4 (¾-inch-thick) boneless center-cut pork loin chops

2 teaspoons lemon pepper

1 tablespoon vegetable oil

½ cup balsamic vinegar

⅓ cup chicken broth

2 tablespoons light brown sugar

- Sprinkle pork chops evenly with lemon pepper. In a heavy skillet over medium-high heat, heat oil until hot. Add pork chops and cook 3 minutes per side or until browned and cooked to desired doneness. Remove pork chops from skillet; keep warm.

- In the same skillet, combine vinegar, broth, and brown sugar, stirring to loosen any browned bits from pan. (This is called "deglazing".) Cook over medium-high heat 4 minutes or until mixture begins to reduce and starts to thicken slightly. Spoon sauce over pork chops and serve.

STICKY FINGERS SPARERIBS

I love, love, love spareribs. So when I say that these are better than good, you know they have to be pretty amazing. (It's all about the homemade sauce!) Just so you know – they're tender, they're saucy, and they're fun to eat. Just make sure you have a whole stack of napkins nearby, 'cause you're going to need them. (If no one's watching, you might be able to get away with licking those sticky fingers!)

Serves 2 to 3

- 1 (2-½- to 3-pound) rack pork spareribs, cut into 3 sections
- ¼ cup vegetable oil
- ¼ cup soy sauce
- 1 tablespoon molasses
- 2 tablespoons packed brown sugar
- 1 teaspoon garlic powder
- 1 teaspoon dry mustard
- 1 teaspoon ground ginger
- 1 teaspoon salt
- ½ teaspoon black pepper

- Place spareribs in a large pot and add just enough water to cover. Over medium-high heat, boil ribs 35 to 40 minutes or until fork-tender; drain well. Let cool slightly, then cut into individual ribs (between each bone).

- Meanwhile, in a large bowl, combine remaining ingredients; mix well. Place ribs in sauce and toss until evenly coated. Preheat air fryer to 390 degrees F.

- Coat air fryer basket with cooking spray. Reserving remaining sauce, place ribs in basket in a crisscross fashion. (This way the air can easily circulate around them, and they cook evenly.) Air-fry 5 minutes, then brush with sauce. Turn ribs over and brush with remaining sauce. Continue to cook 4 to 5 more minutes or until sauce begins to caramelize.

I love that my air fryer has so many uses. Who would've thought that I could make ribs without turning on the oven or firing up the grill? Plus, clean-up is much easier with this method! If you don't have an air fryer, you can cook these in a 400 degree oven on a rimmed baking sheet for about 5 to 8 minutes or until the sauce begins to caramelize.

MCM

PORK TENDERLOIN WITH CREAMY MUSTARD SAUCE

One of the most underutilized cuts of meat in the supermarket has to be pork tenderloin. Once you realize how tender it is and how quick it cooks, there's no doubt you'll be adding it to your weekly shopping list. I cook with it at least a few times a month! While I've prepared it a number of ways, this is one of my favorites. The homemade creamy mustard sauce adds a fancy flair to this dish (which makes it a good one for impressing company, too!).

Serves 3 to 4

1 pound pork tenderloin

¾ teaspoon salt, divided

½ teaspoon black pepper, divided

3 tablespoons butter

1 tablespoon vegetable oil

¼ cup dry white wine

¾ cup chicken broth

1-½ tablespoons Dijon mustard

½ cup heavy cream

½ teaspoon dried tarragon

- Preheat oven to 350 degrees F. Coat a rimmed baking sheet with cooking spray. Sprinkle pork with ½ teaspoon salt and ¼ teaspoon black pepper.

- In a large skillet over medium-high heat, melt butter with oil until hot. Brown pork on all sides. Place pork on baking sheet. Roast 18 to 20 minutes for medium doneness.

- Meanwhile, in the same skillet, add wine and chicken broth; stir, making sure to scrape any bits from bottom of pan. Whisk in Dijon mustard, remaining ¼ teaspoon salt and ¼ teaspoon black pepper, the heavy cream, and tarragon. Simmer 4 to 5 minutes or until thickened. Serve cream sauce with pork.

When it comes to shopping for the Dijon mustard, go for the best you can afford. Since I'm half French I know a thing or two about Dijon mustard, so this is no place to skimp.

MCM

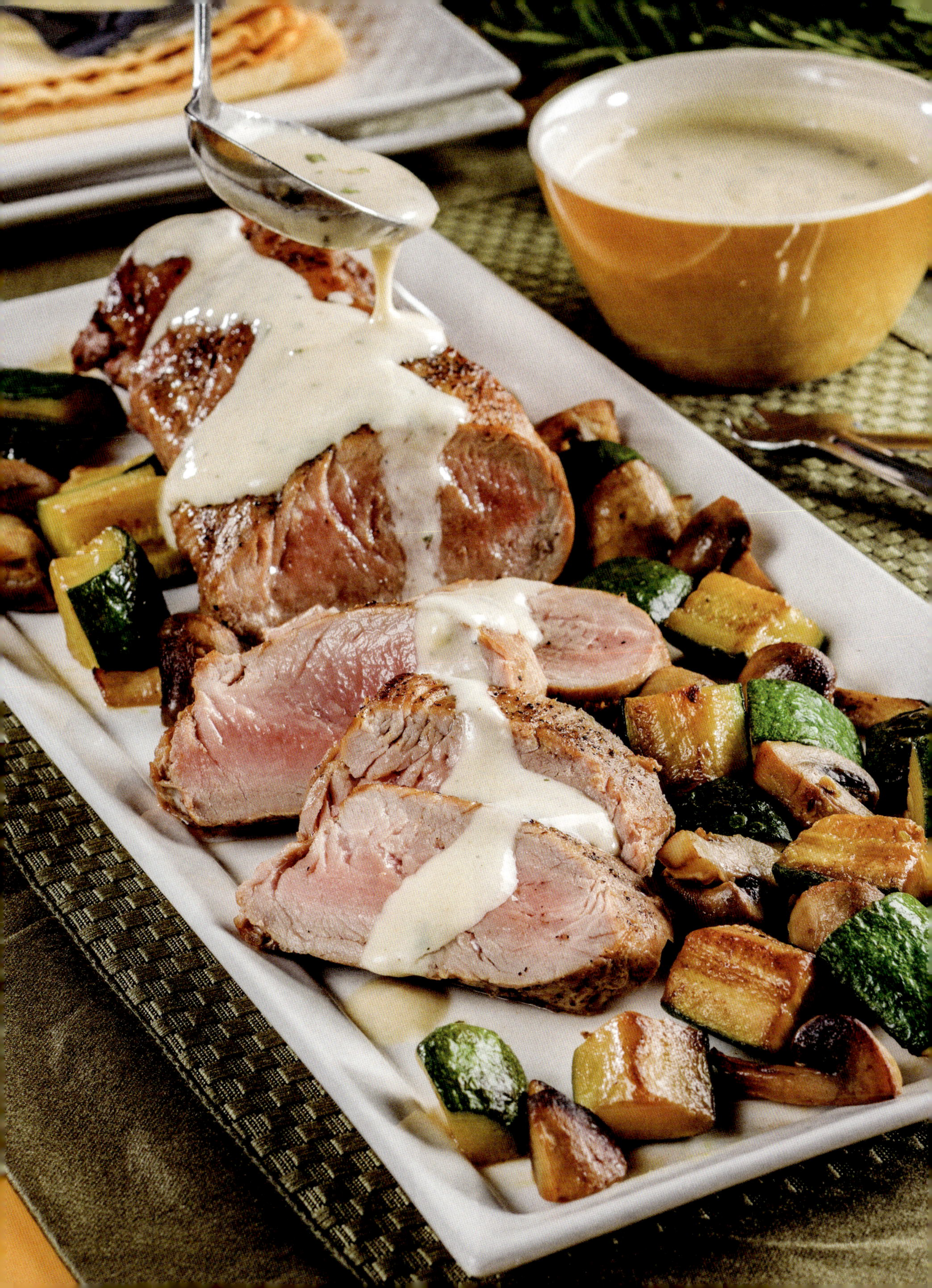

"*Fresh lobsta' rolls need to start with fresh lobster. And if you've never cooked one at home, I'm going to tell you a little secret -- it's not as hard as you'd think. By the way, what do you think of my keto-friendly pizza (see page 164 for the recipe)?*"

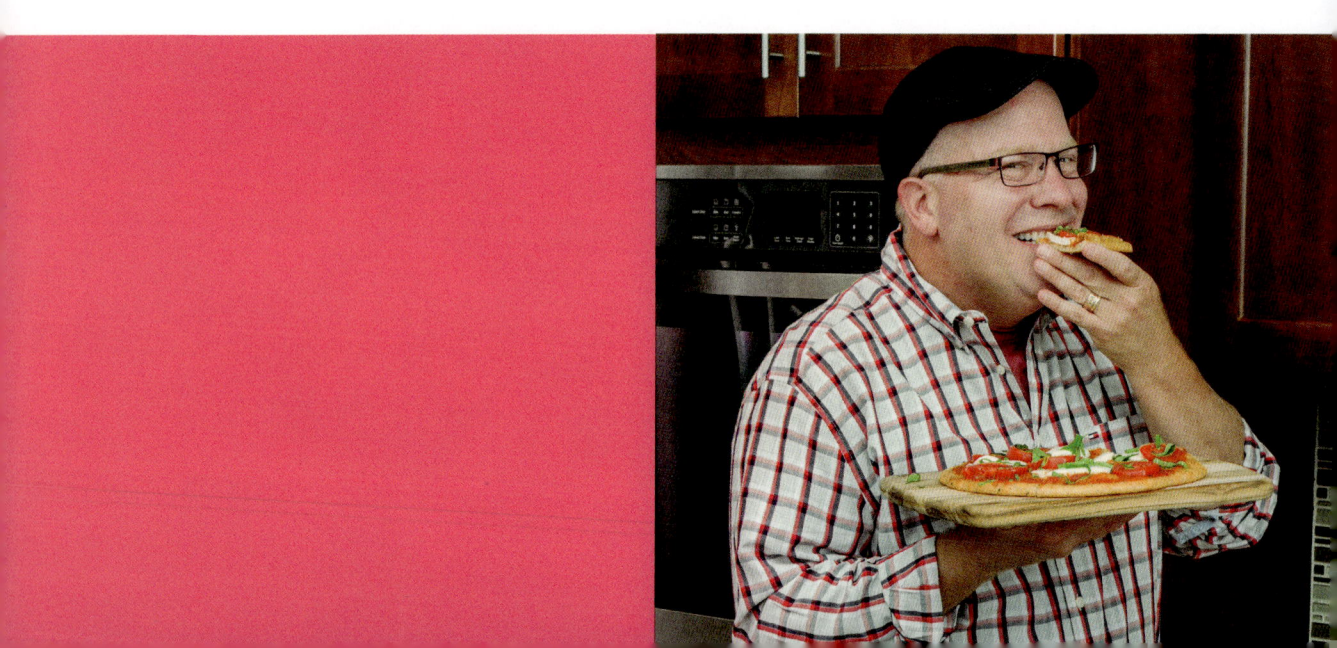

SEAFOOD, PASTA, & MORE

Greek-Style Salmon in Phyllo 142

Ready-in-20 Baked Fish 144

Blackened Catfish & Tropical Slaw 145

Lemon-Butter Parmesan Tilapia 146

Curried Shrimp Pasta Bowl 148

N'awlins Shrimp Gumbo 149

Shrimp & Kale Pasta Toss 150

Rustic Steamed Mussels 152

Scallops & Mushroom Risotto 153

New England Lobster Rolls 154

The Real Deal Crab Cakes 156

Easy Cheesy Ravioli Lasagna 157

Mac 'n' Cheese with Pretzel Confetti 158

Orecchiette with Vodka Sauce 160

Tuscan-Style Sausage Rigatoni 161

Not-Your-Nonna's "Meatballs" 162

Low-Carb, Keto Margherita Pizza 164

The Better Veggie Burger 166

GREEK-STYLE SALMON IN PHYLLO

Anything that requires multiple "butter brushings" is likely to get my seal of approval, and that includes this phyllo-wrapped fish dish. If you've ever had spanakopita or baklava, then you're already familiar with this crispy and flaky pastry—it's used a lot in Greek cuisine. Here, I've paired it with salmon and some tasty Greek flavors to make a winning combo. Don't forget to keep your fingers damp and your dough covered, so it doesn't dry out!

Serves 4

1 (9-ounce) package frozen chopped spinach, thawed and squeezed dry

½ cup crumbled feta cheese

½ cup Greek salad dressing

½ a (16-ounce) package frozen phyllo dough, thawed

½ stick butter, melted

4 (4-ounce) skinless salmon fillets

- Preheat oven to 425 degrees F. Coat a baking sheet with cooking spray.

- In a medium bowl, combine spinach, feta cheese, and Greek dressing; mix well and set aside.

- On a cutting board, lay out 1 phyllo sheet and brush lightly with butter. Place another sheet on top and brush with butter. Repeat with 2 more sheets, brushing each with butter. Place 1 salmon fillet along the short side of phyllo. Top salmon with ¼ of spinach mixture. Fold in long sides of phyllo, then roll up envelope-style and place seam-side down on baking sheet. Lightly brush top with butter and cut 2 slits in top of phyllo. (This helps any steam escape.) Repeat with remaining phyllo and salmon fillets.

- Bake 15 to 18 minutes or until phyllo is golden brown and fish flakes easily with a fork.

To make things even better, I often whip up a quick throw-together tzatziki sauce (also known as a cucumber sauce) to serve with the fish. It's made by mixing together ½ cup plain yogurt, ½ cup shredded cucumber, 1 teaspoon lemon juice, 1 clove garlic, minced, ¼ teaspoon salt, and ⅛ teaspoon black pepper. MCM

SEAFOOD, PASTA, & MORE

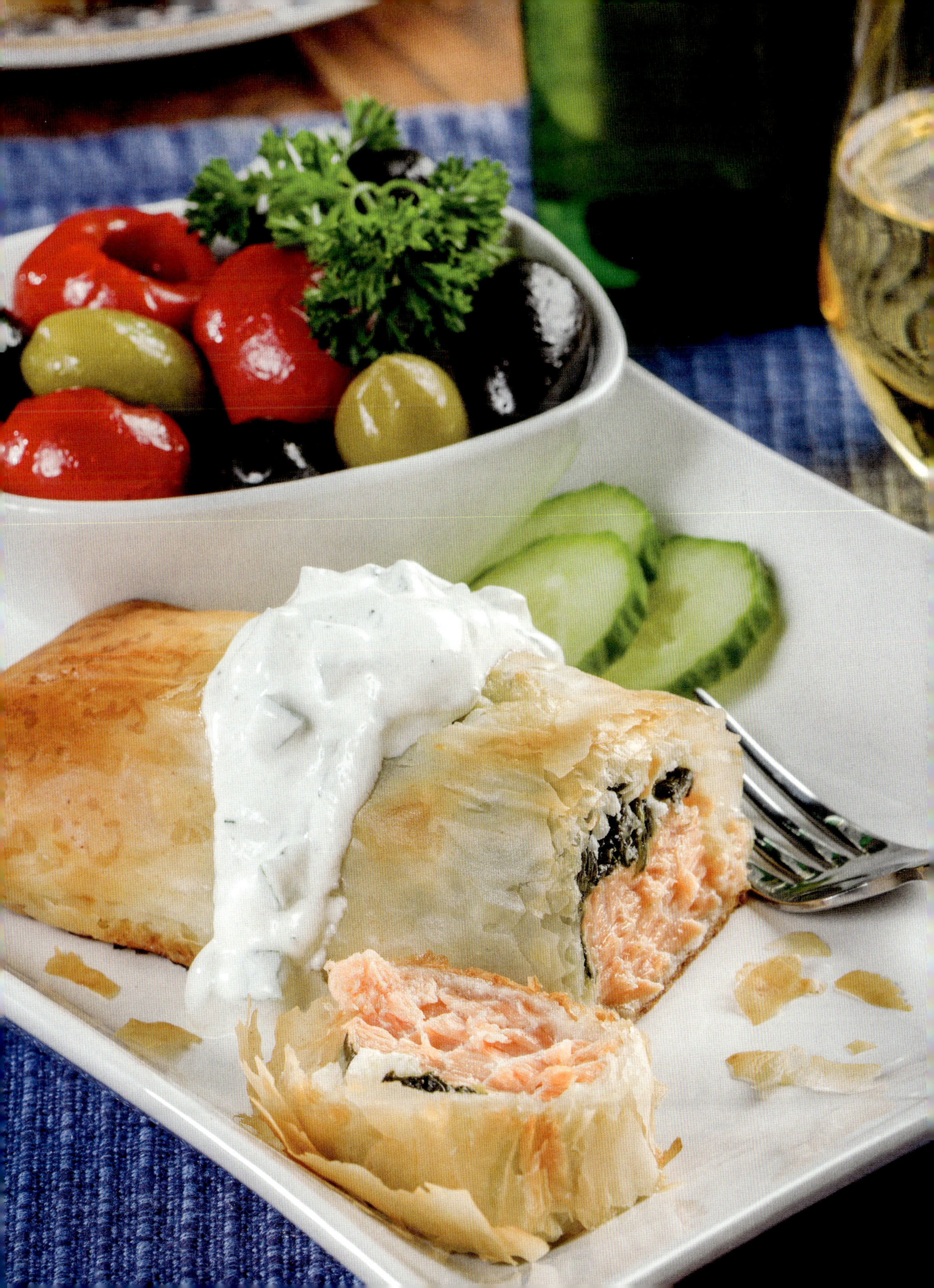

READY-IN-20 BAKED FISH

Pull out your timer. Ready? Get set. Go! You'll have dinner on the table in no time with this mouthwatering recipe. While the creamy, cheesy fish is baking in the oven, you can get working on the side dishes (maybe my Crispy-Crunchy Carrot Pancakes or Farm Fresh Potato Salad?) and setting the table. Just make sure you hurry, because it'll be ready in 20!

Serves 4 to 5

1-½ pounds white-fleshed fish fillets

1 cup sour cream

¼ cup shredded Parmesan cheese

½ teaspoon paprika

¼ teaspoon salt

¼ teaspoon black pepper

2 tablespoons Italian-style bread crumbs

2 tablespoons butter, melted

- Preheat oven to 350 degrees F. Coat a 9- x 13-inch baking dish with cooking spray. Place fillets in baking dish in a single layer; set aside.

- In a medium bowl, combine sour cream, Parmesan cheese, paprika, salt, and pepper; mix well. Spread mixture evenly over fillets, sprinkle with bread crumbs, and drizzle with butter.

- Bake 20 to 25 minutes or until fish flakes easily with a fork.

Cod, tilapia, and haddock are all great fish options, but you can use another white-fleshed fish if you prefer. You'll probably want to start by checking what's freshest or on sale.

MCM

SEAFOOD, PASTA, & MORE

BLACKENED CATFISH & TROPICAL SLAW

I'll be honest with you—I haven't always been a big fan of catfish. I think for a lot of people, catfish has a bad rap. But after learning more about farm-raised catfish and how fresh-tasting and versatile it is, I was hooked (pun intended). Now I love finding new ways to make it at home. This blackened version is A+, especially when it's topped with my tropical coleslaw. You get the perfect balance of sweet and heat!

Serves 4

TROPICAL SLAW

3 cups coleslaw mix

¼ cup diced red bell pepper

2 tablespoons chopped red onion

1 (8-ounce) can crushed pineapple, drained

1 tablespoon sugar

¼ cup rice wine vinegar

1 tablespoon vegetable oil

2 tablespoons butter

4 (6-ounce) catfish fillets

4 tablespoons blackened seasoning

- To make Tropical Slaw, in a medium bowl, combine coleslaw mix, red bell pepper, onion, pineapple, sugar, vinegar, and oil; mix well and set aside.

- In a large skillet over medium heat, melt butter. While that's heating up, coat both sides of fish fillets with blackened seasoning. Sauté 5 to 6 minutes per side or until fish flakes easily with a fork; remove to a platter.

- Top blackened fish with slaw and serve.

LEMON-BUTTER PARMESAN TILAPIA

If you're not eating fish once or twice a week, you could be missing out on some serious brainpower. I don't know if you've heard, but there's a lot of science out there that proves that fish is brain food and can improve memory. Whether or not it's true, I figure I have nothing to lose! Plus, it gives me another excuse to cook up yummy, buttery fish.

Serves 4

½ cup panko bread crumbs

¼ cup grated Parmesan cheese

½ teaspoon garlic powder

¼ teaspoon black pepper

4 tilapia fillets

3 tablespoons butter, melted

1 tablespoon lemon juice

- Preheat oven to 375 degrees F. Coat a rimmed baking sheet with cooking spray.

- In a small bowl, combine bread crumbs, Parmesan cheese, garlic powder, and pepper; mix well.

- Place fish on baking sheet and cover each with 2 tablespoons of Parmesan mixture.

- In a small bowl, combine butter and lemon juice; mix well and drizzle evenly over fish. (This makes it buttery-delicious, so no skimping here.)

- Bake 15 to 20 minutes or until fish flakes easily with a fork and crust is golden.

Make sure you use a good refrigerated Parmesan cheese that's freshly grated and not the shaker-can type. Trust me, it makes a big difference! MCM

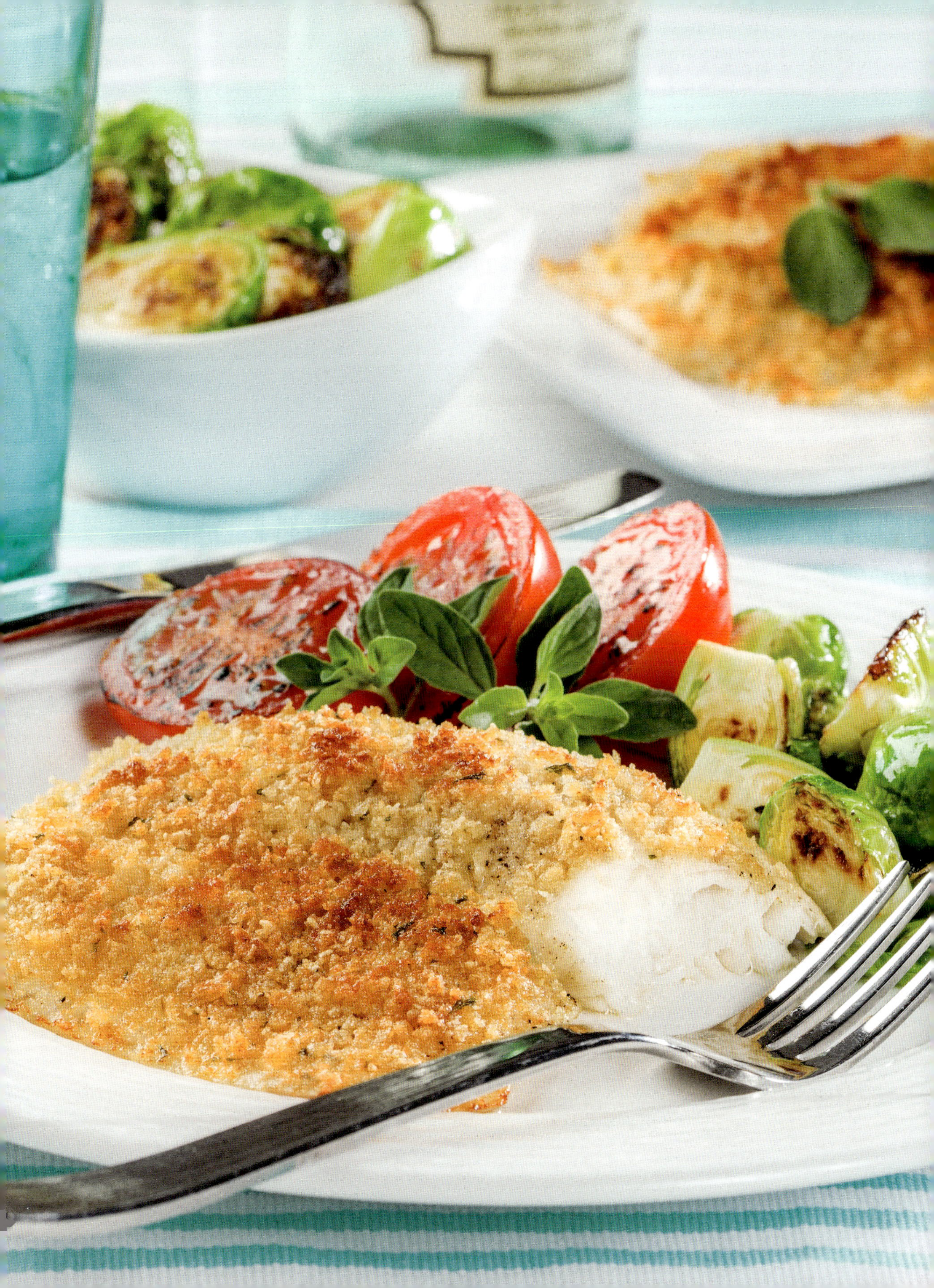

CURRIED SHRIMP PASTA BOWL

Lately, I've been doing a little more experimenting in my kitchen, especially with ethnic flavors and cuisines. It's been a great way for me to introduce my taste buds to something new while learning a little more about other cultures. This is an Indian-inspired shrimp dish that I like to serve over spaghetti. (It's hard to resist my Italian side!) It's easy to whip up and has so much great flavor. I can't wait to hear what you think!

Serves 4 to 5

1 pound spaghetti
2 tablespoons butter
2 onions, chopped
2 cloves garlic, minced
1 (15-ounce) can coconut milk
4 teaspoons curry powder
2 tablespoons lime juice
2 tablespoons honey
1 pound raw large shrimp, peeled, deveined, and tails removed
2 tablespoons chopped fresh basil

- Prepare spaghetti according to package directions; drain, remove to a serving bowl, and cover to keep warm.

- Meanwhile, in a large skillet over medium heat, melt butter. Add onions and garlic, and sauté until tender. Add coconut milk, curry powder, lime juice, and honey; bring to a boil.

- Add shrimp and cook 3 to 4 minutes or until shrimp are pink. Pour over spaghetti and sprinkle with chopped basil.

I like to serve this with some warm naan bread, which is an Indian flatbread, similar to a pita. I use it to sop up every drop of flavorful sauce. MCM

N'AWLINS SHRIMP GUMBO

You don't have to wait for Mardi Gras to serve this. This one-pot Bayou favorite has become one of my new weeknight go-to's. It cooks up in no time and makes plenty, so there's always enough left over for lunch the next day. Most importantly, it tastes incredible. I once served this to a friend who said, "It brings some South to your mouth!"

Serves 5 to 6

- 1 stick butter
- 1 cup sliced celery
- 1 green bell pepper, chopped
- 1 cup chopped onion
- 1 teaspoon chopped garlic
- 2 tablespoons all-purpose flour
- 1 teaspoon salt
- 1 teaspoon chili powder
- ¼ teaspoon cayenne pepper
- 2 (14.5-ounce) cans diced tomatoes, undrained
- 1 cup frozen okra, thawed
- 1 cup water
- 1 pound raw large shrimp, peeled, deveined, and tails removed

■ In a soup pot over medium heat, melt butter. Add celery, green pepper, onion, and garlic, and cook 5 minutes or until vegetables are tender, stirring occasionally. Stir in flour, salt, chili powder, and cayenne pepper, and cook 1 minute. (It's okay if the butter starts to brown a bit; it will add to the flavor.)

■ Add tomatoes with their juice, okra, and water and simmer 8 to 10 minutes, stirring occasionally.

■ Add shrimp and cook 4 to 5 minutes or until shrimp are pink. Serve immediately.

If you're sensitive to spicy foods, don't be scared off by the cayenne pepper. Just start by adding a little bit at a time until you get it just the way you like it. MCM

SEAFOOD, PASTA, & MORE

SHRIMP & KALE PASTA TOSS

This pasta toss is "shrimply" the best! No, really! It's fresh-tasting and filling while still being light and bright. I love how the lemon complements the tender-cooked kale and adds its own zest to the dish. Of course, you can't have zest without a little zing, and that's exactly what the buttery shrimp brings to the bowl. Toss them both in some penne and you've got yourself a winning meal.

Serves 4 to 5

- 8 ounces penne pasta
- ½ stick butter
- 2 tablespoons olive oil
- 1 pound raw extra-large shrimp, peeled and deveined
- ½ teaspoon salt
- ¼ teaspoon black pepper
- 4 cloves garlic, minced
- ¼ teaspoon red pepper flakes
- 4 cups kale, ribs removed, chopped
- 1 lemon, zested
- 2 tablespoons lemon juice

- ■ Cook pasta according to package directions; drain, reserving ½ cup of pasta water; set aside.

- ■ Meanwhile, in a large skillet over medium-high heat, melt butter and oil; add shrimp, salt, and black pepper, and sauté 2 to 3 minutes or until shrimp turn pink, stirring occasionally. Remove shrimp mixture to a bowl.

- ■ Add garlic and red pepper flakes to skillet and cook 1 minute. Add kale, lemon zest, lemon juice, and reserved pasta water. Cook 3 minutes or until kale is tender. Return shrimp mixture and pasta to skillet, toss to coat, and simmer until heated through. Serve immediately.

The reason why I use both butter and olive oil in this recipe is that the butter adds a rich, creamy taste, while the olive oil allows me to cook everything just the way I like it without it burning. (Good quality olive oils have a high smoke point.) MCM

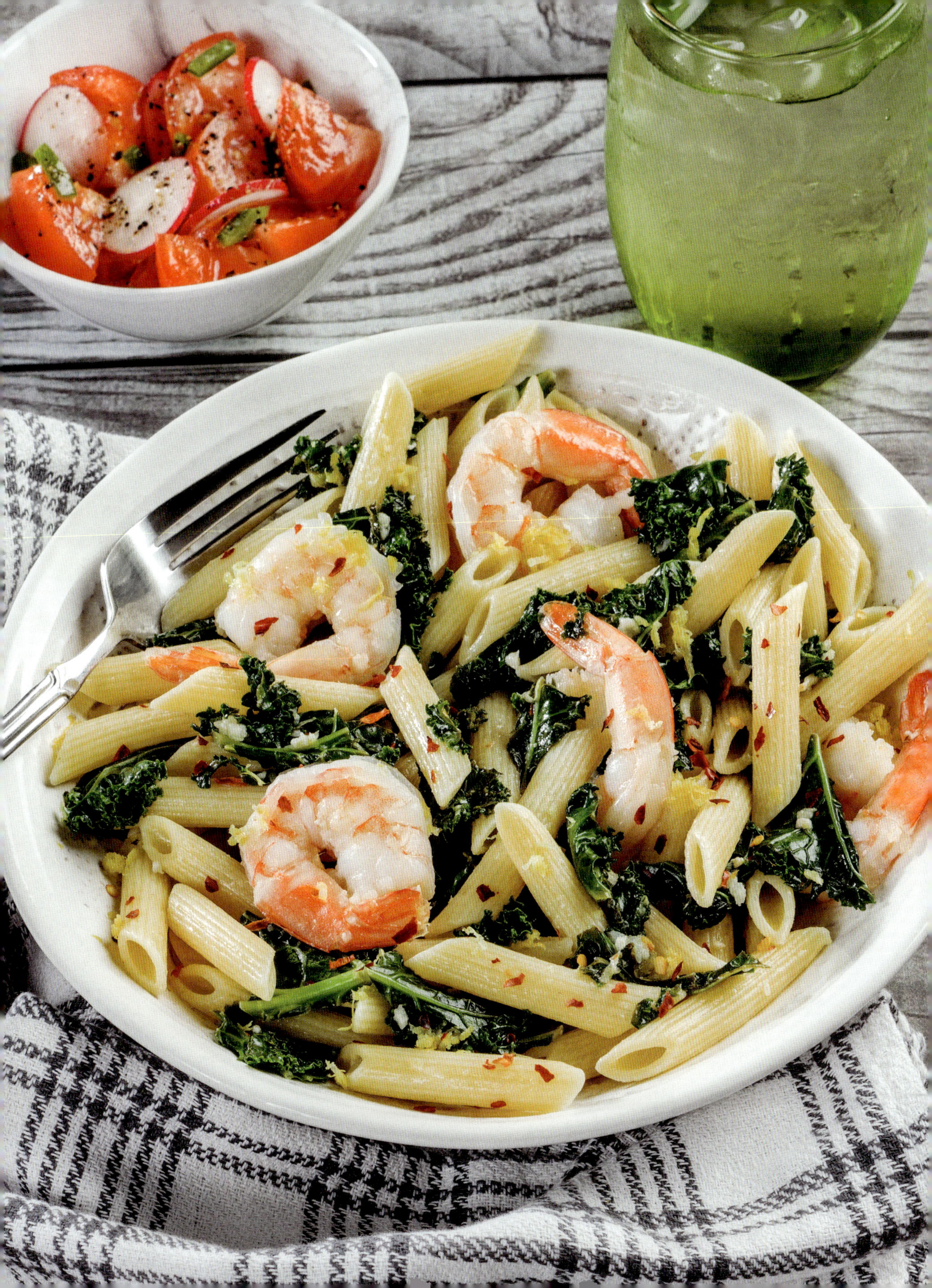

RUSTIC STEAMED MUSSELS

After losing some weight over the past year, I tried to add some healthy bulk with a little strength training. Let me tell you—it's not easy to build "mussel" at my age. Fortunately, it's easy to enjoy mussels at any age, especially when they're prepared like this! (I hope that gave you a good laugh!) These are cooked rustic-style, with white wine and stewed tomatoes. They're so good, you won't be leaving any behind!

Serves 3 to 4

- 2 pounds fresh mussels, cleaned
- 1 (14.5-ounce) can diced tomatoes, juice reserved
- ¼ cup dry white wine
- ½ teaspoon dried oregano
- 1 teaspoon salt
- ¼ teaspoon black pepper

- In a large pot, combine all ingredients (including the juice from the tomatoes). Cover and bring to a boil over high heat.

- Reduce heat to low and simmer 6 to 8 minutes or until mussels open. Do not overcook. Discard any mussels that don't open. Remove to a serving platter or individual bowls and serve.

I'm not about to leave behind any of the flavor-packed sauce. That's why I serve these in big bowls and use the empty shells as a scoop. That's right, spoons are optional. — MCM

SEAFOOD, PASTA, & MORE

SCALLOPS & MUSHROOM RISOTTO

As I've mentioned before, I'm a "fun guy," but I'm not down with the "fungi" (darn allergies!), so this dish is one I make for the mushroom lovers in my life. (If I make it for myself, I use cut asparagus rather than mushrooms.) I'm not sure why restaurants charge so much for risotto, considering it's so easy to make. Sure, the scallops add a few dollars, but they're worth it!

Serves 4 to 5

1 pound fresh sea scallops (or frozen and thawed), patted dry

¼ teaspoon salt

½ teaspoon black pepper, divided

6 tablespoons butter, divided

3 cups chicken or vegetable broth

1-½ cups sliced mushrooms

½ cup finely chopped onion

1 cup uncooked Arborio rice

1 teaspoon minced garlic

⅓ cup white wine

¼ cup grated Parmesan cheese

1 tablespoon chopped fresh parsley

- Sprinkle scallops evenly with salt and ¼ teaspoon pepper. In a large skillet over medium-high heat, melt 3 tablespoons butter; sauté scallops 3 to 4 minutes per side or until browned and firm in center. Remove to a platter and cover to keep warm.

- In a saucepan over medium heat, bring broth to a simmer, but do not boil. Keep warm over low heat.

- Meanwhile, in a large saucepan over medium-high heat, melt 2 tablespoons butter. Add mushrooms and onion and sauté 4 to 5 minutes or until softened. Stir in rice, garlic, and wine; cook until wine is absorbed. Add 1 cup hot broth, stirring constantly until liquid is nearly absorbed. Repeat process, adding remaining broth 1 cup at a time, stirring constantly until broth is absorbed each time. (This process will take about 15 minutes and is worth every minute as it will make the rice nice and creamy.)

- Remove from heat. Stir in remaining 1 tablespoon butter, the Parmesan cheese, parsley, and remaining ¼ teaspoon pepper. Serve immediately, topped with scallops.

NEW ENGLAND LOBSTER ROLLS

I love New England, especially Cape Cod. It's got such a great laid back vibe and the food is amazing. One of my favorites is the classic lobster roll—I could eat one every day I'm there. Unfortunately, with my busy schedule at QVC, I don't get to go there as often as I'd like. But there's a bright side! I've found a way to bring the taste of the Cape back home, and now you can too.

Makes 4

1 (1 to 1-¼ pound) live lobster (see note)

¼ cup mayonnaise

½ cup chopped celery

½ teaspoon dried tarragon

1 tablespoon lemon juice

¼ teaspoon salt

¼ teaspoon black pepper

2 tablespoons butter, melted

4 New England-style top-split hotdog rolls

■ Fill a soup pot with water about ¾ of the way full and bring to a boil over high heat. Place lobster into the pot, claws first, cover and return to a boil. Cook 10 to 15 minutes or until lobster turns bright red. Carefully remove from pot and let cool.

■ Using a seafood cracker, remove meat from lobster and cut into 1-inch chunks. (Be careful, lobster shells are sharp!)

■ In a medium bowl, combine mayonnaise, celery, tarragon, lemon juice, salt, and pepper; mix well. Toss dressing with lobster meat and refrigerate until ready to use.

■ Brush butter on outside of rolls and lightly toast in a skillet. Fill rolls evenly with lobster mixture and serve.

If cooking a whole fresh lobster isn't for you -- no worries. Most supermarket fish departments will steam them for you. And if you ask nicely, many will even remove the meat for you too! MCM

SEAFOOD, PASTA, & MORE

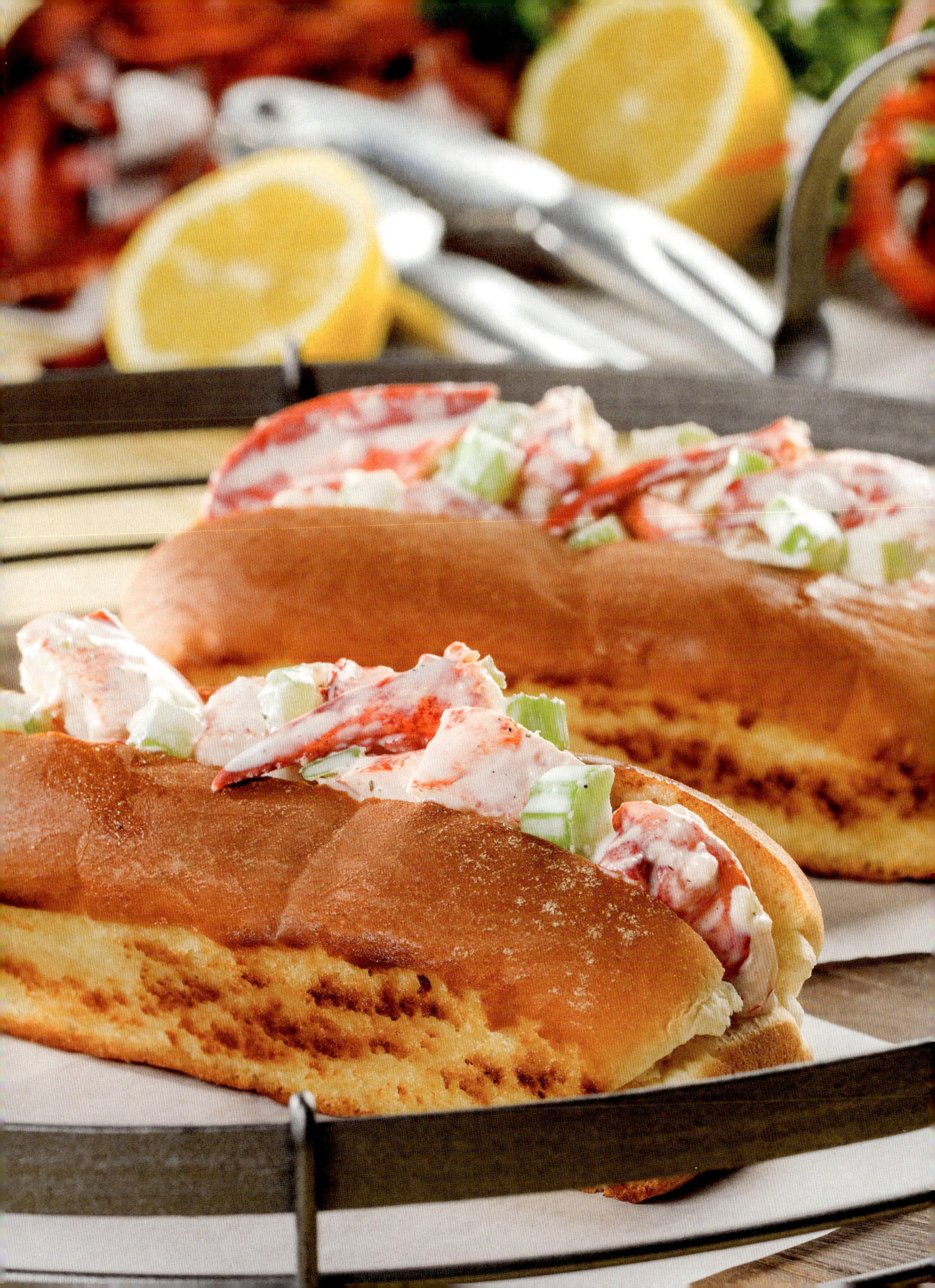

THE REAL DEAL CRAB CAKES

If you know me, you know that I love crab cakes. If a menu has crab cakes on it, I'll give them a try. From all of this taste-testing, I've come to know what I like and what I don't like. At its most basic, a great crab cake should have lots of chunky crab without a ton of fillers. And the best of the best are formed by hand, not compressed by a machine. Now, I hope you'll enjoy my take on a simple, but delicious crab cake.

Makes 8

1 egg
1 tablespoon mayonnaise
1 teaspoon Dijon mustard
1 teaspoon seafood seasoning (like Old Bay®)
8 saltine crackers, crushed
1 pound jumbo lump crabmeat
2 tablespoons vegetable oil

- In a large bowl, lightly beat egg. Add mayonnaise, mustard, seafood seasoning, and crushed crackers; mix well.

- Gently stir in crabmeat until thoroughly combined. Using an ice cream scoop, scoop into 8 equal portions onto a baking sheet; lightly flatten with your hand. (Do not pack them firmly.)

- In a skillet over medium heat, heat oil until hot. Sauté crab cakes about 3 to 4 minutes per side or until golden and heated through.

If you prefer, you can cook these in an air fryer. Simply brush them with a bit of oil and pop them in a 350 degree air fryer for about 10 to 12 minutes, flipping them halfway through cooking time. MCM

EASY CHEESY RAVIOLI LASAGNA

I know that lasagna can be a little intimidating for some people (all those layers!), which is why I wanted to share a super easy way for you to make it at home. The great thing about this is that it's unique. Just use ravioli instead of having to add both the traditional lasagna noodles and ricotta! Not only is it easy, but every bite delivers cheesy goodness! Oh, and did I mention you get triple the cheese with this recipe?

Serves 8 to 10

2 (20-ounce) bags frozen square cheese ravioli

2 (28-ounce) jars spaghetti sauce

1 cup cooked crumbled sausage

3 tablespoons grated Parmesan cheese

3 cups (12 ounces) shredded mozzarella cheese

■ Preheat oven to 350 degrees F. In a large pot of boiling salted water, cook ravioli until just tender (don't overcook); drain.

■ Spoon 1-¼ cups spaghetti sauce on bottom of a 9- x 13-inch baking dish. Place ⅓ ravioli in a single layer over sauce, sprinkle with ⅓ sausage, then sprinkle with 1 tablespoon Parmesan cheese. Pour 1-¼ cups sauce over Parmesan cheese, then top with 1 cup mozzarella cheese. Repeat layers two more times.

■ Bake 35 to 40 minutes or until heated through and cheese is melted and bubbly. Let rest 5 minutes before serving, to allow it to set.

If you're not a sausage lover, you can just leave it out or substitute with cooked and crumbled ground beef. MCM

MAC 'N' CHEESE WITH PRETZEL CONFETTI

In my *Easy Everyday Favorites* cookbook, I introduced you to the mac 'n' cheese I normally make for my kids. It was so well-loved that I decided to go back into the kitchen and see if I could whip up another tasty version. Well, here it is—a blond version of my extra-cheesy, ooey-gooey, yummy macaroni. And this time, I've added a bit of Philly flair to it with a sprinkling of crunchy snack pretzels!

Serves 6 to 8

- 1 pound medium shell-shaped pasta
- ½ stick butter
- ¼ cup all-purpose flour
- 3 cups milk
- 1 (8-ounce) block sharp white cheddar cheese, shredded
- 1 (8-ounce) block Muenster cheese, shredded
- 1-½ teaspoons dry mustard
- 1 teaspoon salt
- ½ teaspoon black pepper
- ½ cup cubed mozzarella cheese
- ¼ cup chopped pretzels

■ In a soup pot, cook pasta according to package directions; drain and set aside.

■ In the same pot over medium heat, melt butter, then stir in flour. Gradually stir in milk and cook 5 minutes or until thickened, stirring frequently. Add cheddar cheese and Muenster cheese, dry mustard, salt, and pepper, and stir 3 to 5 minutes or until cheeses are melted.

■ Add cooked pasta and cubed mozzarella cheese to pot; mix until evenly coated. Cook on low heat 2 to 3 minutes or until heated through, stirring constantly. Sprinkle with pretzels. Serve immediately.

Make this mac and cheese all your own by adding in your hometown favorites. You can do anything from bacon and sliced jalapeños to peas and carrots. Have fun and personalize yours to fit your family's tastes! MCM

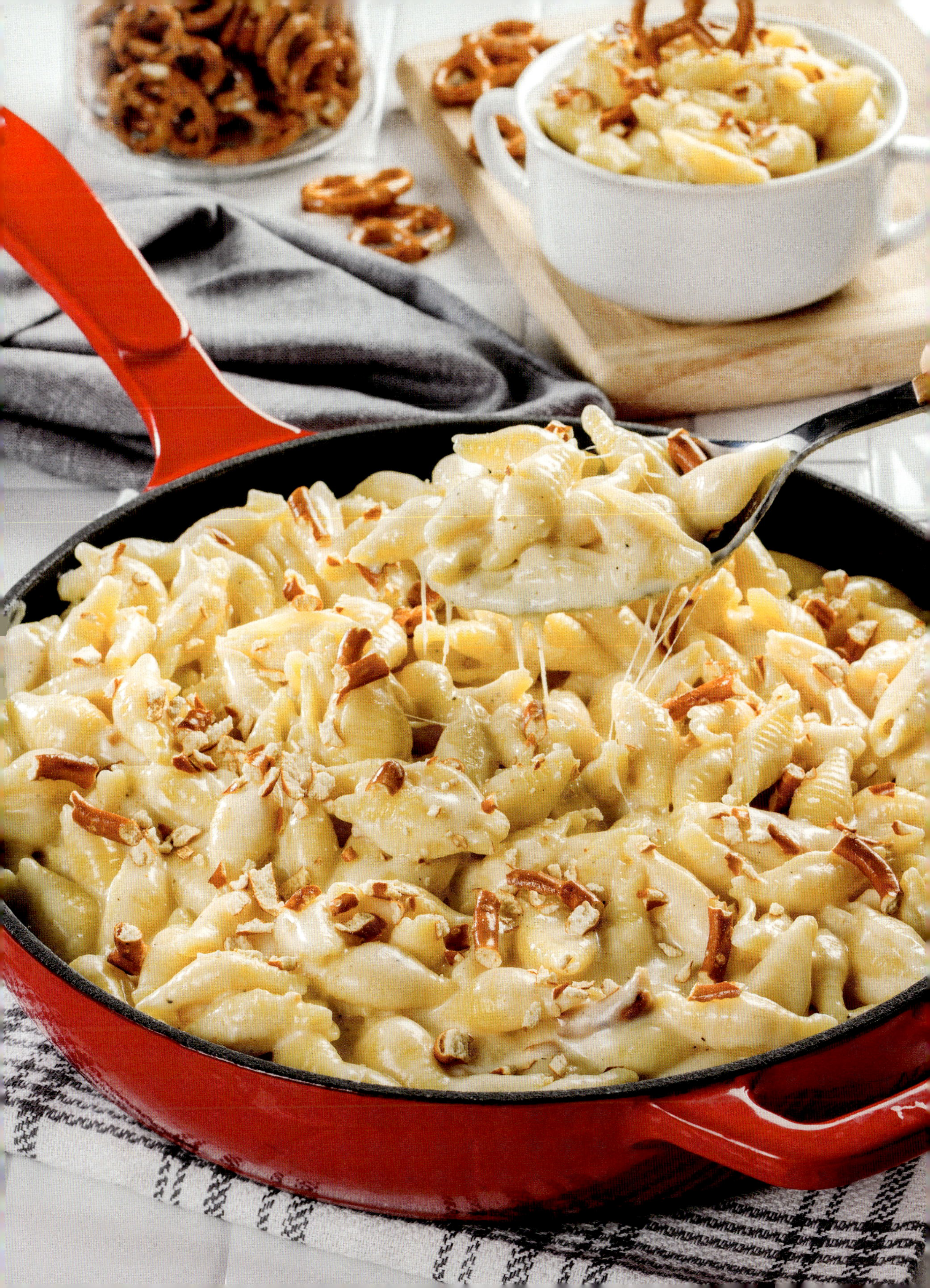

ORECCHIETTE WITH VODKA SAUCE

I've made many versions of vodka sauces over the years, and this one is honestly the best of the best. The secret is the mascarpone cheese. It makes the sauce so rich and creamy; you'll literally want to lick your plate clean. Since you might not want to do that in front of everyone else seated around the table, make sure you set out a basket of crusty bread to help you out.

Serves 3 to 4

1 tablespoon olive oil

1 tablespoon chopped garlic

¼ cup vodka

2 (14.5-ounce) cans diced tomatoes, undrained

12 ounces orecchiette pasta

1 (8-ounce) container mascarpone cheese

2 tablespoons coarsely chopped fresh basil

1 teaspoon salt

1 teaspoon black pepper

■ In a medium saucepan over medium heat, heat oil. Add garlic and sauté 1 to 2 minutes, just until browned. Add vodka and tomatoes with their juice; bring to a boil. Reduce heat to low and simmer 15 minutes.

■ Meanwhile, cook pasta according to package directions. Drain and return pasta to pot; cover to keep warm.

■ Add remaining ingredients to tomato mixture and stir until thoroughly combined and cheese is melted. Pour over pasta and stir until combined, rewarming over low heat, if necessary. Serve immediately.

TUSCAN-STYLE SAUSAGE RIGATONI

My summer trips to Italy are spent exploring as much of the country as possible, and that includes tasting all of the wonderful dishes that are unique to each region. In Tuscany, olive oil is king, beans are fairly common, and the food is simple, but still very impressive. Inspired by everything I've seen and eaten during these yearly visits, I've come up with a pasta dish that celebrates some of my favorite Tuscan flavors.

Serves 4 to 5

- 8 ounces rigatoni pasta
- 1 tablespoon olive oil
- 1 pound turkey sausage, with casing removed
- 1 cup coarsely chopped onion
- 3 cloves garlic, minced
- 1-¾ cups chicken broth
- 1 (15.5-ounce) can cannellini beans, undrained
- 1 teaspoon dried thyme leaves
- ½ teaspoon salt
- ¼ teaspoon black pepper
- 5 cups packed baby spinach
- ¼ cup sliced sundried tomatoes in oil

◼ Cook pasta according to package directions; drain and set aside.

◼ Meanwhile, in a large skillet over medium-high heat, heat oil until hot. Cook sausage, onion, and garlic 8 minutes or until browned. Add broth, beans, thyme, salt, and pepper and cook 5 minutes.

◼ Stir in cooked pasta, spinach, and sundried tomatoes. Cook 3 to 4 minutes or until heated through. Serve immediately.

I call for turkey sausage in this recipe, but I've definitely made this with other sausage varieties too, so go ahead and use a traditional pork sausage or a specialty sausage you've found at your supermarket. And if you don't have cannellini beans at home, you can toss in a can of undrained garbanzo beans instead. MCM

SEAFOOD, PASTA, & MORE

NOT-YOUR-NONNA'S "MEATBALLS"

Fair warning—if you've got an Italian grandmother (like my nonna on my father's side), then you might want to prepare for some backlash the first time you tell her you're making these. Why? Well, because there's no meat in these meatballs, and you know how nonna can be about her meatball recipe (mine sure was particular!). The good news is, once you get her to agree to a taste of these "meaty" eggplant meatballs, she's going to be sold. They're unbelievably good.

Makes 18

1 tablespoon olive oil

1 large eggplant, unpeeled and cut into 1-inch chunks

1/3 cup water

1-1/2 cups Italian bread crumbs

1/4 cup grated Parmesan cheese plus extra for sprinkling

1 egg, beaten

3 cloves garlic, minced

2 tablespoons chopped fresh basil

1/2 teaspoon salt

1/4 teaspoon black pepper

1 pound spinach fettucine pasta

1 cup ricotta cheese

1 (24-ounce) jar spaghetti sauce, warmed

- Preheat oven to 375 degrees F. Coat a rimmed baking sheet with cooking spray.

- In a large skillet over medium heat, heat oil until hot. Add eggplant and water and cook 10 minutes or until tender, stirring occasionally.

- Place eggplant in a food processor and pulse 4 to 5 times or until eggplant is broken up. In a large bowl, combine eggplant, bread crumbs, Parmesan cheese, egg, garlic, basil, salt, and pepper; mix well. Form mixture into 18 balls, rolling tightly, and place on baking sheet. Bake 15 to 20 minutes or until firm and browned.

- Meanwhile, cook pasta according to package directions; drain well. Place pasta on a serving plate, and dollop with ricotta cheese. Place "meatballs" on top of ricotta cheese and top with pasta sauce and a sprinkle of Parmesan cheese.

Check out the photo for an elegant and easy serving idea. Just twirl the pasta with a fork to make the nests, set the "meatballs" on top, and top each one with a little spaghetti sauce. Now it's restaurant fancy! MCM

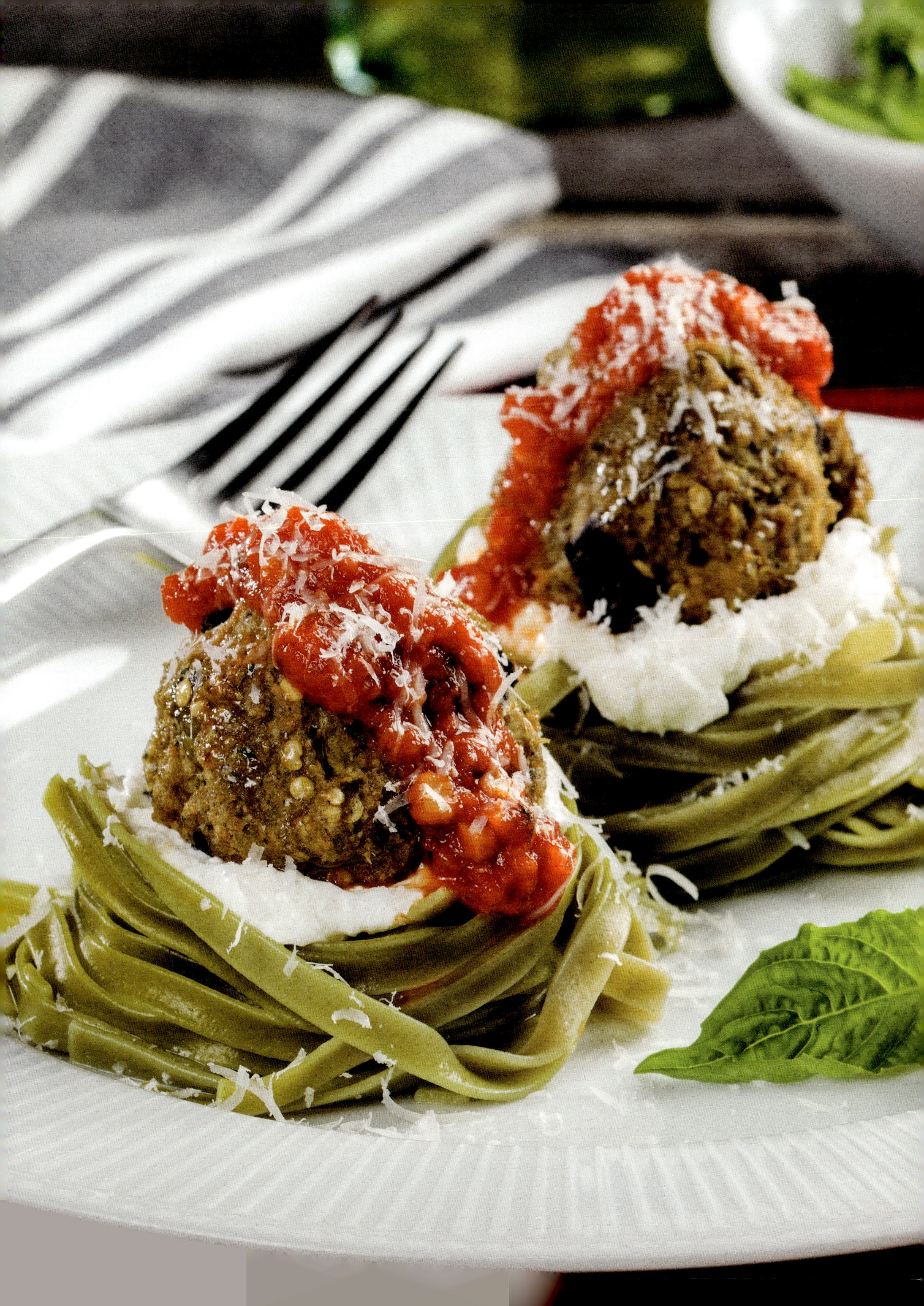

LOW-CARB KETO MARGHERITA PIZZA

The keto diet is popular these days, so of course, when I was working on losing a few pounds, I tried to follow some of its guidelines. No, I didn't adopt a keto-lifestyle, but I did successfully reduce the amount of carbs I was eating. At first, I wasn't sure I'd be able to give up traditional pizza. But then I discovered the world of low-carb keto pizza! While it might not be what you're used to, I promise it's really, really tasty (and cheesy!).

Serves 2 to 4

- 1-½ cups shredded mozzarella cheese
- 2 tablespoons cream cheese
- ¾ cup almond flour
- ½ teaspoon dried Italian seasoning
- ½ teaspoon garlic powder
- ½ teaspoon salt
- ¼ teaspoon black pepper
- 1 egg
- ¼ cup marinara sauce
- 2 plum tomatoes, sliced
- ¼ pound fresh mozzarella cheese, sliced ¼-inch thick
- 3 to 4 fresh basil leaves, thinly sliced
- Olive oil for drizzling

- Preheat oven to 400 degrees F. Coat a baking sheet with cooking spray.

- In a large nonstick skillet over medium heat, combine shredded mozzarella cheese and cream cheese, and stir constantly until melted. Remove from heat and let sit 30 seconds. Add almond flour, Italian seasoning, garlic powder, salt, pepper, and egg; mix until thoroughly combined and a dough is formed.

- On a flat surface, place dough on parchment paper. Place another piece of parchment paper over dough. Using a rolling pin, roll out dough to a 9-inch circle. (If you don't have a rolling pin, just coat the palms of your hands with cooking spray and press out dough into a thin round.) Slide dough off parchment paper onto baking sheet. Prick dough all over with a fork. Bake 10 minutes.

- Remove from oven and spread marinara sauce over crust. Top with tomato slices and fresh mozzarella cheese. Return to oven and bake 7 to 9 minutes or until crust is golden and cheese is melty. Top with basil and a drizzle of olive oil.

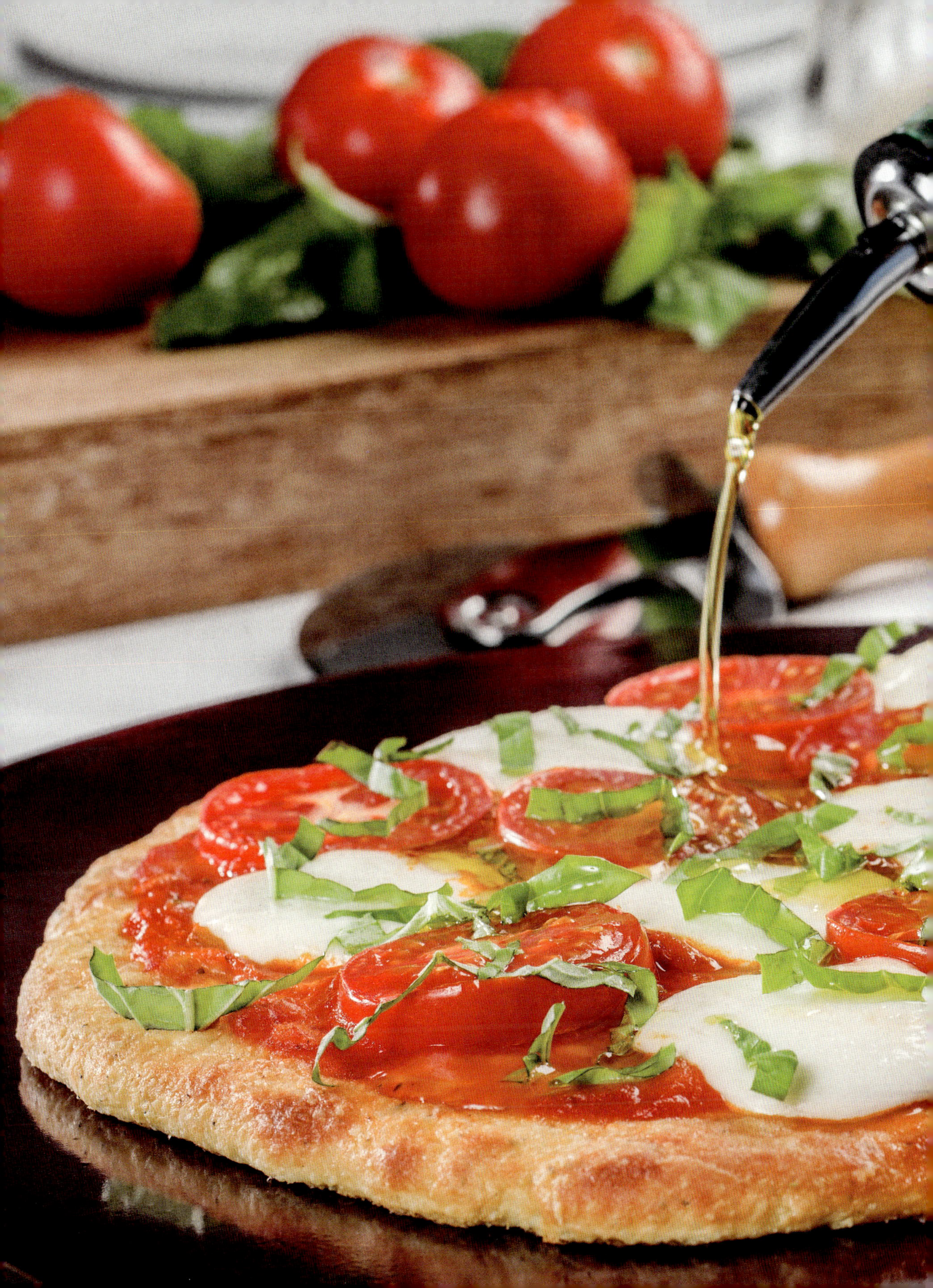

THE BETTER VEGGIE BURGER

Up until I made this, I was never a fan of bean or veggie burgers. They just never satisfied my tastes for a burger. I spent a long time trying to come up with these, and trust me, it took several attempts. But it was all worth it once I finally found the right combination of ingredients. These are quite spectacular and deliver the "beefiness" that I love and crave.

Makes 5

- 1 (15-ounce) can black beans, rinsed and drained, divided
- 2 cups chopped Portobello mushrooms
- 1 cup chopped fresh broccoli florets
- ¾ cup frozen corn, thawed
- ¼ cup chopped onion
- 1 teaspoon garlic powder
- ¼ teaspoon black pepper
- 2 eggs, beaten
- 1 tablespoon Worcestershire sauce
- 1 cup panko bread crumbs
- ¼ cup grated Parmesan cheese
- 1 tablespoon canola oil
- 5 pretzel rolls

■ In a large bowl, mash 1 cup of black beans. Add remaining whole black beans, the mushrooms, broccoli, corn, onion, garlic powder, and pepper; mix well. Add eggs, Worcestershire sauce, bread crumbs, and Parmesan cheese; mix just until combined.

■ Form mixture into 5 equal-sized patties. In a large skillet over medium heat, heat oil until hot. Cook burgers 4 to 5 minutes per side or until golden brown and heated through.

■ Place each burger on a pretzel roll and serve.

Top these with a quick dressing made with 1/2 cup buttermilk ranch dressing and 1 teaspoon hot sauce mixed together. It may sound simple, but it really makes the burger even better. Also, if you're looking for a low-carb option, try swapping iceberg lettuce leaves for the rolls. MCM

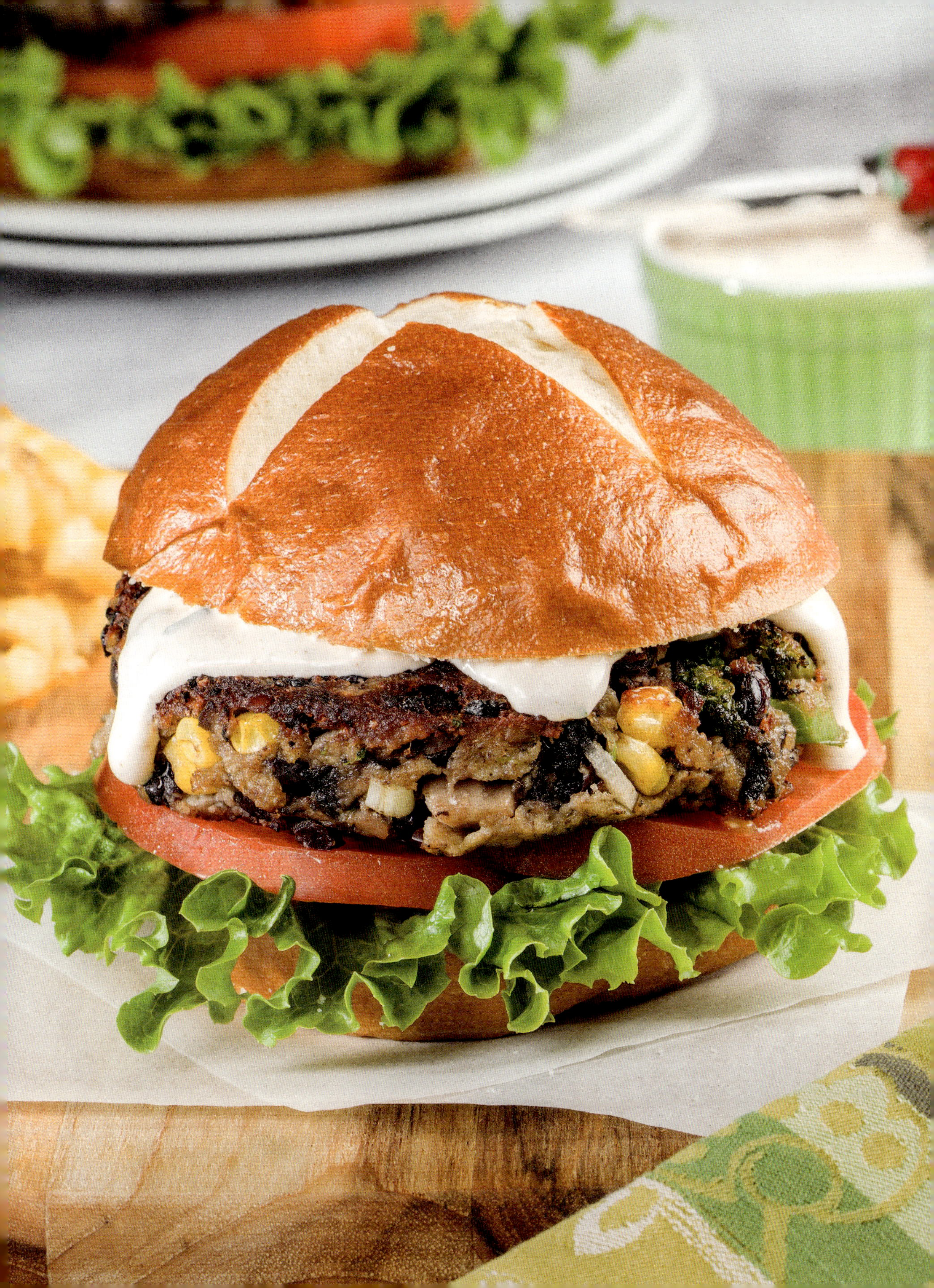

> "It's ok if you call me Bugs, since I love fresh carrots! Actually, I love any kind of fresh veggies as they add lots of color and nutrition to almost everything I make."

SIDE DISHES

Crispy-Crunchy Carrot Pancakes 170

Cauliflower Steaks with Romesco 172

Bacon-Parmesan Creamy Spinach 174

Sweet Onion Petal Crisps 175

Simply Nutty Broccoli Toss 176

Sheet Pan Root Veggies 178

Cheddar Cheesy Rice Bake 179

Heavenly Havarti Orzo Cups 180

Christmas Tree Holiday Stuffing 182

Buttery Potato Skillet 184

Grandma's Special Mashed Potatoes 186

Secret Ingredient Sweet Potato Bake 187

Feta & Kale Quick Bread 188

Farm-Fresh Potato Salad 190

Sweet Pickle Coleslaw 191

CRISPY-CRUNCHY CARROT PANCAKES

I've been making potato pancakes for years, and boy, do I love them. One day, I said to myself, "Hey MarkCharles, why don't you try making the same concept with another tasty veggie?" Well guys, as it turns out, I give myself good advice. My new carrot pancakes are so good, I think I like them even better than my potato ones. Give them a try and let me know what you think!

Makes 8

- 1 pound carrots, grated
- 2 eggs
- ¼ cup all-purpose flour
- ½ cup bread crumbs
- ½ teaspoon garlic powder
- ½ teaspoon onion powder
- ½ teaspoon ground nutmeg
- ½ teaspoon salt
- ¼ teaspoon black pepper
- 2 tablespoons vegetable oil

■ In a large bowl, combine carrots, eggs, flour, bread crumbs, garlic powder, onion powder, nutmeg, salt, and pepper; mix well.

■ Measure about ¼ cup carrot mixture and form into a patty. Repeat with remaining mixture.

■ In a large skillet over medium heat, heat oil until hot. Cook carrot pancakes, in batches, 3 to 4 minutes per side or until golden. Drain on a paper towel-lined platter; serve warm.

These can be made ahead of when you want to serve them and simply warmed up in the oven or air fryer. (P.S. They freeze really well!) *MCM*

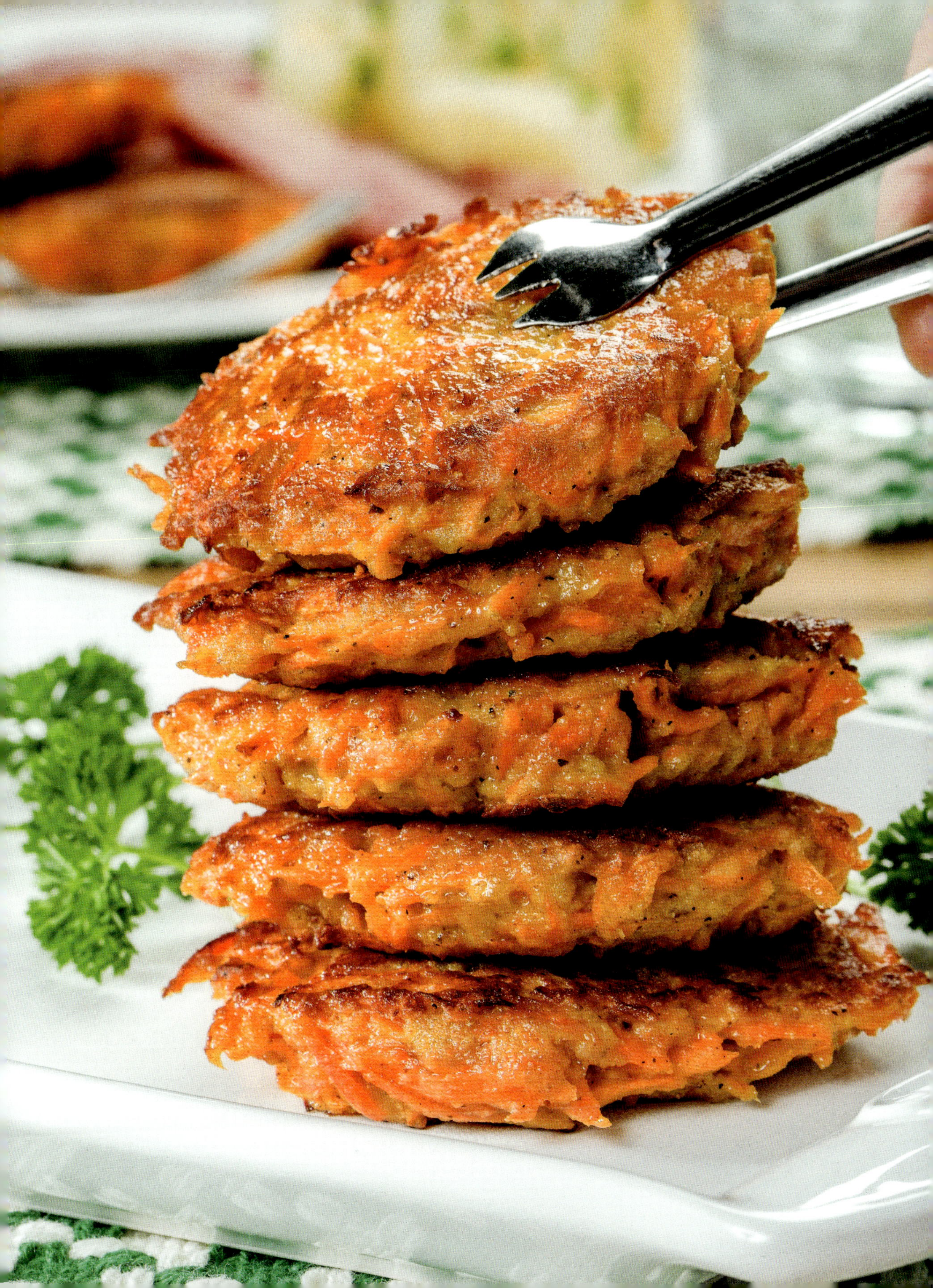

CAULIFLOWER STEAKS WITH ROMESCO

Is it possible to have "steaks" for dinner without ever going to the butcher or stopping in the meat department? The answer is yes. The next time you're at the produce counter, pick up a head of cauliflower and give these a try. I have to admit that I was surprised by how tasty these turned out. The tomato-based, homemade Romesco sauce makes them even better.

Serves 4

1 large head cauliflower

2 tablespoons olive oil

Salt for sprinkling

Black pepper for sprinkling

ROMESCO SAUCE

1 plum tomato, cut into quarters

½ cup almonds

1 (12-ounce) jar roasted red peppers, drained

2 cloves garlic

¼ cup olive oil

1 tablespoon red wine vinegar

1 teaspoon salt

1 teaspoon smoked paprika

¼ cup fresh parsley

■ Preheat oven to 425 degrees F. Trim bottom stem of cauliflower and place head of cauliflower stem-side down on a cutting board. Using a sharp knife, cut cauliflower head vertically into 4 (1-inch thick) "steaks."

■ Arrange cauliflower steaks in a single layer on a rimmed baking sheet and brush both sides with olive oil. Sprinkle evenly with salt and pepper. Roast 20 minutes. Turn each steak over and cook 10 more minutes or until edges are browned and cauliflower is tender.

■ Meanwhile, to make the Romesco sauce, in a food processor, combine all sauce ingredients and process until smooth.

■ Place cauliflower steaks on a serving platter and spoon sauce evenly over top. Serve immediately.

Over the last couple of years, cauliflower has become a favorite go-to veggie. Aside from cutting it into steaks, like I did here, I also boil and smash it like potatoes, grate it so it looks and tastes like rice, or add some cheese and shape it into tasty tots. (If you're watching your carbs, this is a great option!)

MCM

SIDE DISHES

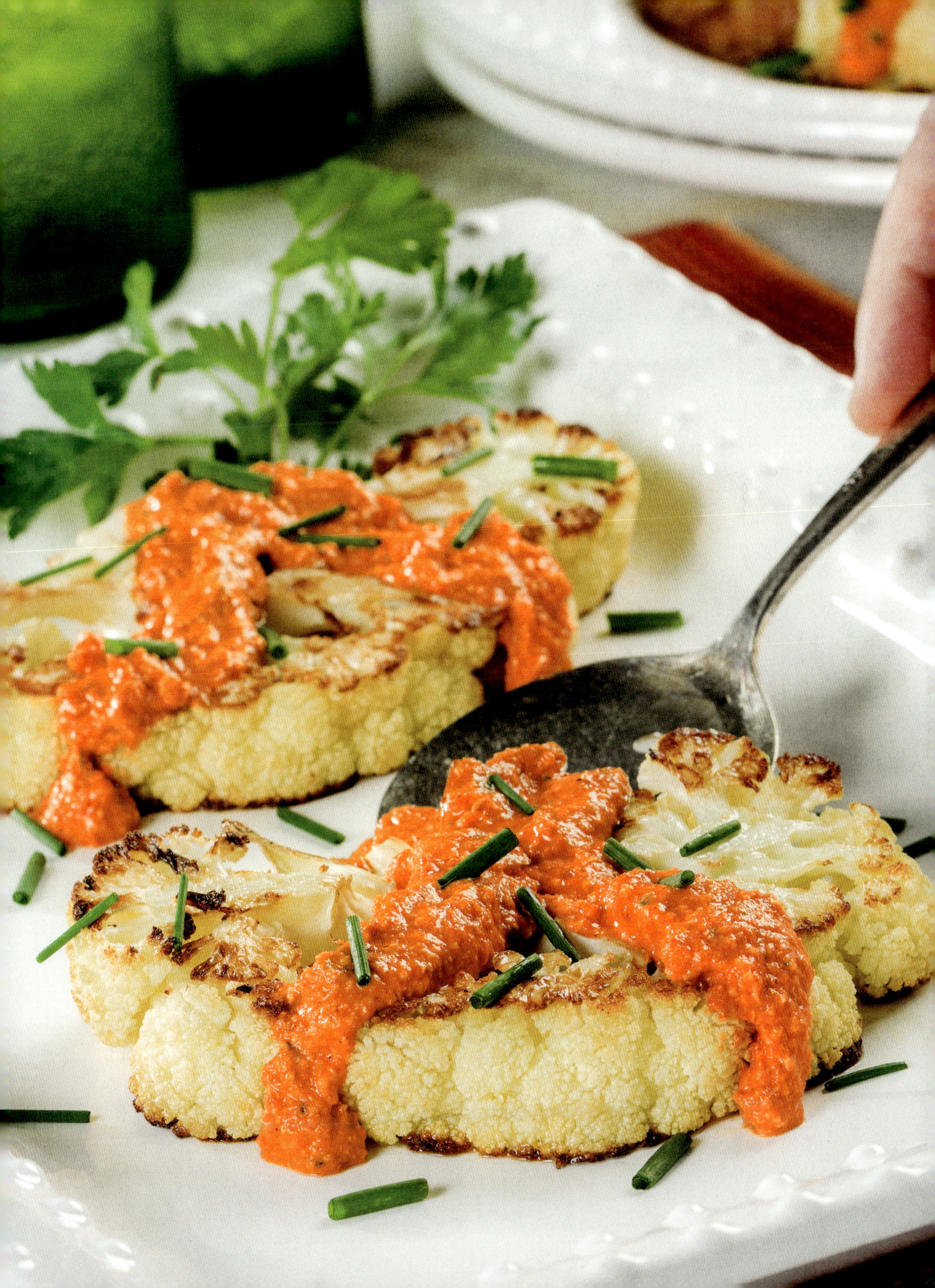

BACON-PARMESAN CREAMY SPINACH

I love creamed spinach. It's something I guess I picked up from my dad, who ordered it wherever it was offered. There's just something about all those creamy ingredients coming together. Here, you've got the trio: cream cheese, butter, and sour cream—how could you go wrong? Best part is, this dish goes with just about everything, from grilled steak to roast chicken or fish. And since it's so creamy, it's pretty easy to get the kids to eat it too!

Serves 4 to 6

4 ounces cream cheese, softened

½ stick butter, softened

¼ cup sour cream

¼ cup finely chopped onion

¼ teaspoon garlic powder

¼ teaspoon salt

¼ teaspoon black pepper

2 (10-ounce) packages frozen chopped spinach, thawed and well drained

2 tablespoons grated Parmesan cheese

2 tablespoons chopped cooked bacon

- Preheat oven to 350 degrees F. Coat a 1-½ quart baking dish with cooking spray; set aside.

- In a large bowl, combine cream cheese, butter, sour cream, onion, garlic powder, salt, and pepper; mix well. Add spinach; mix well. Spoon mixture into baking dish. Sprinkle with Parmesan cheese and chopped bacon.

- Bake 30 to 35 minutes or until heated through and top is golden.

The best part of this dish is the topping. The combo of grated Parmesan and bacon makes it irresistible! MCM

SWEET ONION PETAL CRISPS

You won't find these petals growing on any garden-variety flower. These are a cross between an onion ring and a blooming onion. But they're even better, because they're much easier to make and eat. The key to amazing and crispy petals is to start with large sweet onions. You also want to ensure your oil is hot, but not to the point where it starts smoking. By the way, I take full responsibility for your new sweet onion addiction.

Serves 6 to 8

2 large sweet onions

1 cup buttermilk

1 cup all-purpose flour

½ teaspoon baking soda

¼ teaspoon cayenne pepper

¾ teaspoon salt

½ teaspoon black pepper

2 cups vegetable oil

- Cut onions in half crosswise, remove peel, and trim off both ends. Cut each onion half into quarters and separate layers with your hands, so the pieces look like petals of a flower.

- In a large bowl, combine onions and buttermilk. In a shallow dish, combine remaining ingredients, except oil.

- In a large skillet over medium heat, heat oil until hot, but not smoking.

- Using tongs, remove onions from buttermilk, a few at a time, and place into flour mixture, coating evenly. Gently place in oil and fry 2 to 3 minutes or until golden. Drain on a paper towel-lined platter. Repeat with remaining onions; serve hot.

You already know I'm a dipper. And when it comes to these, my go-to dip is a good quality 1000 Island dressing. You can use the bottled kind or mix up a quick batch by combining 1 cup mayo, 1/4 cup ketchup and a 1/4 cup of sweet pickle relish. Happy dipping! MCM

SIDE DISHES

SIMPLY NUTTY BROCCOLI TOSS

I guess you could say, I'm kind of a nutty guy. Not that I've lost my head (although sometimes it sure does feel like it!), but more that I'm a big fan of foods that feature nuts—it's all about that crunch! I love things like fish almondine and pasta with pesto. Although there's only a small amount of pine nuts in this, they add the perfect buttery crunch.

Serves 3 to 4

- 2 tablespoons olive oil
- 4 cloves garlic, thinly sliced
- 4 heaping cups broccoli florets
- ¼ cup sun-dried tomatoes, cut into thin strips
- 1 tablespoon pine nuts
- ¼ teaspoon salt

- ■ In a large wok or skillet over medium-high heat, heat olive oil until hot. Add garlic and broccoli; cook 3 to 4 minutes or until broccoli is bright green, stirring occasionally.

- ■ Stir in sun-dried tomatoes, pine nuts, and salt. Cook 2 more minutes or until heated through.

Sometimes I leave out the salt and add a shake or two of soy sauce to give this side dish an Asian flair. Other times, I'll add about a tablespoon of grated Parmesan cheese because it adds its own nutty taste to it. Have fun and make it your own! MCM

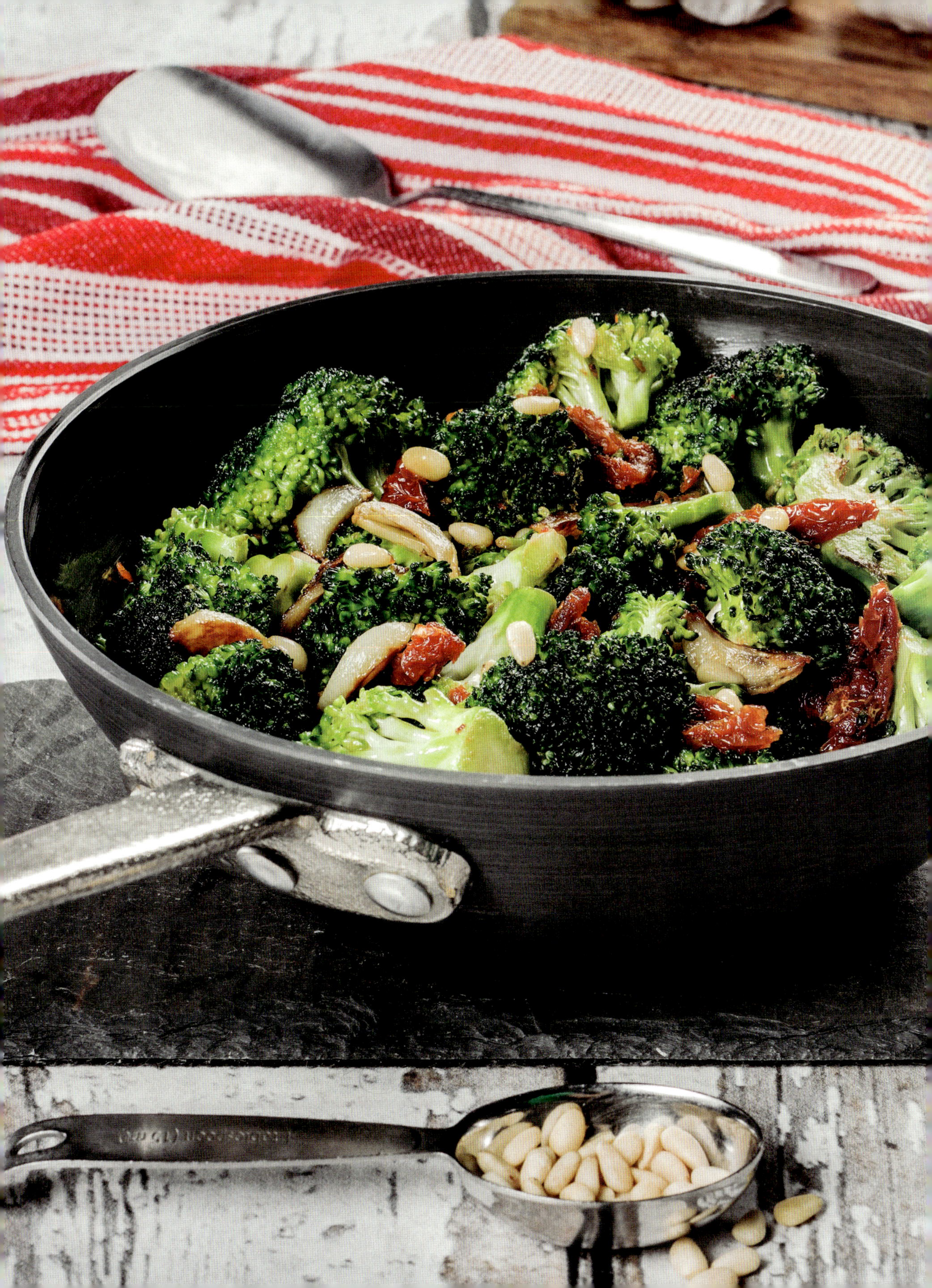

SHEET PAN ROOT VEGGIES

I'm all about making the most of my time spent in the kitchen (that's what a lot of my kitchen gadgets do!), so sheet pan cooking is something I can get behind. After some quick prep, all you have to do is throw it on a sheet pan, pop it in the oven, and go about getting other things done while it cooks. Then you just wait for the timer to ring. Wouldn't it be great if everything in life were this easy?

Serves 4 to 6

¼ cup olive oil

1 teaspoon garlic powder

1 teaspoon salt

¼ teaspoon black pepper

1 sprig of rosemary, coarsely chopped

3 parsnips, peeled and cut into 2-inch chunks

3 carrots, peeled and cut into 2-inch chunks

3 white potatoes, cut into 2-inch chunks

1 red onion, peeled and sliced into half moons

8 ounces Brussels sprouts, trimmed and cut in half

- Preheat oven to 425 degrees F.
- In a large bowl, combine oil, garlic powder, salt, pepper, and rosemary; mix well. Add vegetables and toss until evenly coated. Place vegetables in a single layer on 2 rimmed baking sheets.
- Roast 40 to 45 minutes or until vegetables are fork-tender.

CHEDDAR CHEESY RICE BAKE

Cheddar cheese is the star of this creamy rice casserole, which is unbelievably good. While this works as a side dish to just about anything, I occasionally turn it into an all-in-one meal by adding cooked turkey or chicken. (Put those leftovers to use!) I just dice it and add it to the layers of cheese.

Serves 3 to 4

- 2 cups sour cream
- 1 tablespoon sugar
- 1 teaspoon salt
- ¼ teaspoon black pepper
- 3 scallions, chopped
- 3 cups (12 ounces) shredded cheddar cheese
- 3 cups cooked rice, divided

- Preheat oven to 425 degrees F. Coat a 2-quart casserole dish with cooking spray.
- In a medium bowl, combine sour cream, sugar, salt, and pepper. In a large bowl, combine scallions and cheese.
- Place ⅓ rice in casserole dish. Layer ⅓ sour cream mixture over rice, then ⅓ cheese mixture. Repeat layers two more times, ending with a layer of cheese mixture.
- Bake 25 to 30 minutes or until bubbly and brown around the edges.

HEAVENLY HAVARTI ORZO CUPS

This is the quickest way to wow your family without having to do a whole lot. I came up with these on a whim one day while experimenting in the kitchen. I had some great Havarti cheese on-hand and I wanted to make something new and tasty. Fortunately, the results were a success. This doesn't just look like something you'd order at a restaurant; it tastes like it too.

Serves 6

1 cup uncooked orzo pasta

1 (8-ounce) block Havarti cheese, shredded

½ cup finely chopped roasted red peppers

2 eggs

1 cup milk

½ teaspoon salt

⅓ cup pesto sauce

- Preheat oven to 350 degrees F. Coat 6 (8-ounce) ramekins with cooking spray.

- Cook orzo according to package directions for al dente; drain well.

- In a large bowl, combine orzo, Havarti cheese, and peppers; mix well. Spoon mixture evenly into ramekins or custard cups and place on a baking sheet. In a medium bowl, whisk eggs, milk, and salt; pour over orzo mixture.

- Bake 30 to 35 minutes or until set in center and golden. Let stand 5 minutes, then run a knife around sides of ramekins and invert onto serving plates. (Careful, they will be hot!) Top with pesto sauce and serve.

If you don't have ramekins, you can bake these in foil cupcake liners. Just make sure you spray them with cooking spray. And be gentle handling them; they're very delicate, but so worth it. MCM

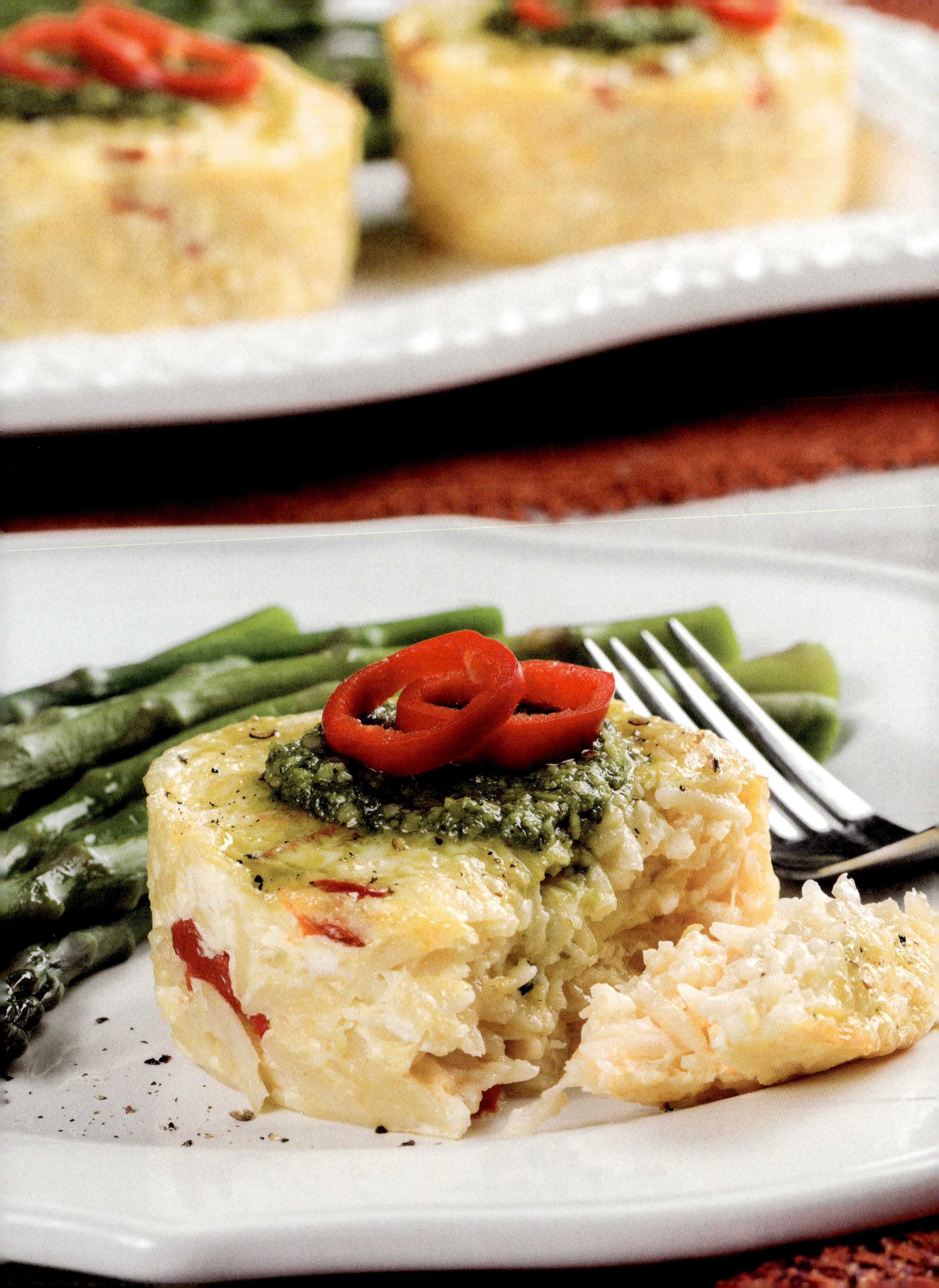

CHRISTMAS TREE HOLIDAY STUFFING

There's nothing like a great holiday stuffing, and this one is just perfect. I dress up a bag of herbed stuffing mix with some tasty veggies, buttery walnuts, and dried cranberries for sweetness. Then I bake it up in a Christmas-tree shaped pan to add some additional holiday flair. It makes the stuffing the talk of the table and it's so easy to do!

Serves 6 to 8

1 stick butter

1 cup chopped onion

1 cup chopped celery

1 cup dried cranberries

½ cup chopped walnuts

2-½ cups chicken broth

½ teaspoon ground sage

1 (14-ounce) bag herb-seasoned stuffing

- Preheat oven to 350 degrees F. Spray a 3-quart baking dish (see note) with cooking spray.

- In a large saucepan, melt butter over medium-high heat. Add onion and celery and cook 6 to 8 minutes or until tender. Add cranberries, walnuts, broth, sage, and stuffing; gently stir until well combined.

- Spoon into casserole and bake, covered, 30 minutes. Uncover and continue to bake 10 to 15 more minutes or until heated through.

If you bake your stuffing in a Christmas tree-shaped pan, like I do, then after flipping it over onto a serving platter, you can decorate it with additional cranberries and fresh thyme. It'll be the tastiest tree on the block! MCM

SIDE DISHES

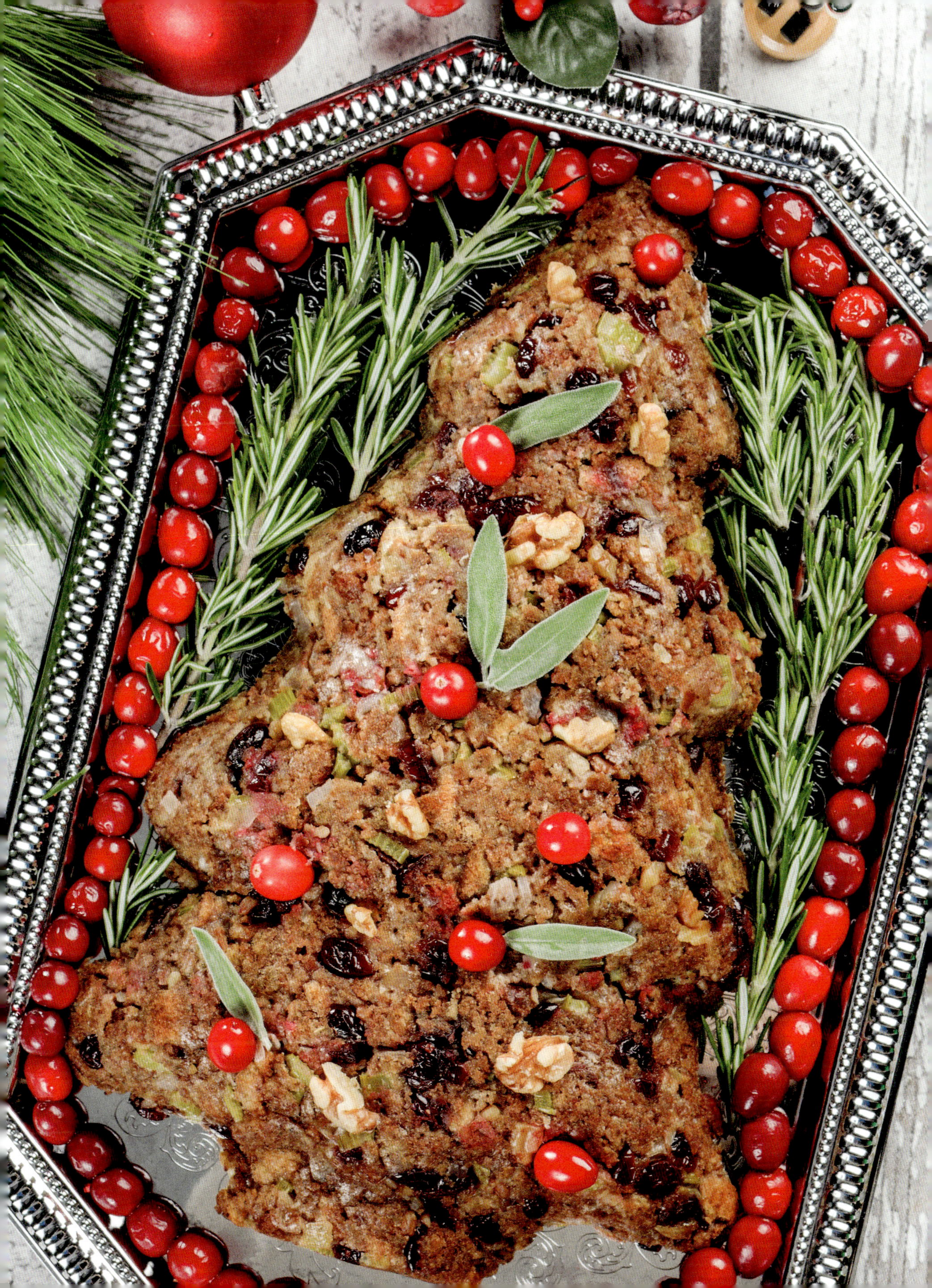

BUTTERY POTATO SKILLET

Pinch me! How could four simple ingredients taste so good? What I love about this recipe is that it proves that you can make a family-favorite dish with just a few basic ingredients. The trick to cooking these perfectly is to make sure the potatoes are all cut to the same thickness. I get it done with the help of a mandoline slicer. Enjoy all the buttery deliciousness!

Serves 6 to 8

1 stick butter, melted

2 pounds small russet potatoes, peeled, very thinly sliced

Salt for sprinkling

Black pepper for sprinkling

- Preheat oven to 425 degrees F.

- Pour 1 tablespoon butter in bottom of a cast iron skillet. Arrange potato slices in an overlapping pattern in a single layer in bottom of skillet. Sprinkle with salt and pepper, and drizzle with a little butter. Repeat with remaining potatoes, sprinkling salt and pepper and drizzling with butter between each layer. Pour any remaining butter over top and cover.

- Over low heat, cook potatoes 10 minutes; do not stir. Uncover skillet and place in oven. Bake 30 to 35 minutes or until potatoes are tender in center and browned and crisp around edges. Let sit 5 minutes, then slice and serve.

These potatoes are buttery-good on their own, but sometimes I like to sprinkle them with some crumbled bacon and sliced scallions for the last 5 or 10 minutes of cooking. MCM

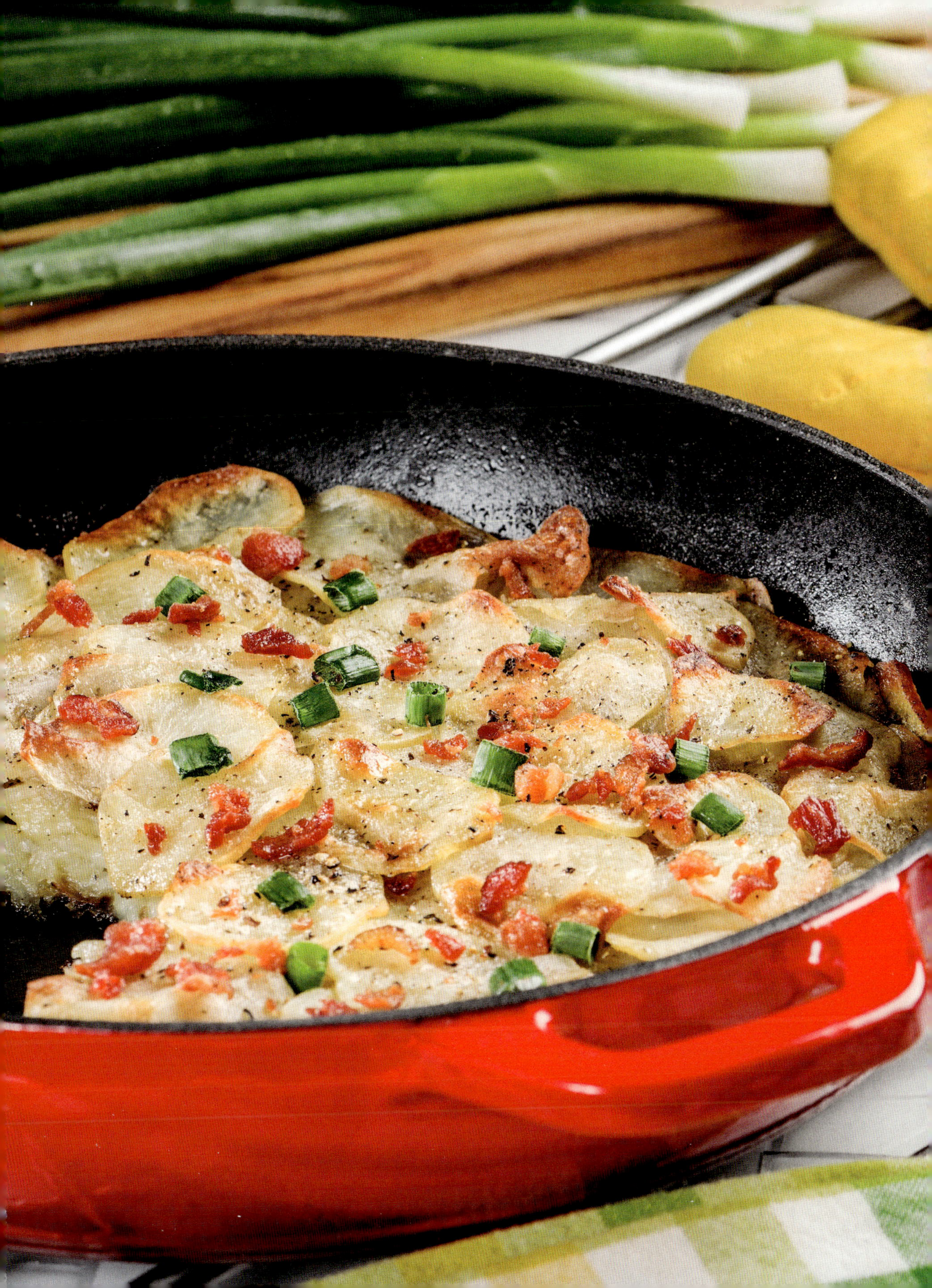

GRANDMA'S SPECIAL MASHED POTATOES

Anything my grandmother ever made for me was special. That's because she always put lots of TLC into all her cooking. These mashed potatoes are no exception. They're creamy, buttery, and go with anything. In fact, I'm guilty of eating a bowl before they even make it to the dinner table. I just can't help it—they call to me!

Serves 4 to 6

- 2-½ pounds russet potatoes, peeled and cut into 2-inch chunks
- ½ stick butter, softened
- 4 ounces cream cheese
- ¼ cup milk
- 4 scallions, thinly sliced
- 1 teaspoon salt
- ¼ teaspoon black pepper

■ Place potato chunks in a soup pot and add just enough water to cover.

■ Bring to a boil over high heat and cook 20 to 25 minutes or until tender. Drain well and return potatoes to pot. Place back on heat 1 minute to make sure all water is gone. (Trust me, this is what turns good potatoes into great potatoes.)

■ Add remaining ingredients and beat with an electric mixer until desired texture. Serve immediately.

To fancy up your mashed potatoes, try serving them in martini glasses. You probably never use them much to begin with, and it's such a trendy way to show off grandma's recipe. MCM

SIDE DISHES

SECRET INGREDIENT SWEET POTATO BAKE

If you don't have a baby at home, chances are you've probably been skipping the baby food aisle at your supermarket. Well it's time to take your shopping cart to uncharted destinations, because baby food is the secret ingredient I use to make this moist and fluffy sweet potato bake. It's sweet, it's easy, and it's ready to surprise everyone. They'll go ga-ga for it!

Serves 6 to 9

- 3 (4-ounce) jars sweet potato baby food
- 1 stick butter, melted
- 3 eggs
- 1 cup all-purpose flour
- 1 cup packed light brown sugar
- 1 teaspoon vanilla extract
- 1 teaspoon baking soda
- 1 teaspoon baking powder
- ¼ teaspoon salt

- Preheat oven to 350 degrees F. Coat an 8-inch-square baking dish with cooking spray.
- In a large bowl, combine sweet potato and butter; mix well. Add remaining ingredients; mix until well blended, then pour into baking dish.
- Bake 35 to 40 minutes or until a toothpick inserted in center comes out clean. Cut into squares and serve.

Here's an idea … don't tell your guests what the secret ingredient is in this recipe. After they enjoy it, let them try to guess! MCM

SIDE DISHES

FETA & KALE QUICK BREAD

Since I'm not the kind of guy who spends hours in the kitchen waiting for dough to rise, you can probably appreciate how much I love this mix-it-up-and-bake-it bread recipe. There's no proofing and no kneading. And since it's loaded with a bunch of tasty, Mediterranean-inspired ingredients, including feta, walnuts, and olive oil, it was even easier for me to fall in love with it.

Makes 1 loaf

- 2-½ cups all-purpose flour
- 1 tablespoon baking powder
- 1 teaspoon garlic powder
- 1 teaspoon salt
- 2-½ cups shredded kale
- 1 cup crumbled feta cheese
- ½ cup plus 1 tablespoon dried cranberries, divided
- ½ cup olive oil
- 2 eggs
- ¾ cup plain Greek yogurt
- ¾ cup milk
- ¼ cup chopped walnuts

- Preheat oven to 350 degrees F. Coat a 9- x 5-inch loaf pan with cooking spray.
- In a large bowl, combine flour, baking powder, garlic powder, and salt. Add kale, feta cheese, and ½ cup cranberries; stir until combined.
- In a medium bowl, whisk oil, eggs, yogurt, and milk. Pour into dry ingredients and mix until well combined. Pour batter into loaf pan and sprinkle with walnuts and remaining 1 tablespoon cranberries.
- Bake 45 to 50 minutes or until a toothpick inserted in center comes out clean. Let sit 10 minutes, then remove to a wire rack to cool completely.

If you like giving homemade food gifts for the holidays, keep this recipe close by! Bake a bunch of loaves, wrap them in cellophane, and fancy them up with a bow. *MCM*

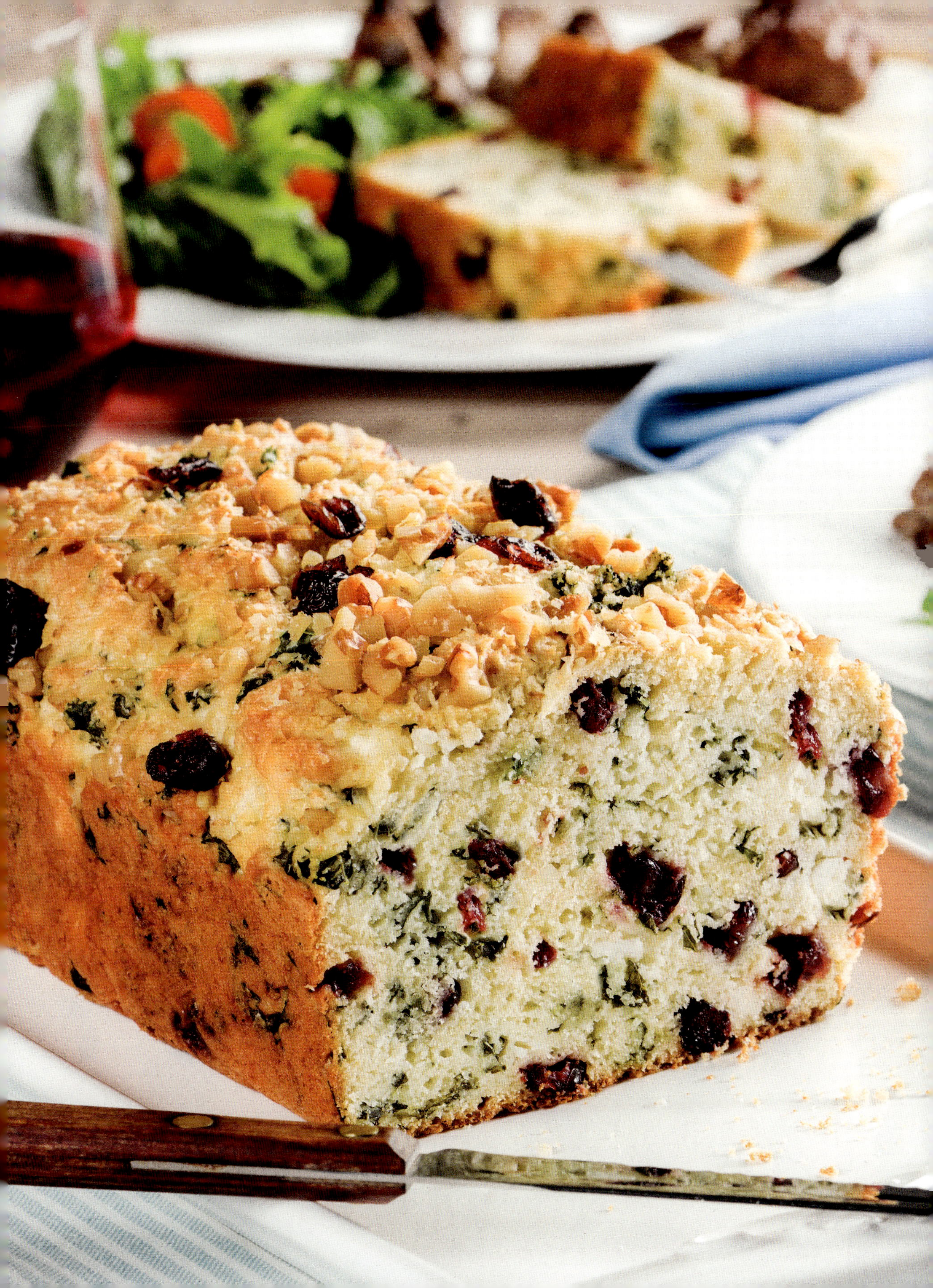

FARM-FRESH POTATO SALAD

This isn't your traditional, mayo-based potato salad. I wanted to share a lighter and brighter version that really showcases the flavors of all the fresh produce. Here, you've got red potatoes, spinach, tomatoes, and red onion all dressed up with simple seasonings, some olive oil, lemon, and vinegar. To get the full farm-fresh experience, why not shop at your local farmer's market for some of these ingredients?

Serves 6 to 8

3 pounds red potatoes, cut into 1-½-inch chunks

½ cup olive oil

3 tablespoons red wine vinegar

3 tablespoons fresh lemon juice

3 cloves garlic, minced

1 teaspoon salt

½ teaspoon black pepper

2 cups spinach, coarsely chopped

1 cup cherry tomatoes, cut in half

½ cup chopped red onion

1 teaspoon lemon zest

- Place potatoes in a large pot with enough water to cover them. Bring to a boil over high heat and cook 15 to 20 minutes or until fork-tender. Drain and let cool; place in a large bowl.

- In a medium bowl, whisk oil, vinegar, lemon juice, garlic, salt, and pepper.

- Add spinach, tomatoes, onion, and lemon zest to the potatoes. Pour vinaigrette over mixture and toss until evenly coated. Serve immediately or cover and refrigerate until ready to serve.

This is great to bring to a backyard picnic or barbecue. Since it doesn't have any mayo in it, you don't need to worry too much about it sitting in the heat. MCM

SWEET PICKLE COLESLAW

Pickle lovers, meet the game-changing recipe that's going to become your favorite summer side dish. This coleslaw doesn't just feature pieces of pickle—the pickle juice is mixed in too. That means every bite is going to deliver the sweet tang of pickles. And if that's still not enough for you, try serving this coleslaw with pickle-flavored potato chips. Yum!

Serves 5 to 6

1 cup mayonnaise

¼ cup chopped sweet pickles

3 tablespoons pickle juice

1 tablespoon vinegar

1 teaspoon sugar

½ teaspoon celery seed

½ teaspoon salt

1 (16-ounce) package coleslaw mix

- In a large bowl, combine mayonnaise, pickles, pickle juice, vinegar, sugar, celery seed, and salt; mix well. Add coleslaw mix and toss until evenly coated.

- Serve or refrigerate 1 hour before serving.

If you'd rather cut your own cabbage, instead of using a mix, go ahead. You can cut it into thin shreds or keep it more coarse based on your preferences. Hey, you can even add some grated carrots if you want to add some color. MCM

SIDE DISHES

"*You can tell by looking at my face that nothing is more heavenly to me than these rainbow cookies. Well -- my lemon-filled cream puffs are a close runner up. Choosing a favorite dessert is like choosing a favorite child -- you just can't do it!*"

DESSERTS

Happy Memories Ice Cream Cake	194
Naked Velvet Christmas Cake	196
Double Coconut Layer Cake	198
Cherry-licious Chocolate Cake	199
Cookie Butter Dump Cake	200
Dreamy Orange Poke Cake	202
The Best Brunch Coffee Cake	203
Irish Cream Cheesecake	204
Pumpkin Pie Cheesecake Squares	206
Cape Cod Cranberry Bundt	207
Salted Caramel Cookie Wedges	208
Summer-Sweet Strawberry Pie	210
Banana Banana Cream Pie	211
Pink Lemonade Cream Cheese Pie	212
From-Scratch Pecan Brownies	214
Pistachio Cranberry Biscotti	216
The Ultimate Chocolate Chip Cookies	217
Italian-Style Rainbow Cookies	218
Old-Fashioned Mud Hen Bars	220
Weeknight-Easy Blueberry Crisp	222
Amish Country Apple Dumplings	223
Luscious Lemon Cream Puffs	224
Crazy-Good Peanut Toffee	226
No-Bake Peanut Butter Balls	227
Kitchen Sink Chocolate Bark	228
Cinnamon-Sugar Air "Fried" Dough	230

HAPPY MEMORIES ICE CREAM CAKE

You don't need to spend hours and hours trying to recreate some fancy dessert just to make something memorable. This super simple ice cream cake is the kind of treat kids (and grownups like me!) love. Not only does it feature the sweet surprise of yummy ice cream sandwiches, but it's easy to customize too. Serve this cake at birthday celebrations, pool parties, and everything in between, and get ready to make some very happy memories.

Serves 10 to 12

1 (4-ounce) package sugar cones (about 12), coarsely crushed to cornflake-sized pieces

1 quart vanilla ice cream, softened

5 to 6 ice cream sandwiches

1 quart chocolate ice cream, softened

Frozen whipped topping, thawed, for garnish

- Place crushed ice cream cones in the bottom of a 10-inch springform pan. Spoon vanilla ice cream over crushed cones and gently spread, creating an even layer.

- This might sound kind of odd, but randomly place 5 or 6 ice cream sandwiches on top of the vanilla ice cream layer and gently press into ice cream.

- Top with a layer of chocolate ice cream, making sure to press ice cream in and around ice cream sandwiches, creating a smooth top. Freeze at least 4 hours or until ice cream is solid.

- Right before you're ready to serve, remove ring from springform pan. Garnish with whipped topping and serve.

To add even more fun to this dessert, I suggest dressing it up with some of your favorite toppings. As you can see, I was feeling pretty colorful the last time I made this cake.

MCM

DESSERTS

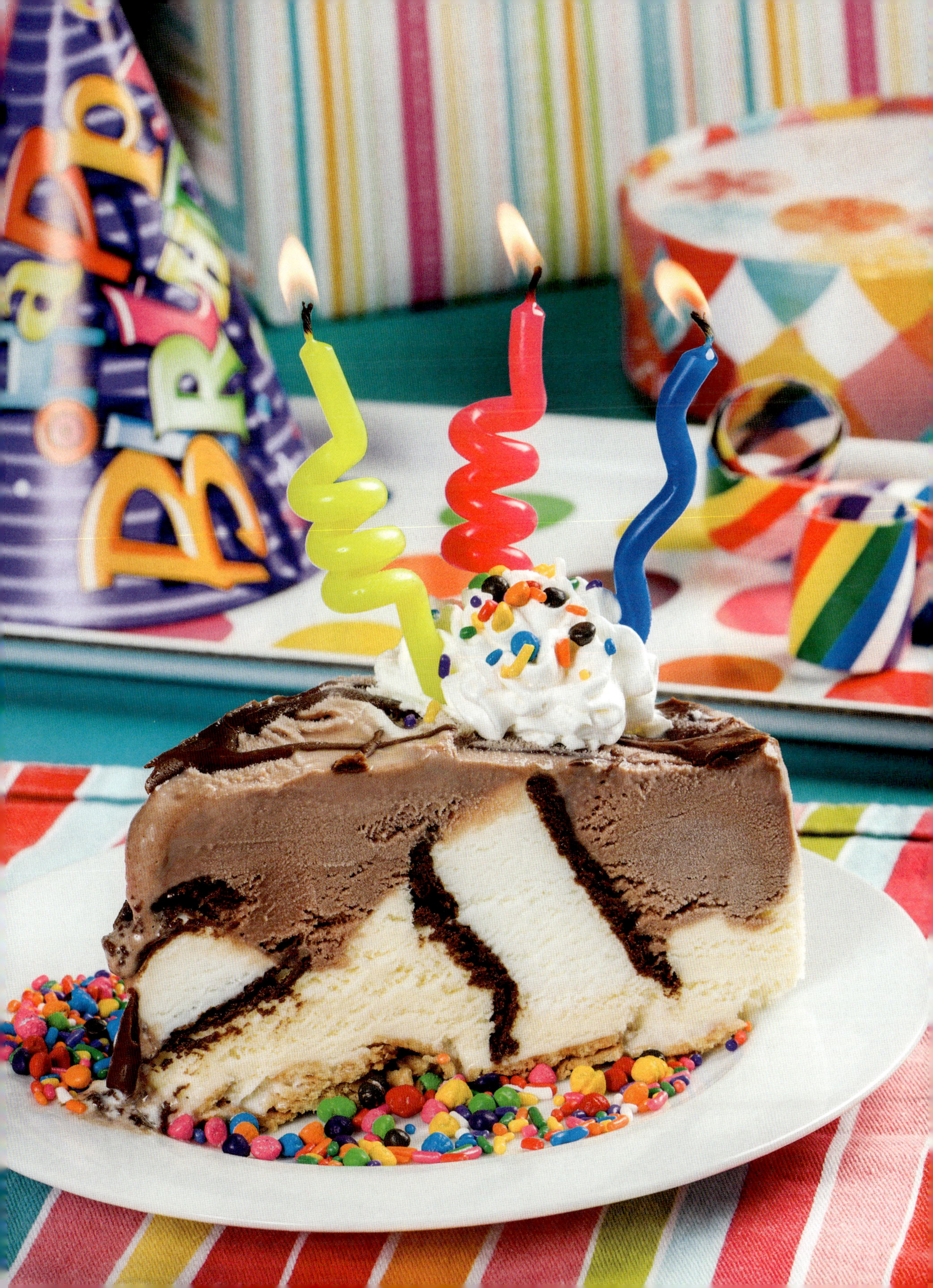

NAKED VELVET CHRISTMAS CAKE

In the last couple of years, "naked cakes" have been on-trend. A naked cake is simply a cake with little to no frosting on the sides, which allows you to get a glimpse of all the layers and fillings the cake has. This year, I invite you to get "naked" for the holidays (your cake, not you—get your mind out of the gutter; it's the holidays, for goodness sake!). This velvety-rich cake is sure to help you spread some holiday cheer.

Serves 12 to 14

1 package red velvet cake mix, batter prepared according to package directions

1 (8-ounce) package cream cheese, softened

½ cup powdered sugar

1 (16-ounce) container frozen whipped topping, thawed

1 (10-ounce) jar red maraschino cherries, with 6 reserved for garnish; drain and chop remaining cherries

1 (6-ounce) jar green maraschino cherries, with 6 reserved for garnish; drain and chop remaining cherries

■ Preheat oven to 350 degrees F. Coat 2 (8-inch) round cake pans with cooking spray. Divide batter evenly between pans.

■ Bake 30 to 32 minutes or until a toothpick inserted in center comes out clean. Let cool 10 minutes, then remove to a wire rack to cool completely. When cool, use a long, serrated knife to cut each layer in half horizontally, creating 4 thin layers.

■ In a large bowl with an electric mixer, beat cream cheese and powdered sugar until smooth. Gently fold in whipped topping and chopped red and green cherries.

■ Place 1 cake layer on platter and evenly spread one-quarter of cream cheese mixture over top of it (not on sides). Repeat with remaining cake layers and finish with cream cheese mixture on top. Garnish with reserved cherries.

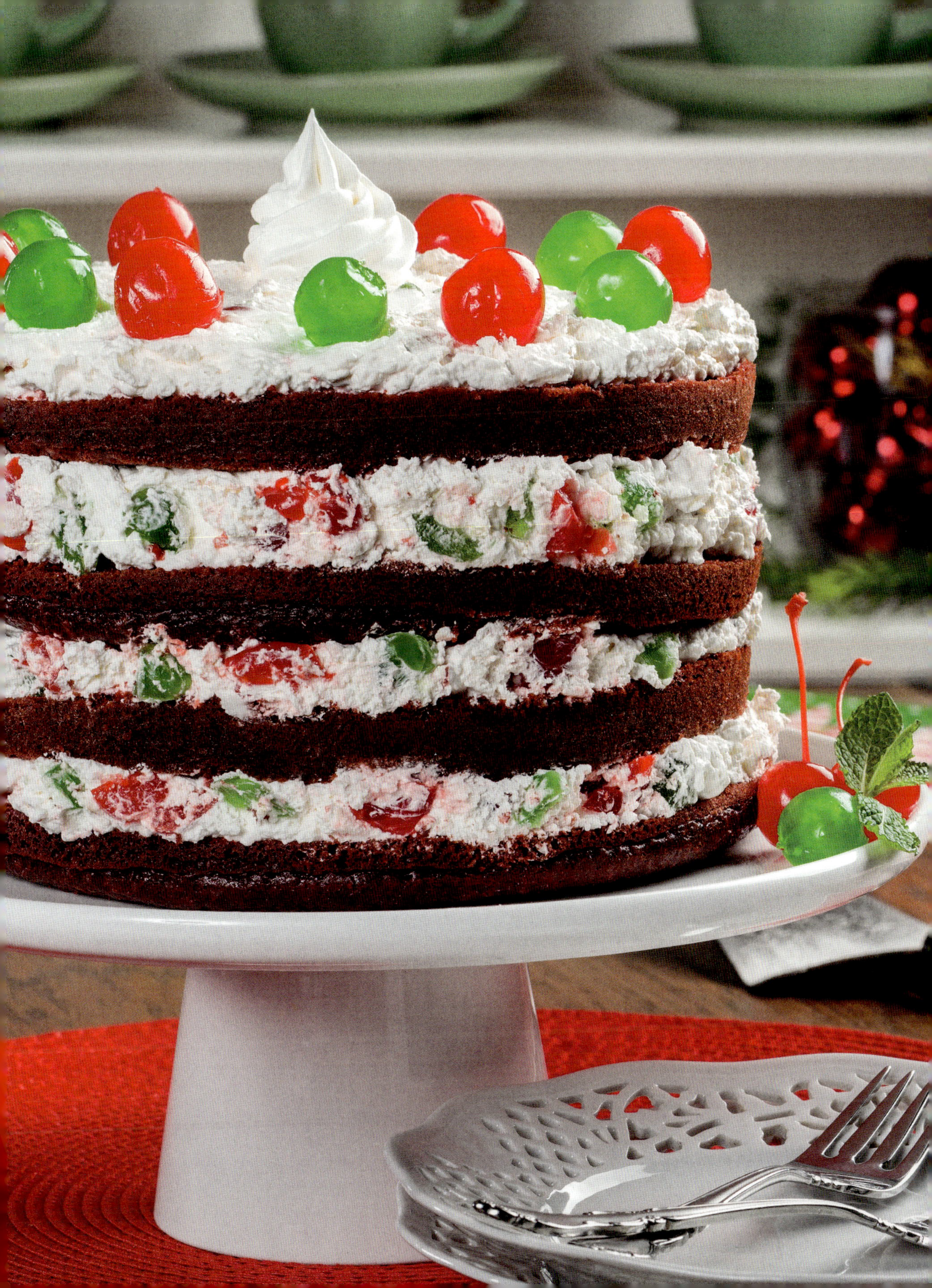

DOUBLE COCONUT LAYER CAKE

If you're crazy about coconut like I am, then hello and welcome to your new cake obsession. This cake has a whole package of sweet, shredded coconut in it! That's right, you're putting coconut into the batter AND into the frosting, so every bite delivers all the coconut goodness you desire. And if you want even more coconut, then who's to stop you from serving each slice on a bed of toasted coconut? Not me. Go on and enjoy yourself.

Serves 12 to 14

1 package white cake mix, batter prepared according to package directions

1 (12- to 14-ounce) package sweetened shredded coconut, divided

2 sticks unsalted butter, softened

2 cups powdered sugar

1 (6-ounce) package white baking bars, melted

- Preheat oven to 350 degrees F. Coat 2 (9-inch) round cake pans with cooking spray.
- Stir 2 cups of coconut into batter. Divide batter evenly between pans.
- Bake 20 to 25 minutes or until a toothpick inserted in center comes out clean; let cool 10 minutes, then remove to a wire rack to cool completely.
- To make frosting, in a large bowl with an electric mixer, beat butter, powdered sugar, and melted baking bars until fluffy and doubled in size. Slowly add remaining coconut and mix gently until thoroughly combined.
- Place 1 cake layer on a serving platter and frost top. Place second layer over first and frost top and sides. Cover loosely and chill at least 2 hours before serving.

Just because you're trying to trim down, doesn't mean you can't enjoy a treat from time to time. Something I like to do, when there's cake leftovers after a party, is to wrap the cake well and pop it in the freezer. Then if I get a craving, I just cut off a small slice without feeling like I need to finish whatever's left because I'm worried it'll go bad.

MCM

CHERRY-LICIOUS CHOCOLATE CAKE

You can bake something really special without ever breaking a sweat, thanks to a couple of supermarket shortcuts. This cake delivers on all counts—it's super-moist, chocolaty, and packed with sweet cherry goodness. Oh yeah, and it's coated in a homemade chocolate glaze that's so good, it's hard to resist licking the bowl clean. I don't know about you, but I could go for a slice right about now...

Serves 12 to 15

1 package devil's food cake mix with pudding

1 (21-ounce) can cherry pie filling

2 eggs

1 teaspoon almond or vanilla extract

CHOCOLATE GLAZE

1 cup sugar

1/3 cup butter

1/3 cup milk

1 cup (6 ounces) semisweet chocolate chips

- Preheat oven to 350 degrees F. Coat a 9- x 13-inch baking dish with cooking spray.

- In a large bowl with an electric mixer, beat cake mix, pie filling, eggs, and almond extract; mix until well combined. Pour into baking dish. Bake 30 minutes or until a toothpick inserted in center comes out clean. Cool in pan on a wire rack.

- Meanwhile, to make Chocolate Glaze, in a small saucepan, combine sugar, butter, and milk. Bring to a boil, stirring constantly. Reduce heat to low and simmer 1 minute, stirring constantly. Remove from heat; stir in chocolate chips until melted.

- Pour chocolate glaze over cake; let stand until set. Allow cake to cool and garnish as desired.

If you want to fancy things up, top each piece with a dollop of whipped cream, some mini chocolate chips, and a cherry; it'll really add a WOW factor. MCM

COOKIE BUTTER DUMP CAKE

Cookie butter is the stuff sweet dreams are made of. For those who still haven't tried it, it's a dessert spread made from European-style, spiced cookies called "speculoos" (kind of like gingerbread cookies). It's got the consistency of peanut butter, which is typically what it's next to in the supermarket. Cookie butter is so addictive, you could eat it by the spoonful, but if you're looking for something more shareable, this dessert really takes the cake.

Serves 12 to 15

- 1 (14-ounce) jar cookie butter
- 1 (14-ounce) can sweetened condensed milk
- 3 eggs
- ½ teaspoon ground cinnamon
- 1 (14-ounce) pouch white chocolate macadamia nut cookie mix
- 1-½ sticks butter, melted

- Preheat oven to 350 degrees F. Coat a 9- x 13-inch baking dish with cooking spray.
- In a large bowl, combine cookie butter, sweetened condensed milk, eggs, and cinnamon. Stir until thoroughly combined. Spread mixture evenly into baking dish.
- Sprinkle dry cookie mix evenly over batter. Drizzle top evenly with melted butter.
- Bake 35 to 38 minutes or until a toothpick inserted in center comes out clean.
- Let cool, cut into squares, and dig in.

A big scoop of ice cream and a drizzle of chocolate sauce, and all of a sudden, nothing else seems to matter. MCM

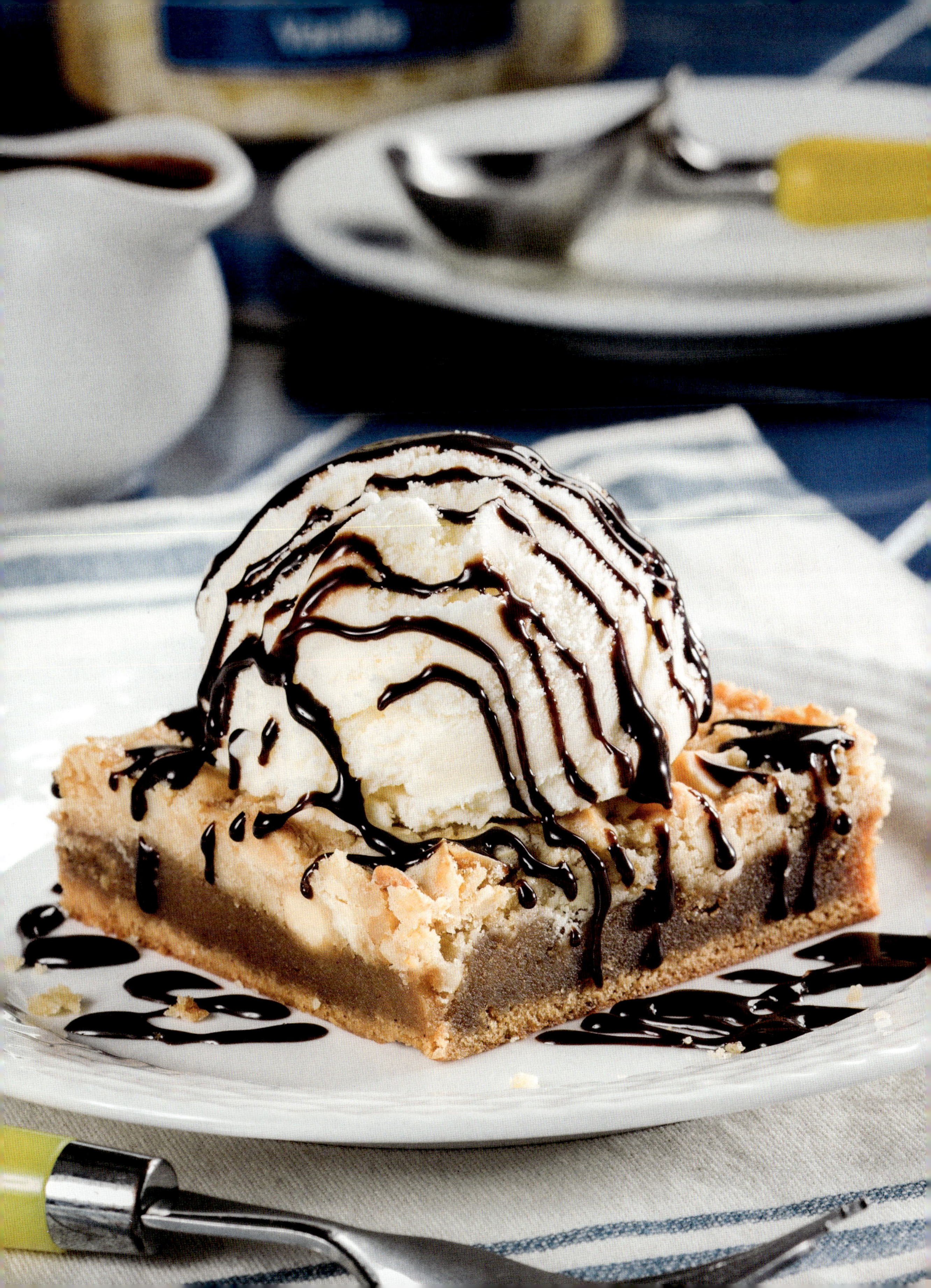

DREAMY ORANGE POKE CAKE

One of my all-time favorite flavor combos is orange and vanilla—especially in the summertime. Anytime I visit the famous Kohr Brothers frozen custard shop on the Jersey shore I order the swirled orange and vanilla custard. It's so creamy and light! Inspired by that yummy summer treat, I came up with this easy, dreamy poke cake the whole family can enjoy.

Serves 12 to 15

1 package white cake mix

1 cup orange juice

1 (5.3-ounce) container orange & cream blended yogurt

3 eggs

1 (4-serving-size) package instant vanilla pudding and pie filling mix

1-¼ cups milk

1 (8-ounce) package cream cheese, softened

½ cup powdered sugar

1 (8-ounce) container frozen whipped topping, thawed

½ cup sour cream

1 teaspoon vanilla extract

Zest from ½ an orange

- Preheat oven to 350 degrees F. Coat a 9- x 13-inch baking dish with cooking spray.

- In a large bowl with an electric mixer, beat cake mix, orange juice, yogurt, and eggs until thoroughly combined. Pour batter into baking dish.

- Bake 30 to 32 minutes or until a toothpick inserted in center comes out clean. Let cool 20 minutes, then poke about 20 holes in top of cake using the handle of a wooden spoon; set aside.

- Meanwhile, in a medium bowl, whisk pudding mix and milk until slightly thickened. Slowly pour mixture into holes and spread evenly over top of cake; chill 1 hour.

- In a large bowl with an electric mixer, beat cream cheese until smooth. Add powdered sugar, whipped topping, sour cream, and vanilla; mix well. Stir in orange zest. Spread mixture gently over pudding. Chill 2 hours or until ready to serve.

Before you start poking your cake, spray the handle of your spoon with cooking spray. This will help keep the moist cake from sticking to the handle. *MCM*

THE BEST BRUNCH COFFEE CAKE

Skip the crowds at Sunday brunch and create your own brunch experience at home. Maybe start things off with my Hot 'n' Hearty Breakfast Casserole (see page 10) and end on a sweet note with this amazing chocolate chip coffee cake? And to make it a truly memorable experience, I suggest setting up a coffee and juice station (mimosas, anyone?) for your friends and family to sip on while savoring every decadent bite.

Serves 15 to 18

2 cups all-purpose flour

1 cup granulated sugar

2 teaspoons baking powder

¼ teaspoon salt

½ stick butter, softened

¾ cup milk

1 egg

1 teaspoon vanilla extract

CHOCOLATE CHIP CRUMB TOPPING

1 cup all-purpose flour

½ cup light brown sugar

½ cup granulated sugar

1 cup chocolate chips, chopped

1 stick butter

2 teaspoons ground cinnamon

- Preheat oven to 350 degrees F. Coat a 10- x 15-inch rimmed baking sheet with cooking spray.

- In a large bowl, combine 2 cups flour, 1 cup granulated sugar, the baking powder, salt, ½ stick softened butter, the milk, egg, and vanilla. Spread batter evenly into baking sheet.

- In a medium bowl, add Chocolate Chip Crumb Topping ingredients. Using a fork or pastry cutter, combine until coarse crumbs form. Evenly sprinkle over batter.

- Bake 15 to 20 minutes or until a toothpick inserted in center comes out clean. Let cool before serving.

When you make the topping, make sure you chop the chocolate chips. You can do this with a knife or toss them in a food processor and give them a pulse or two. MCM

IRISH CREAM CHEESECAKE

I may not be Irish, but I love a good St. Paddy's Day celebration as much as the next guy. Every year, I look forward to a classic meal of corned beef and cabbage (see my recipe on page 116), soda bread, and some form of Irish cream dessert. This cheesecake is one of my favorites. In fact, no matter how full I am after feasting on those hearty Irish comfort foods, I always manage to make room for a slice (or two).

Serves 12 to 14

1-¾ cups chocolate sandwich cookie crumbs (about 20 cookies)

½ stick butter, melted

3 (8-ounce) packages cream cheese, softened

1 cup sugar

3 eggs

½ cup Irish cream liqueur

1 teaspoon vanilla extract

¼ cup all-purpose flour

CHOCOLATE GANACHE

2 cups semi-sweet chocolate chips

¾ cup heavy cream

- Preheat oven to 350 degrees F.

- In a medium bowl, mix cookie crumbs with melted butter; press mixture into a 9-inch springform pan. Wrap bottom of pan with aluminum foil and bring foil up the sides (to prevent water from getting in during baking process); set aside.

- In a large bowl with an electric mixer, beat cream cheese and sugar until smooth. Add eggs, Irish cream, vanilla, and flour; beat until well combined. Pour batter into pan. Place springform pan in a roasting pan. Fill roasting pan about a quarter of the way with hot water. Bake 50 to 55 minutes or until cheesecake is slightly jiggly in center.

- Remove springform pan from water bath and set on a wire rack to cool. Remove aluminum foil and refrigerate at least 6 hours or overnight. Run a thin knife around the edge and remove ring from springform pan.

- To make Chocolate Ganache, in a medium bowl, place chocolate chips. In a small saucepan over medium heat, bring heavy cream to a boil, stirring constantly. Pour over chocolate chips and stir until mixture is smooth and slightly thickened. Pour ganache over cake and let drizzle down sides. Refrigerate 30 minutes or until ready to serve.

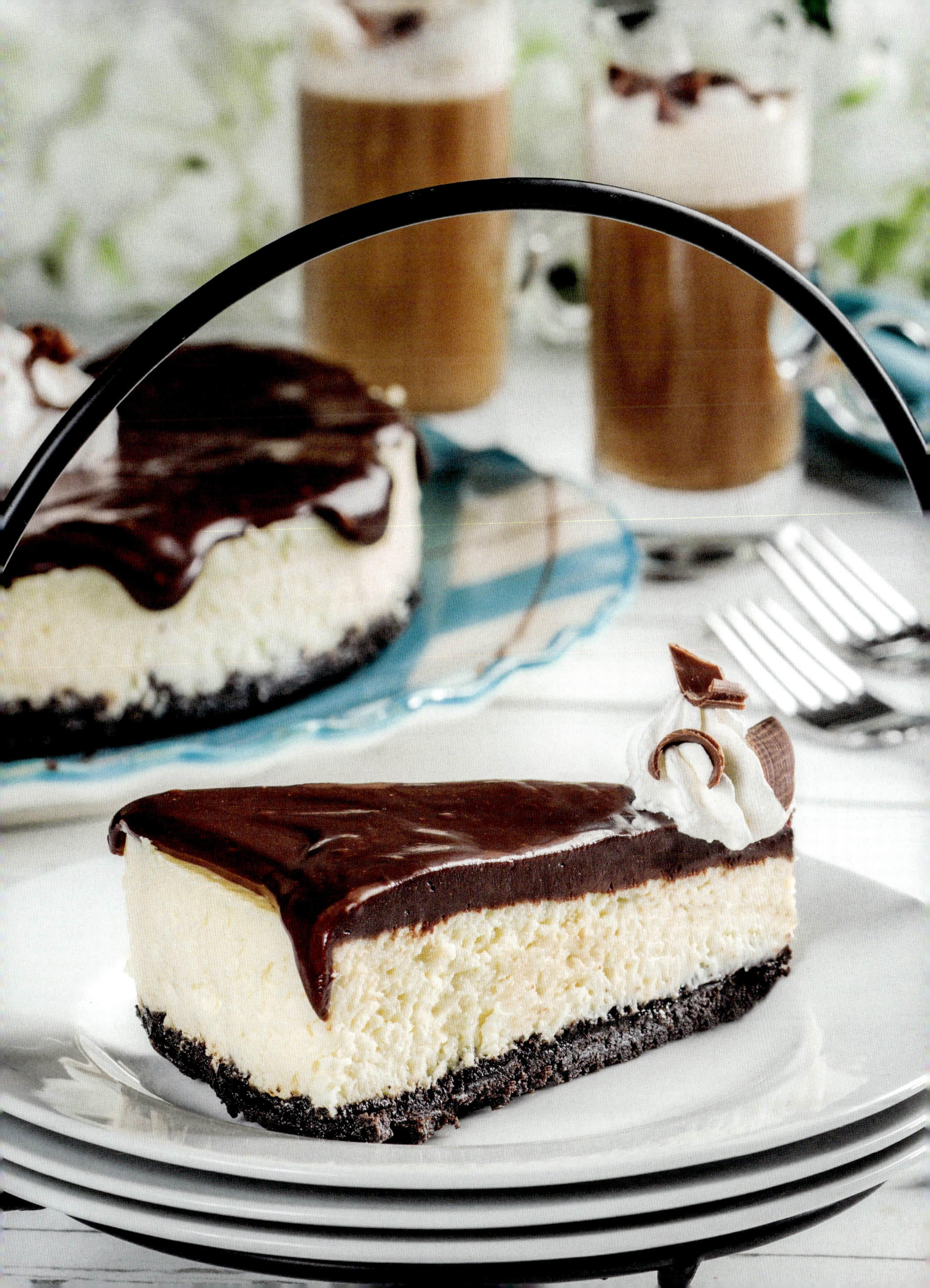

PUMPKIN PIE CHEESECAKE SQUARES

Fall is my favorite season. In addition to the great weather, there are so many other things to celebrate, including the arrival of some of my favorite produce and comforting, spiced treats. Like most other people who love fall, I'm a big fan of pumpkin everything—I even love their color. (My front door is pumpkin-colored!) These perfect pumpkin pie squares are a great way to celebrate the season.

Makes 24

- 1 package pound cake mix (see note)
- 4 teaspoons pumpkin pie spice, divided
- 3 eggs, divided
- 2 tablespoons butter, melted
- 1 (8-ounce) package cream cheese, softened
- 1 (15-ounce) can pure pumpkin
- 1 (14-ounce) can sweetened condensed milk
- ½ teaspoon salt
- 1 cup chopped pecans

- Preheat oven to 350 degrees F. Coat a 10- x 15-inch rimmed baking sheet with cooking spray.

- In a large bowl with an electric mixer, beat cake mix, 2 teaspoons pumpkin pie spice, 1 egg, and the melted butter until crumbly. Press dough into baking sheet.

- In a medium bowl, beat cream cheese at medium speed until creamy. Add remaining 2 teaspoons pumpkin pie spice, remaining 2 eggs, the pumpkin, condensed milk, and salt; beat until combined. Pour over crust; sprinkle with pecans.

- Bake 30 minutes or until set. (By now your house should smell amazing!) Cool completely in pan on a wire rack. Cover and chill, then cut into squares.

You can find pound cake mix in the same aisle as the other cake mixes. It's a great blank canvas for yummy desserts like this one! MCM

CAPE COD CRANBERRY BUNDT

If you've ever been to a cranberry bog, then this cake will bring back lots of memories. If not, one forkful of this will make you want to head to Cape Cod to see one for yourself. I know, I know, I'm using canned cranberry sauce rather than fresh cranberries, but the canned sauce is easier to work with and also features some added sweetness that complements the tart cranberries. Trust me, this cake is a treat!

Serves 12 to 14

- 1 stick butter, softened
- 1-¼ cups granulated sugar
- 2 eggs
- 2 cups all-purpose flour
- 1 teaspoon baking soda
- 1 teaspoon baking powder
- ½ teaspoon salt
- 1 cup sour cream
- 1-½ teaspoons almond extract
- ½ cup chopped walnuts
- 1 (14-ounce) can whole berry cranberry sauce
- Powdered sugar for sprinkling

- Preheat oven to 350 degrees F. Coat a 10-inch Bundt pan with cooking spray.

- In a large bowl with an electric mixer, beat butter and granulated sugar until creamy. Add eggs and beat until smooth.

- In a medium bowl, combine flour, baking soda, baking powder, and salt; gradually add to egg mixture and mix well. Add sour cream, almond extract, and walnuts, and continue mixing until batter is smooth.

- Pour half the batter into Bundt pan. Spoon half the can of cranberry sauce on top of batter and swirl with a knife. Cover with remaining batter. Spoon remaining cranberry sauce on top and swirl.

- Bake 55 to 60 minutes. Let cool 15 minutes, then turn out onto a wire rack to cool completely. Sprinkle with powdered sugar and serve.

If you know me, you know I like to make things look really special. So in the case of this cake, I start by spooning a puddle of extra cranberry sauce on each dessert plate before topping it with a slice. Not only does it look pretty, but the cranberry sauce acts like a glue to keep the cake slice from tumbling over. MCM

SALTED CARAMEL COOKIE WEDGES

I'm not trying to alarm you, but I hope your sweet tooth is ready for a flavor explosion. Here, you've got a dessert so good, you're going to find yourself dreaming (and drooling) about it all day long. It's an odd combo of textures and ingredients (cookie dough, pie crust, gooey caramel), but it works in all the best ways. Welcome to salted caramel heaven!

Serves 10 to 12

1 refrigerated rolled pie crust (from a 14.1-ounce package)

⅓ cup chocolate-flavored hazelnut spread

½ cup miniature semisweet chocolate chips

½ (16.5-ounce) roll refrigerated sugar cookie dough, cut into small pieces

¼ cup toffee bits

10 caramels

1 tablespoon water

¼ teaspoon sea salt

■ Preheat oven to 350 degrees F.

■ Unroll pie crust on an ungreased baking sheet; prick generously with a fork. Bake 5 minutes, just until it sets. Remove from oven. Spread hazelnut spread evenly over crust, leaving a ¼-inch edge all around the crust. Sprinkle with chocolate chips.

■ Place cookie dough pieces over chocolate hazelnut spread, about 1-inch apart. Sprinkle with toffee bits. Bake 20 to 25 minutes or until pie crust edges are golden; let cool.

■ In a small saucepan over medium low heat, melt caramels with water until smooth, stirring constantly. Drizzle caramel over top and sprinkle with salt, then cut into wedges.

If you're making this a day before you plan on serving it, I suggest holding off on the caramel drizzle and sea salt sprinkle until right before serving time. MCM

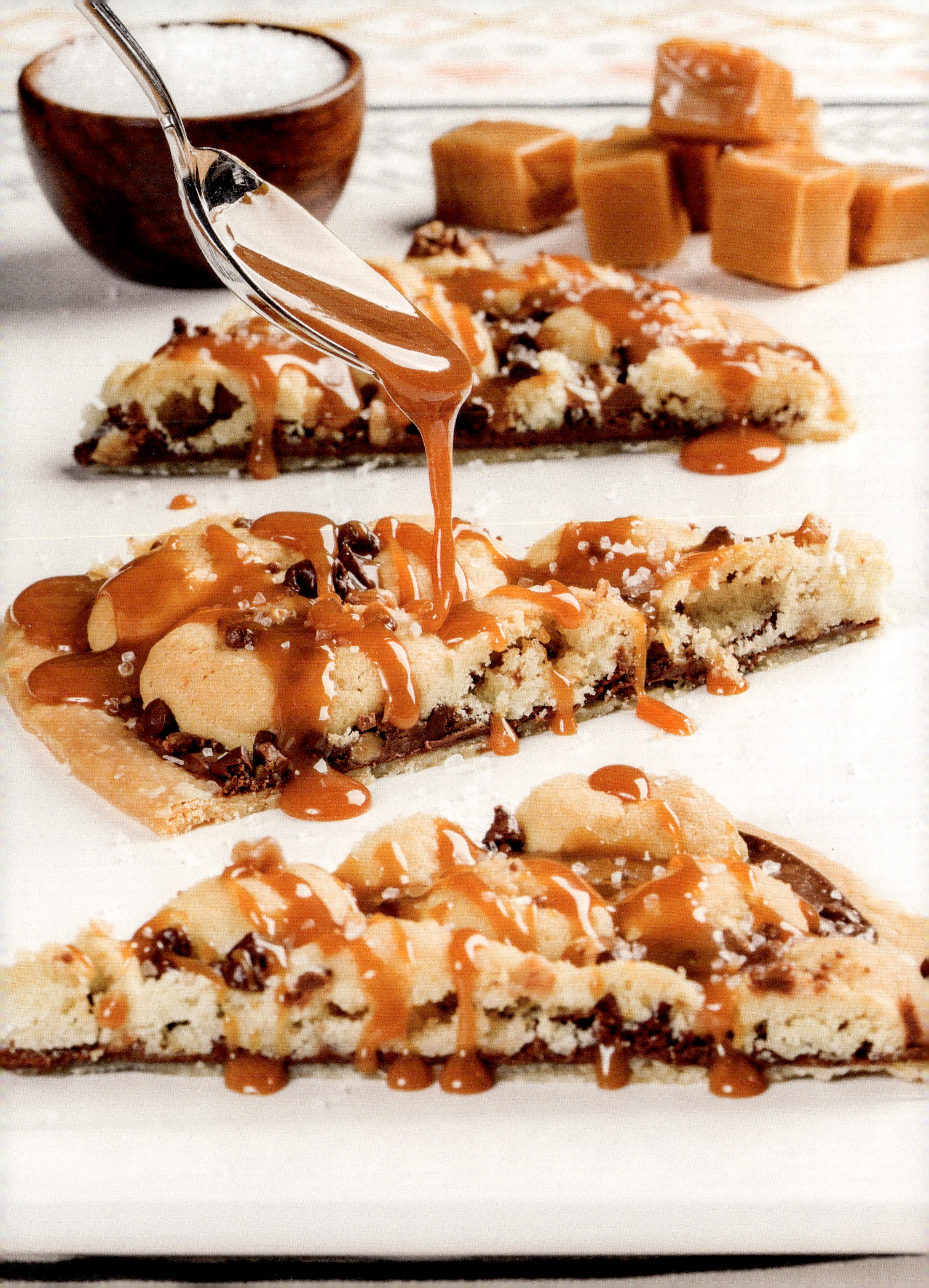

SUMMER-SWEET STRAWBERRY PIE

This isn't your run-of-the-mill strawberry pie. Instead of baking the strawberry filling (which breaks the berries down), I like to add fresh strawberries after the crust is baked. This really lets the strawberries shine—and the glaze helps too! Make this during the summer when strawberries are at their sweetest and top with a dollop of whipped cream for a refreshingly delicious dessert.

Serves 6 to 8

1 refrigerated rolled pie crust (from a 14.1-ounce package)

1 cup water

1 cup sugar

3 tablespoons cornstarch

¼ cup (from a 4-serving-size package) strawberry-flavored gelatin

5 cups fresh strawberries, trimmed and cut in half

Whipped cream or frozen whipped topping, thawed (optional)

- Preheat oven to 450 degrees F. Place pie crust in a 9-inch deep-dish pie plate. Flute edges and prick bottom and sides with a fork. Bake 10 to 12 minutes or until lightly browned; let cool.

- Meanwhile, in a medium saucepan over medium heat, bring water, sugar, and cornstarch to a boil; cook 1 minute or until thickened, stirring constantly.

- Stir in gelatin until dissolved. Remove from heat; let cool 8 to 10 minutes.

- Place strawberries in a large bowl and pour gelatin glaze over them. Toss gently until evenly coated, then spoon evenly into pie crust. Cover and chill 4 hours. Serve with whipped cream, if desired.

BANANA BANANA CREAM PIE

Why is this pie called "Banana Banana"? Well traditionally, banana cream pie features sliced bananas and rich vanilla cream. While that's good, I wanted to give you something new. My version of a banana cream pie features even more banana flavor, thanks to the addition of banana pudding mix in the cream. Yeah, that's right, you get double the banana goodness. I know what you're thinking, "MarkCharles, that's bananas!" Maybe, but it's darn tasty.

Serves 6 to 8

1 refrigerated rolled pie crust (from a 14.1-ounce package)

2 (4-serving-size) packages cook-and-serve banana cream pudding mix

4 cups milk

2 bananas, peeled and sliced, with extra for garnish

1 (12-ounce) container frozen whipped topping, thawed

- Preheat oven to 450 degrees F.
- Place pie crust in a 9-inch deep-dish pie plate. Flute edges and prick bottom and sides with a fork. Bake 10 to 12 minutes or until lightly browned; let cool.
- In a medium saucepan over medium heat, combine pudding mix and milk; cook until thickened, stirring constantly. Remove from heat, cover pudding with wax paper (to prevent it from developing a skin on top), and let cool slightly.
- Place bananas on bottom of pie crust. Spoon pudding mixture evenly over bananas. Chill 1 hour.
- Spoon whipped topping over pudding mixture. Cover and chill at least 3 more hours or until ready to serve. Garnish with extra banana slices right before serving.

To turn this into a coconut-banana pie, just add a handful of shredded or flaked coconut to the filling. Yum! MCM

DESSERTS

PINK LEMONADE CREAM CHEESE PIE

If you've been to a fair or any outdoor event in the summer, I'm sure you've seen your share of lemonade stands. Lemonade is the classic, cool-you-down, thirst-quencher on sunny summer days and it's also the inspiration for this pucker-up pie. It's light, it's creamy, and it's pretty, so call up your friends and invite them over. Heck, go all out and serve with homemade pink lemonade too!

Serves 8 to 10

1 (8-ounce) package cream cheese, softened

1 (6-ounce) container frozen lemonade concentrate, thawed

6 drops neon pink or red food color

1 (8-ounce) container frozen whipped topping, thawed, divided

1 (9-inch) prepared shortbread pie crust

- In a large bowl with an electric mixer, beat cream cheese until smooth. Add lemonade concentrate and food color; beat until well combined. Set aside ½ cup of the whipped topping and fold remaining whipped topping into cream cheese mixture until thoroughly combined.

- Spoon mixture into pie crust and freeze at least 4 hours or until firm. When ready to serve, dollop with reserved whipped topping.

If you'd rather use a graham cracker crust instead of shortbread, go for it! MCM

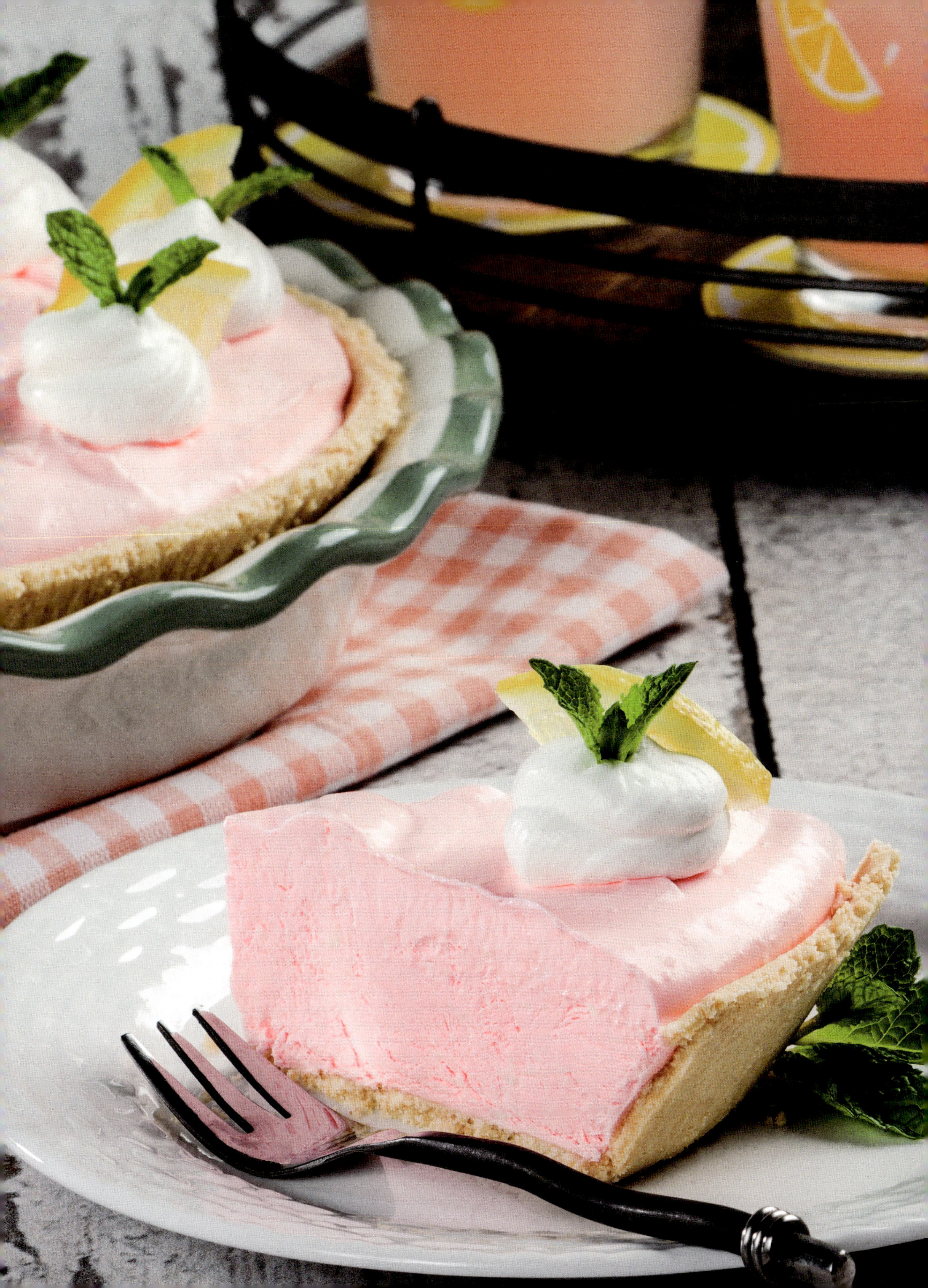

FROM-SCRATCH PECAN BROWNIES

I'll admit it, I'm no stranger when it comes to using a box of brownie mix. However, when I want something a little more extra-special, this is one of my go-to recipes. Every bite of these chocolaty brownies delivers the soft, buttery crunch of pecans. Make these for your favorite neighbors, a group of friends, your family or honestly, just for yourself—they're incredible!

Serves 9 to 12

1 stick butter, melted

1 tablespoon vegetable oil

1-¼ cups sugar

2 eggs

1-½ teaspoons vanilla extract

½ cup cocoa powder

½ cup all-purpose flour

¼ teaspoon salt

¾ cup chopped pecans, divided

- Preheat oven to 350 degrees F. Coat an 8-inch-square baking dish with cooking spray.

- In a large bowl, combine butter, oil, and sugar; whisk until creamy. Add eggs and vanilla; mix until thoroughly combined. Stir in cocoa powder, flour, salt, and ½ cup pecans until just combined.

- Pour batter into baking dish, smoothing top evenly. Top with remaining ¼ cup pecans.

- Bake 20 to 25 minutes or until a toothpick inserted in center comes out with moist crumbs. Let cool, then cut into squares.

To bring out the best taste in the pecans, I like to toast them for about a minute in a skillet before I chop them up. Doing this brings out their natural oils, which makes them even more spectacular. MCM

214 DESSERTS

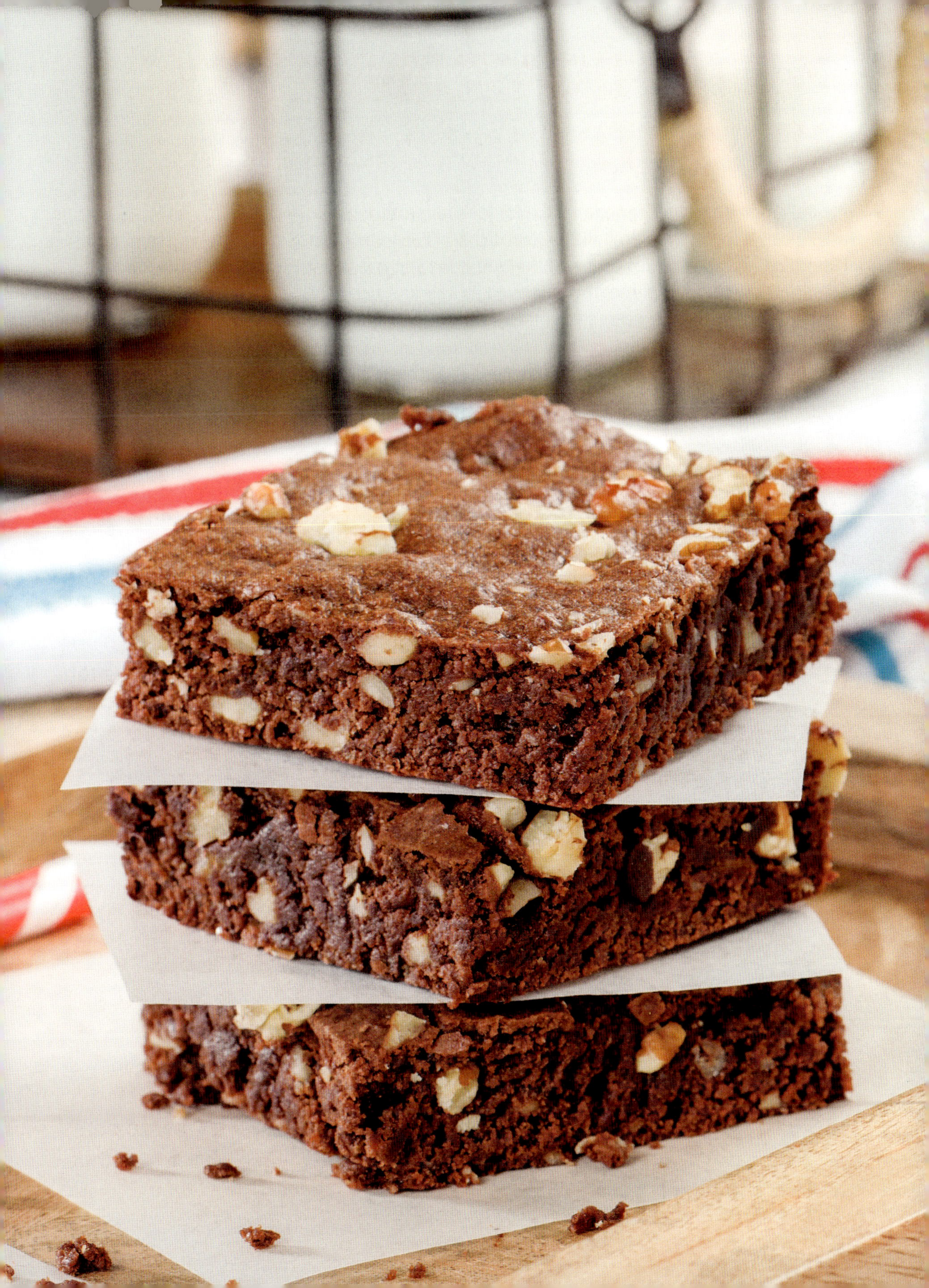

PISTACHIO CRANBERRY BISCOTTI

My Italian grandmother (nonna) baked a lot of biscotti, especially during the holidays. Even as a little boy, I loved being with her in the kitchen. When she'd bake these, she'd let me add the pistachios and cranberries to the batter and hand me a big wooden spoon for mixing. While I'd stir and stir, she'd tell me how she used to help out her nonna in the kitchen. Those are the memories I get to relive every time I make this recipe.

Makes 36

2 eggs

⅓ cup sugar

2 tablespoons butter, softened

1-½ teaspoons vanilla extract

1 cup all-purpose flour

1 teaspoon baking powder

⅓ cup sweetened, dried cranberries

⅓ cup shelled pistachios

- Preheat oven to 350 degrees F. Coat 2 baking sheets with cooking spray.

- In a large bowl with an electric mixer, beat eggs and sugar until frothy. Add butter and vanilla; mix 30 seconds, then add flour and baking powder, and mix well. Gently stir in cranberries and pistachios.

- Divide dough evenly on baking sheets. Form each into a slightly rounded 3- x 9-inch loaf. Bake 15 minutes; remove from oven and allow to cool 5 minutes.

- While still warm, cut each loaf into 18 (½-inch-thick) slices. Place slices cut-side down on baking sheets and bake an additional 10 minutes or until crisp. Cool before serving; store in an airtight container.

THE ULTIMATE CHOCOLATE CHIP COOKIES

I truly believe that the world is a better place since the creation of the first chocolate chip cookie. Whether you eat them right out of the oven, sandwiched with a scoop of ice cream, or at the end of the day with a tall glass of cold milk, chocolate chip cookies have a way of making more people smile than any other treat I know. While I know you have lots of options when it comes to chocolate chip cookie recipes, trust me when I say—these are amazing.

Makes about 3 dozen

- 2 cups all-purpose flour
- 1 teaspoon baking soda
- ½ teaspoon baking powder
- ½ teaspoon salt
- 1 cup shortening
- 1 cup firmly packed brown sugar
- 1 cup granulated sugar
- 2 eggs
- 1 teaspoon vanilla extract
- 1 cup rolled oats
- 2 cups chocolate chips (see note)

- Preheat oven to 350 degrees F. Coat baking sheets with cooking spray.
- In a medium bowl, sift together flour, baking soda, baking powder, and salt; set aside.
- In a large bowl with an electric mixer, cream shortening, sugars, eggs, and vanilla until light and fluffy. Add flour mixture and mix well. Stir in oats and chocolate chips. Drop mixture by heaping teaspoonfuls onto baking sheets.
- Bake 12 to 14 minutes or until lightly browned. Remove to a wire rack to cool.

Go ahead and use your favorite kind of chocolate chips. They're YOUR ultimate cookies!

MCM

ITALIAN-STYLE RAINBOW COOKIES

Rainbow cookies are popular in Italian bakeries year-round, but during the holidays many home bakers make these colorful cookies to display on their cookie platters. In my house, these are a long-standing holiday tradition. They take a little more work than a basic slice-and-bake cookie, but they're worth it! Not only do they look impressive, but with all the layers of almond-flavored cake, raspberry jam, and chocolate they taste absolutely decadent!

Makes 4 dozen

2 teaspoons almond extract

1 package yellow cake mix, batter prepared according to package directions

1 teaspoon red food color

1 teaspoon green food color

1 teaspoon yellow food color

1 (12-ounce) jar raspberry jam, melted

1 cup semi-sweet chocolate chips, melted

- Preheat oven to 325 degrees F. Coat 3 separate 9- x 13-inch baking dishes with cooking spray, line with wax paper, and coat again with cooking spray.

- Stir almond extract into cake batter and divide batter evenly into 3 small bowls. Stir red food color into one bowl, green food color into another bowl, and yellow food color into the third bowl. Pour each color batter into a separate baking dish and spread evenly. (The layer of batter will be very thin; that's okay.)

- Bake 15 to 18 minutes or until a toothpick inserted in center comes out clean; let cool completely.

- Place red layer top-side down on a cutting board and remove wax paper. Spread half the raspberry jam evenly over top, then place yellow cake layer top-side down over jam. Remove wax paper and spread remaining jam over yellow layer. Place green cake layer top-side down on top, leaving wax paper in place. Use a baking sheet to gently press layers together.

- Chill 1 hour, then remove from refrigerator and remove wax paper. Spread a thin layer of melted chocolate over top and allow to harden slightly. Cut into 1- x 2-inch bars and serve or cover and chill until ready to serve.

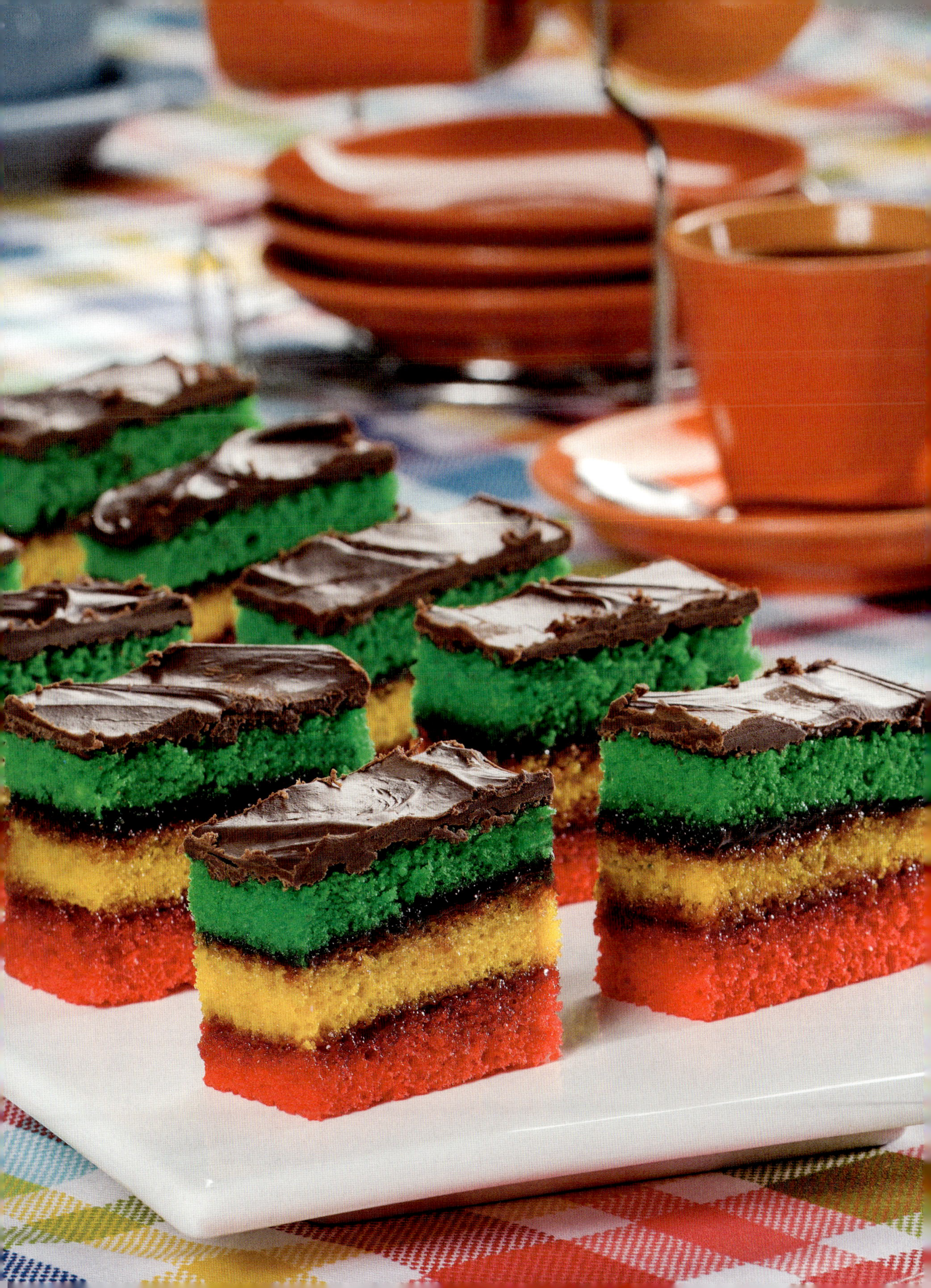

OLD-FASHIONED MUD HEN BARS

They say everything old is new again, and that's definitely the case with these. From what I read, the original recipe dates back more than 100 years! According to some stories, they were named "mud hen bars" because their original creator thought they looked "uglier than a mud hen." Over time, this classic Southern treat has gotten a number of updates, but the name lives on. All I know is, ugly or not, they're deliciously sweet.

Serves 12 to 15

1 stick butter, softened

1 cup granulated sugar

1 whole egg plus 2 separated eggs

1 teaspoon vanilla extract

1-½ cups all-purpose flour

1 teaspoon baking powder

½ teaspoon salt

1 cup semi-sweet chocolate chips

1 cup mini marshmallows

1 cup light brown sugar

¼ teaspoon ground cinnamon

■ Preheat oven to 350 degrees F. Coat a 9- x 13-inch baking dish with cooking spray.

■ In a large bowl with an electric mixer, beat butter, granulated sugar, 1 whole egg plus 2 egg yolks, and vanilla until creamy. Add in flour, baking powder, and salt; mix until just combined. Spread batter in baking dish. Top with chocolate chips and mini marshmallows; set aside.

■ In a medium bowl, beat remaining 2 egg whites for 2 minutes or until stiff peaks form. Fold in brown sugar and cinnamon until combined and no lumps remain. Spread evenly over chocolate chips and marshmallows. Bake 30 to 35 minutes or until a toothpick inserted in center comes out clean and top is golden brown. Allow to cool completely before cutting.

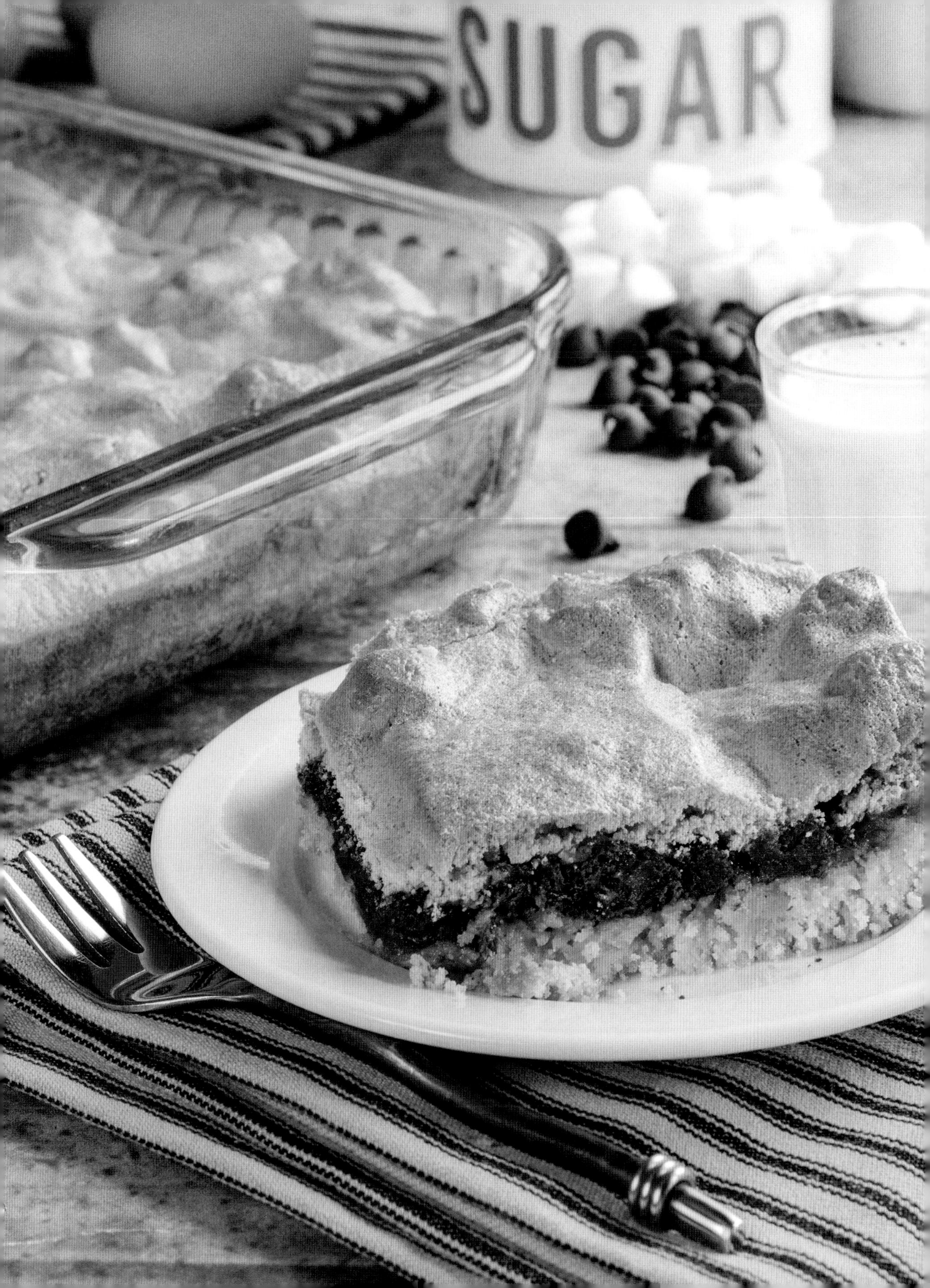
SUGAR

WEEKNIGHT-EASY BLUEBERRY CRISP

If you have a copy of my last book, *Easy Everyday Favorites*, then you know blueberry pie is my all-time favorite dessert. In that book, I shared a from-scratch recipe that's loaded with fresh blueberries. But sometimes, there's just no time to make a homemade pie, which is why I came up with a weeknight-friendly blueberry dessert to help satisfy my cravings. This crisp is easy to throw together and features a buttery-delicious crumb topping.

Serves 6 to 8

1 (21-ounce) can blueberry pie filling

1 cup fresh blueberries

1 tablespoon lemon zest

½ cup quick-cooking oats

3 tablespoons light brown sugar

¼ cup all-purpose flour

2 tablespoons butter

- Preheat oven to 400 degrees F. Coat an 8-inch-square baking dish with cooking spray.

- In a large bowl, combine blueberry pie filling, blueberries, and lemon zest; mix well. Spoon into baking dish; set aside.

- In a medium bowl, combine oats, brown sugar, and flour; mix well. With a fork, blend in butter until crumbly; sprinkle over blueberries.

- Bake 30 to 35 minutes or until golden and bubbly. Serve warm.

Know what goes great with a warm blueberry crisp? A scoop of creamy vanilla ice cream and a dollop of whipped cream! MCM

AMISH COUNTRY APPLE DUMPLINGS

Living in Philadelphia, I've had the pleasure of visiting Amish country more times than I can count. And if there's one thing I've learned during my visits is that the Amish are great bakers. From shoofly pies and lard cakes to friendship breads and oatmeal cookies, there are so many wonderful goodies to enjoy. One of my favorites is the classic apple dumpling. For those of you who can't make it to Amish country as easily as I can, here's my homestyle version.

Makes 4

½ cup water

¼ cup granulated sugar

1 teaspoon vanilla extract

2 tablespoons butter, softened, divided

⅛ teaspoon ground nutmeg

¼ cup light brown sugar

¼ teaspoon ground cinnamon

4 small or 2 medium Granny Smith apples, peeled

1 refrigerated rolled pie crust (from a 14.1-ounce package)

- Preheat oven to 375 degrees F.

- In a small saucepan over high heat, combine water, granulated sugar, vanilla, 1 tablespoon butter, and the nutmeg. Bring to a boil and cook 1 minute; set aside.

- In a small bowl, combine brown sugar, cinnamon, and remaining 1 tablespoon butter; mix well.

- Using an apple corer, core each apple ¾ of the way through. (This will be where all the yummy filling will go.) Stuff each apple with an equal amount of brown sugar mixture and set aside. Unroll pie crust and cut into quarters. Place an apple on each piece of dough. Wrap pie crust up around apples and pinch edges together to completely enclose apples. Place dumplings seam-side down in an 8-inch square baking dish and pour sugar-vanilla mixture over top.

- Bake 45 to 50 minutes or until golden. Serve warm, drizzled with the drippings from the baking dish.

LUSCIOUS LEMON CREAM PUFFS

Up until a few years ago, I never thought that I could make homemade choux pastry puffs. (That's the fancy term for cream puff shells.) Then one day, I challenged myself and discovered that they're a lot easier to make than people let on! Sure, it's still no walk in the park, but if you follow each of my steps carefully you can definitely nail these. To make the reward even sweeter, I fill mine with a luscious lemon cream filling.

Makes 10

1 cup water

½ stick butter, softened

¼ teaspoon salt

1 cup all-purpose flour

4 eggs, at room temperature

1 egg yolk

2 tablespoons milk

2 cups (1 pint) heavy cream

½ cup powdered sugar, plus extra for sprinkling

1 teaspoon vanilla extract

½ cup lemon curd

1 teaspoon lemon zest (optional)

■ Preheat oven to 400 degrees F. In a medium saucepan over medium-high heat, bring water, butter, and salt to a boil. Add flour all at once, and stir quickly until mixture forms a ball; remove from heat. Add 1 egg and mix well with a spoon to blend. Add remaining 3 eggs one at a time, beating well after each addition. (Each egg must be completely blended in before the next egg is added. As you beat mixture, it will change from almost-curdled to a smooth appearance.)

■ Once it's smooth, spoon 10 mounds of dough onto 2 baking sheets. In a small bowl, combine egg yolk and milk; mix well and brush over dough. Bake 25 to 30 minutes or until golden. Remove to a wire rack to cool completely.

■ Meanwhile, in a large bowl with an electric mixer on medium speed, beat heavy cream until soft peaks form. Add ½ cup powdered sugar and the vanilla, and beat until stiff peaks form. Fold in lemon curd and zest, if desired, and beat until thoroughly combined. Cut top third off each pastry puff and spoon or pipe whipped cream filling equally into all shells. Replace tops and sprinkle with powdered sugar. Serve immediately or cover and chill until ready to serve.

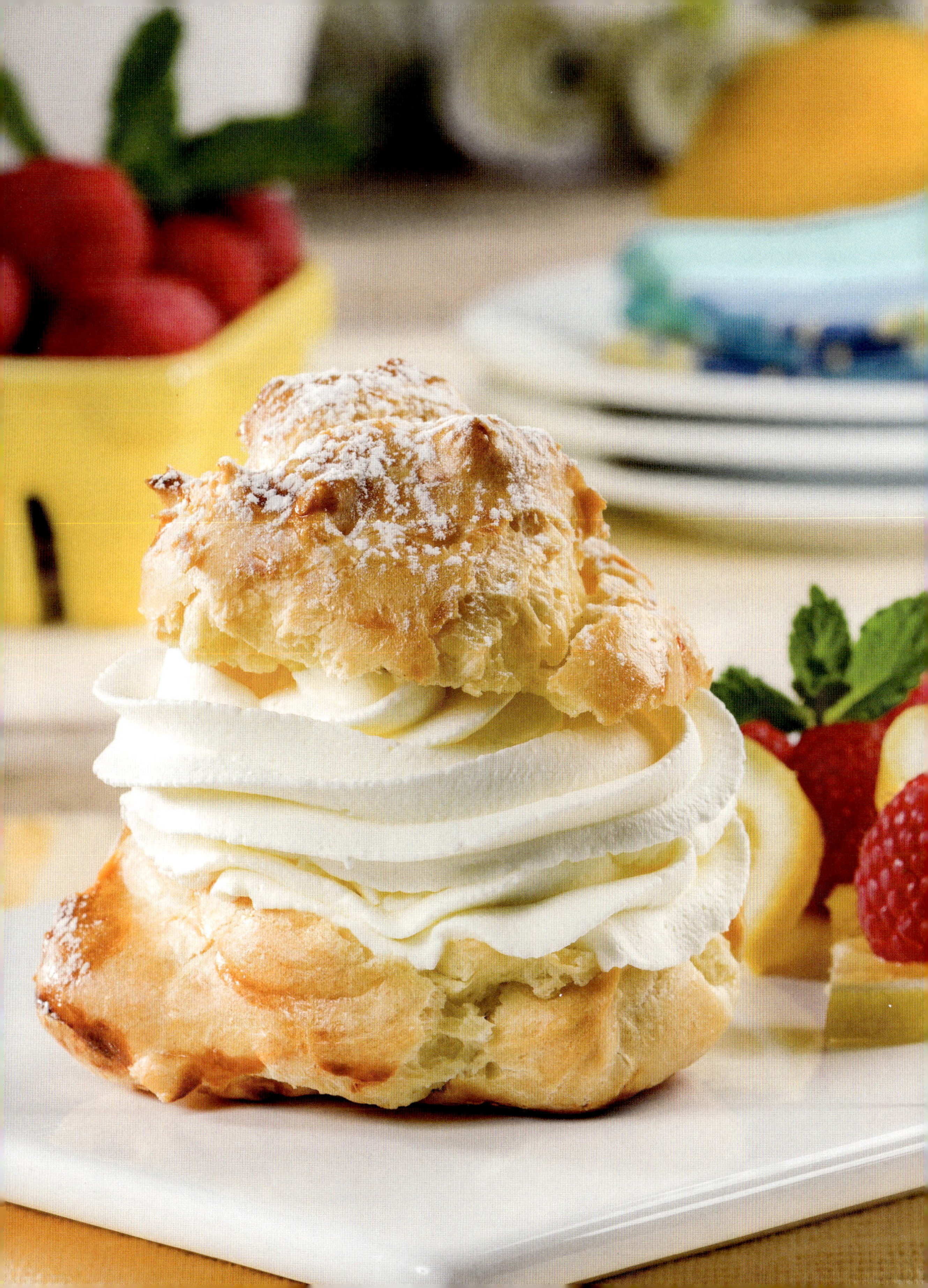

CRAZY-GOOD PEANUT TOFFEE

Spread a little joy at a moment's notice with this crazy-good peanut toffee. It's just the thing to make when you want to let someone know you're thinking of them or that you're thankful for what they do. You can whip up a batch before you leave the house and by the time you return it'll be set and ready to be packed up in a decorative box or canister. Now I can't offer any guarantees, but I'm confident this toffee can put a smile on anyone's face.

Serves 8 to 10

¾ cup finely chopped unsalted peanuts, divided

1 stick butter

1 cup sugar

¼ cup water

½ cup peanut butter chips

½ cup milk chocolate chips

- Lightly coat a 9-inch pie plate with cooking spray. Place ½ cup peanuts into bottom of pie plate.

- Using the stick of butter, coat inside top 2 inches of a 2-½-quart microwave-safe glass bowl. (This will prevent the mixture from bubbling over the top of the bowl.) Place remaining butter in bowl. Add sugar and water to bowl. Do not stir. Microwave on HIGH 8 to 10 minutes or just until mixture begins to turn light brown; carefully pour evenly over peanuts.

- Immediately sprinkle with peanut butter chips and chocolate chips; let stand 1 to 2 minutes or until softened. Spread melted chips evenly over peanut mixture, and sprinkle with remaining ¼ cup peanuts. Chill 2 hours or until firm. Break into bite-sized pieces. Store in an airtight container.

If you don't want to wait 2 hours for this to firm up, place it into the freezer for 30 minutes and you'll be good to go. MCM

NO-BAKE PEANUT BUTTER BALLS

The great thing about being a peanut butter lover is knowing that I'm not alone—many of you are as nutty for the stuff as I am. (It's a reassuring thought on those occasions when I find myself with a spoonful of peanut butter halfway to my mouth!) For those of you who share my feelings, this no-bake recipe is for you. If you're making them for a party, use toothpicks for serving. It's less messy and gives them a "cocktail meatballs" kind of look.

Makes 4 dozen

1 cup creamy peanut butter

2 sticks salted butter

2 teaspoons vanilla extract

1 (16-ounce) package powdered sugar

½ cup white baking chips, melted

2 tablespoons milk

½ cup finely chopped salted peanuts

- In a large saucepan over medium heat, melt peanut butter and butter; stir in vanilla. Add powdered sugar and with a spoon, beat vigorously until well blended. Remove from heat and let cool until mixture can be handled. (See note.)

- Knead mixture 5 minutes or until it gets stiff. Form into 1-inch balls. Place on wax paper.

- In a small saucepan over medium-low heat, melt white baking chips and milk, stirring to combine. Drizzle over peanut butter balls and sprinkle with peanuts. Let sit a few minutes for drizzle to harden before serving.

You want the mixture cool enough so that you don't burn your hands, but warm enough so that it's easy to work with. MCM

DESSERTS

KITCHEN SINK CHOCOLATE BARK

Ever heard the phrase, "everything but the kitchen sink"? It refers to anything that has everything imaginable. (Confused yet?) This chocolate bark has it all—pretzels, cookies, nuts, toffee… you name it. In fact, you can add even more to it if you want! This is a great treat to make and share with the kids too.

Serves 10 to 12

2 cups dark chocolate chips

1 cup mini pretzels

8 cream-filled chocolate sandwich cookies, coarsely chopped

¼ cup toffee bits

¼ cup coarsely chopped roasted, salted almonds

¼ cup coarsely chopped roasted, salted peanuts

Sea salt for sprinkling

- Line a rimmed baking sheet with parchment or wax paper; set aside. (Before you start, make sure all ingredients are chopped, prepped, and ready to go, so that they're ready to be added to the chocolate while it's hot and melty.)

- In a microwave-safe bowl, melt chocolate chips 60 seconds. Stir chocolate and continue to microwave in 15 second intervals, as needed, or until chocolate is melted and smooth. Pour chocolate onto baking sheet and smooth out evenly with a spatula.

- Immediately sprinkle with pretzels, cookie pieces, toffee bits, almonds, and peanuts. Sprinkle with sea salt. Refrigerate 1 hour or until hardened. Break into pieces and serve.

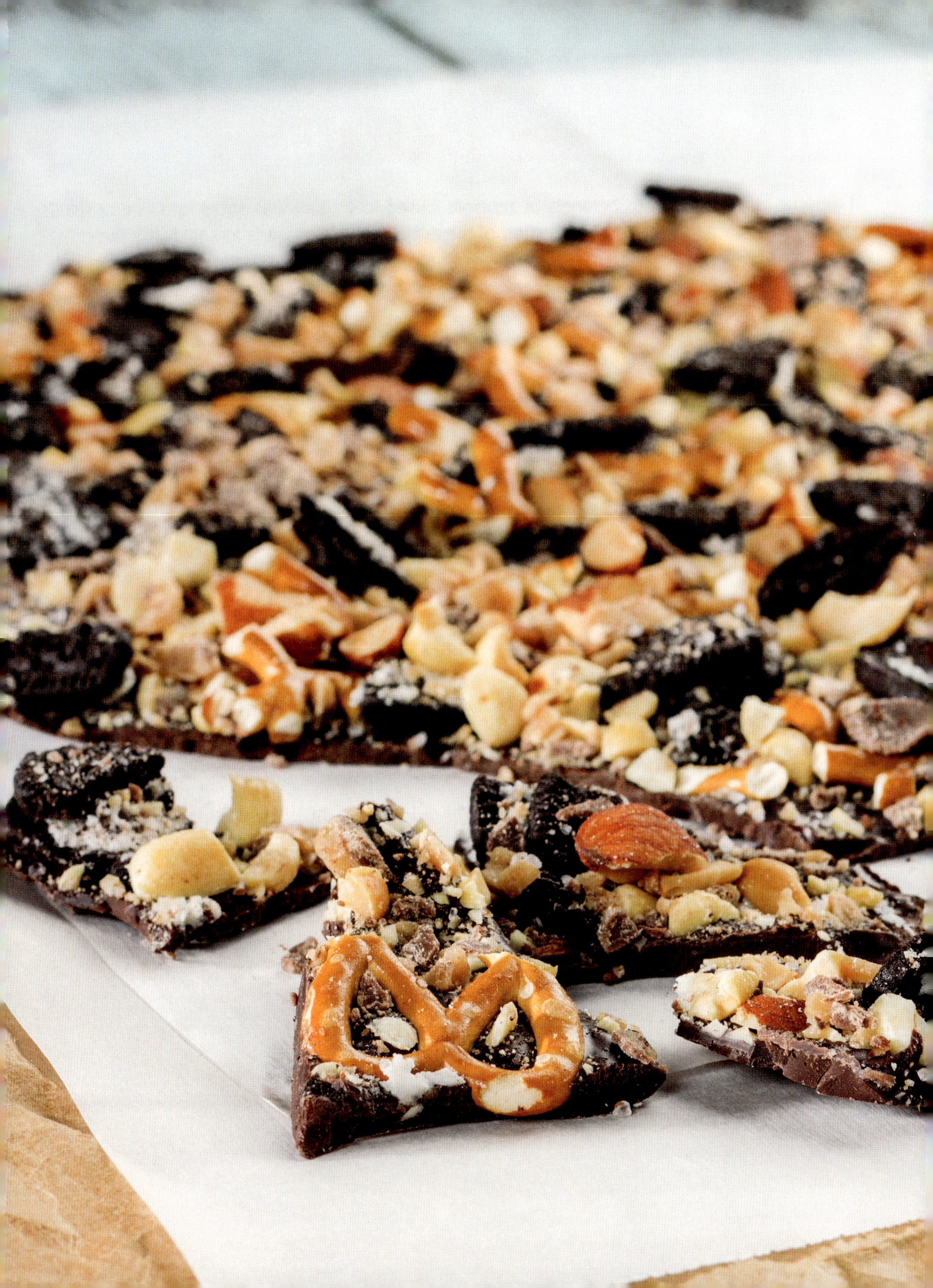

CINNAMON-SUGAR AIR "FRIED" DOUGH

I grew up knowing these as beignets or zeppole. I used to go to Italian street fairs (we called them "feasts") where I'd get some version of these fried dough desserts to satisfy my sweet tooth. They were so good! Here's your chance to make a homemade version that's easier, lighter, and just as tasty; and it's all thanks to the air fryer. Beware, these are addictive!

Makes 4

1/3 cup sugar

1/4 teaspoon ground cinnamon

All-purpose flour for dusting

1 pound store-bought pizza dough, kept at room temperature 30 to 60 minutes to let rise

Cooking spray

■ Preheat air fryer to 400 degrees F. Mix sugar and cinnamon in a shallow dish.

■ Dust a cutting board with flour. Place dough on cutting board and cut into quarters. Using your fingers, form dough into 6-inch circles. Using a fork, prick each piece of dough about 10 times to prevent it from bubbling up while baking. Lightly spray both sides of dough with cooking spray and dip both sides in cinnamon sugar.

■ Coat air fryer basket with cooking spray. Place 1 piece of dough in basket and air-fry 3 minutes. Using tongs, turn over and continue to cook 2 to 3 more minutes or until light golden.

■ Remove "fried" dough and dip in remaining cinnamon sugar, pressing firmly so it sticks to dough. Repeat process with remaining dough. After last piece is "fried," place all pieces back in basket to warm up (because everyone's going to want to eat these while they're still warm).

An easy way to make sure these are coated all around is to place them (straight from the air fryer) in a paper bag that's filled with the remaining cinnamon sugar. Then just shake, shake, shake until they're well coated. MCM

RECIPES IN ALPHABETICAL ORDER

"Classy Café" Avocado Toast 4
"Spaghetti" & Pork Chunks 134
10-Minute Turkey Tacos 110
All-In Game Day Chili 67
All-in-One Meatball Bake 120
Amish Country Apple Dumplings 223
Any Night Soup 58
Artichoke Dip Company Chicken 98
Asian Chicken Noodle Soup 64
Bacon-Parmesan Creamy Spinach 174
Banana Banana Cream Pie 211
Banana Pancakes with Banana Syrup 13
Banana-Walnut Overnight Oats 19
Barbecue Chicken Flatbread 50
BBQ Chicken Party Ring 105
BBQ-Style Deviled Eggs 32
Beefed-Up Cantina Soup 63
Bite-Sized Berry Dutch Babies 14
Black Bean Tex-Mex Hummus 38
Blackened Catfish & Tropical Slaw 145
Blueberry-Lemon Air Fryer Muffins 18
Bread Bowl Buffalo Chicken Dip 46
Bun-less Egg Sandwich 8
Buttery Potato Skillet 184
Cape Cod Cranberry Bundt 207
Cauliflower Steaks with Romesco 172
Cereal-Crusted French Toast 12
Cheddar Cheesy Rice Bake 179
Cheesy BBQ Meatloaf 123
Cheesy Chicken Tortilla Bake 104
Cheesy Sausage & Tots Bake 7
Cherry-licious Chocolate Cake 199
Chicken Caesar Salad Pizza 102
Chopped Greek Salad 79
Christmas Tree Holiday Stuffing 182
Cinnamon Sugar Air "Fried" Dough 230
Cookie Butter Dump Cake 200
Corn Chip Taco Pie 124
Cranberry-Herb Glazed Chicken 84
Crazy-Good Peanut Toffee 226
Creamy Pesto Chicken Rolls 101
Creamy Swiss Fondue Bread 49
Crispy-Crunchy Carrot Pancakes 170
Crispy-Crunchy Fried Chicken 89
Crunchy Cabbage Salad with
 Peanut Dressing 74
Curried Shrimp Pasta Bowl 148
Double Coconut Layer Cake 198
Dreamy Orange Poke Cake 202
Easy Cheesy Ravioli Lasagna 157
Fan-Favorite Mushroom Soup 59
Fantastic Philly Cheesesteak Dip 30
Farm-Fresh Potato Salad 190
Feta & Kale Quick Bread 188
From-Scratch Pecan Brownies 214
Fruity Chicken Friendship Salad 78
Garlicky Lemon Chicken Wings 36
Grandma's Special Mashed Potatoes 186
Greek-Style Salmon in Phyllo 142
Ham 'n' Egg Rollups 16
Happy Memories Ice Cream Cake 194
Hearty Harvest Salad 68
Heavenly Havarti Orzo Cups 180
Honey Butter Chicken Tenders 96
Hot 'n' Hearty Breakfast Casserole 10
Irish Cream Cheesecake 204
Irish Pub Beef Stew 127
Irish-American Corned Beef & Cabbage 116
Italian Hoagie Salad 72
Italian-Style Rainbow Cookies 218
Keep-it-Simple Shrimp Scampi 45
Kinda Quiche-y Salad 76
Kitchen Sink Chocolate Bark 228
Korean Beef Bulgogi 130
Lemon-Butter Parmesan Tilapia 146
Little Italy Antipasto Stack 28
Loaded Potato Bites 39
Low-Carb, Keto Margherita Pizza 164

INDEX 231

RECIPES IN ALPHABETICAL ORDER

Luscious Lemon Cream Puffs 224
Mac 'n' Cheese with Pretzel Confetti 158
Make-Your-Own Oatmeal Cookie Pizza 20
Maple-Pecan Chicken Breasts 100
Munch Madness Snack Mix 52
My Go-To Burgers 126
Naked Velvet Christmas Cake 196
N'awlins Shrimp Gumbo 149
New England Lobster Rolls 154
No-Bake Peanut Butter Balls 227
Not-Your-Nonna's "Meatballs" 162
Old World Sausage 'n' Cabbage 131
Old-Fashioned Mud Hen Bars 220
Orecchiette with Vodka Sauce 160
Overstuffed Omelet for Two 6
Paradise Pineapple Fritters 24
Parmesan-Crusted Pork Milanese 132
Peachy-Keen Cinnamon Bun Bake 22
Pepperoni Pizza Poppers 33
Pimiento Cheese Lollipops 34
Pink Lemonade Cream Cheese Pie 212
Pistachio Cranberry Biscotti 216
Popular Party Meatballs 44
Pork Tenderloin with Creamy Mustard Sauce 138
Pumpkin Pie Cheesecake Squares 206
Quick & Hearty Spanish Paella 93
Ready-in-20 Baked Fish 144
Real Deal Texas Chili 128
Really Classy Chicken 90
Really Sloppy, Sloppy Joes 122
Roasted "Carroflower" Soup 60
Roasted Eggplant Spread 40
Rustic Steamed Mussels 152
Salted Caramel Cookie Wedges 208
Saucy Balsamic Pork Chops 136
Scallops & Mushroom Risotto 153
Secret Ingredient Sweet Potato Bake 187
Semi-Homemade Chicken & Dumplings 106
Sheet Pan Eggs & Corned Beef Hash 2

Sheet Pan Root Veggies 178
Shrimp & Kale Pasta Toss 150
Shrimp Scampi Salad with Goat Cheese 80
Simply Nutty Broccoli Toss 176
Skillet Steak & Potato Wedges 119
Slow Cooker Italian Chicken 88
Slow Cooker Split Pea Soup 66
Soda Fountain Grilled Chicken 92
Spatchcocked Greek Chicken 86
Special Tuscan Tortellini Soup 62
Sticky Fingers Spareribs 137
Summer-Sweet Strawberry Pie 210
Sweet Onion Petal Crisps 175
Sweet Pickle Coleslaw 191
Tex-Mex Chicken Burritos 97
The Best Brunch Coffee Cake 203
The Better Brisket Dinner 118
The Better Veggie Burger 166
The Real Deal Crab Cakes 156
The Ultimate Chocolate Chip Cookies 217
Turkey Cordon Bleu 108
Tuscan-Style Sausage Rigatoni 161
Two-in-One Stuffed Peppers 94
Unstuffed Cabbage Soup 56
Wedge Salad with Chipotle Ranch Dressing 70
Weeknight-Easy Blueberry Crisp 222
Wilted Bistro Salad 73
Wine & Dine Goat Cheese Bites 42
Wrapped-Up Cranberry Brie 48
Yabba Dabba T-Bone Steak 114

RECIPES BY CATEGORY

Air Fryer
- Blueberry-Lemon Air Fryer Muffins 18
- Garlicky Lemon Chicken Wings 36
- Honey Butter Chicken Tenders 96
- Sticky Fingers Spareribs 137
- The Real Deal Crab Cakes 156

Appetizers
- See "Starters" Table of Contents 27

Bacon
- Bacon-Parmesan Creamy Spinach............. 174
- Irish Pub Beef Stew 127
- Kinda Quiche-y Salad 76
- Loaded Potato Bites 39
- My Go-To Burgers 126
- Pimiento Cheese Lollipops 34
- Wilted Bistro Salad 73

Beans
- Black Bean Tex-Mex Hummus 38
- 10-Minute Turkey Tacos 110
- All-In Game Day Chili 67
- Any Night Soup 58
- Tex-Mex Chicken Burritos 97
- The Better Veggie Burger 166
- Tuscan-Style Sausage Rigatoni 161

Beef
- All-In Game Day Chili 67
- All-in-One Meatball Bake......................... 120
- Beefed-Up Cantina Soup 63
- Cheesy BBQ Meatloaf............................. 123
- Corn Chip Taco Pie.................................. 124
- Fantastic Philly Cheesesteak Dip 30
- Irish Pub Beef Stew 127
- Irish-American Corned Beef & Cabbage........................... 116
- Korean Beef Bulgogi................................ 130
- My Go-To Burgers 126
- Popular Party Meatballs 44
- Real Deal Texas Chili 128
- Really Sloppy, Sloppy Joes...................... 122
- Sheet Pan Eggs & Corned Beef Hash 2
- Skillet Steak & Potato Wedges 119
- The Better Brisket Dinner........................ 118
- Unstuffed Cabbage Soup............................ 56
- Yabba Dabba T-Bone Steak...................... 114

Bread
- "Classy Café" Avocado Toast 4
- 10-Minute Turkey Tacos 110
- All-in-One Meatball Bake......................... 120
- Barbecue Chicken Flatbread 50
- BBQ Chicken Party Ring........................... 105
- Blueberry-Lemon Air Fryer Muffins 18
- Bread Bowl Buffalo Chicken Dip................. 46
- Cereal-Crusted French Toast 12
- Cheesy Chicken Tortilla Bake 104
- Chicken Caesar Salad Pizza 102
- Christmas Tree Holiday Stuffing............... 182
- Cinnamon Sugar Air "Fried" Dough 230
- Corn Chip Taco Pie.................................. 124
- Creamy Swiss Fondue Bread 49
- Feta & Kale Quick Bread 188
- Greek-Style Salmon in Phyllo 142
- Hot 'n' Hearty Breakfast Casserole 10
- Italian Hoagie Salad 72
- Kinda Quiche-y Salad 76
- Maple-Pecan Chicken Breasts 100
- My Go-To Burgers 126
- Paradise Pineapple Fritters....................... 24
- Peachy-Keen Cinnamon Bun Bake.............. 22
- Pepperoni Pizza Poppers........................... 33
- Really Sloppy, Sloppy Joes...................... 122
- Semi-Homemade Chicken & Dumplings............................. 106
- Tex-Mex Chicken Burritos 97
- Wine & Dine Goat Cheese Bites................. 42
- Wrapped-Up Cranberry Brie...................... 48

Breakfast
- See "Breakfast & Brunch" Table of Contents...................................... 1

Brownies/Bars
- Old-Fashioned Mud Hen Bars 220
- From-Scratch Pecan Brownies.................. 214
- Italian-Style Rainbow Cookies 218
- Pumpkin Pie Cheesecake Squares 206
- Salted Caramel Cookie Wedges 208

INDEX 233

RECIPES BY CATEGORY

Cakes, Cupcakes & Cheesecakes
Cape Cod Cranberry Bundt 207
Cherry-licious Chocolate Cake 199
Cookie Butter Dump Cake 200
Double Coconut Layer Cake 198
Dreamy Orange Poke Cake 202
Happy Memories Ice Cream Cake 194
Irish Cream Cheesecake 204
Naked Velvet Christmas Cake 196
Pumpkin Pie Cheesecake Squares 206
The Best Brunch Coffee Cake 203

Casseroles
All-in-One Meatball Bake 120
Bacon-Parmesan Creamy Spinach 174
Cheesy Chicken Tortilla Bake 104
Cheesy Sausage & Tots Bake 7
Corn Chip Taco Pie 124
Easy Cheesy Ravioli Lasagna 157
Hot 'n' Hearty Breakfast Casserole 10
Peachy-Keen Cinnamon Bun Bake 22

Cheese
10-Minute Turkey Tacos 110
All-in-One Meatball Bake 120
Artichoke Dip Company Chicken 98
Bacon-Parmesan Creamy Spinach 174
Barbecue Chicken Flatbread 50
BBQ Chicken Party Ring 105
Beefed-Up Cantina Soup 63
Bread Bowl Buffalo Chicken Dip 46
Bun-less Egg Sandwich 8
Cheddar Cheesy Rice Bake 179
Cheesy BBQ Meatloaf 123
Cheesy Chicken Tortilla Bake 104
Cheesy Sausage & Tots Bake 7
Chicken Caesar Salad Pizza 102
Chopped Greek Salad 79
Corn Chip Taco Pie 124
Creamy Pesto Chicken Rolls 101
Creamy Swiss Fondue Bread 49
Dreamy Orange Poke Cake 202
Easy Cheesy Ravioli Lasagna 157
Fantastic Philly Cheesesteak Dip 30
Feta & Kale Quick Bread 188
Grandma's Special Mashed Potatoes 186
Greek-Style Salmon in Phyllo 142
Ham 'n' Egg Rollups 16
Heavenly Havarti Orzo Cups 180
Hot 'n' Hearty Breakfast Casserole 10
Irish Cream Cheesecake 204
Italian Hoagie Salad 72
Kinda Quiche-y Salad 76
Lemon-Butter Parmesan Tilapia 146
Little Italy Antipasto Stack 28
Loaded Potato Bites 39
Low-Carb, Keto Margherita Pizza 164
Mac 'n' Cheese with Pretzel Confetti 158
My Go-To Burgers 126
Naked Velvet Christmas Cake 196
Not-Your-Nonna's "Meatballs" 162
Overstuffed Omelet for Two 6
Parmesan-Crusted Pork Milanese 132
Pepperoni Pizza Poppers 33
Pimiento Cheese Lollipops 34
Pumpkin Pie Cheesecake Squares 206
Ready-in-20 Baked Fish 144
Scallops & Mushroom Risotto 153
Shrimp Scampi Salad
   with Goat Cheese 80
Spatchcocked Greek Chicken 86
Tex-Mex Chicken Burritos 97
The Better Veggie Burger 166
Turkey Cordon Bleu 108
Two-in-One Stuffed Peppers 94
Wine & Dine Goat Cheese Bites 42
Wrapped-Up Cranberry Brie 48

Chocolate
Cherry-licious Chocolate Cake 199
Crazy-Good Peanut Toffee 226
From-Scratch Pecan Brownies 214
Happy Memories Ice Cream Cake 194
Irish Cream Cheesecake 204
Italian-Style Rainbow Cookies 218
Kitchen Sink Chocolate Bark 228
Naked Velvet Christmas Cake 196
Old-Fashioned Mud Hen Bars 220
Salted Caramel Cookie Wedges 208
The Best Brunch Coffee Cake 203
The Ultimate Chocolate Chip
   Cookies 217

RECIPES BY CATEGORY

Cookies
Italian-Style Rainbow Cookies 218
No-Bake Peanut Butter Balls.................... 227
Pistachio Cranberry Biscotti 216
The Ultimate Chocolate Chip
  Cookies.. 217

Desserts
See "Desserts" Table of Contents 193

Eggs
"Classy Café" Avocado Toast 4
BBQ-Style Deviled Eggs............................. 32
Bun-less Egg Sandwich 8
Cereal-Crusted French Toast 12
Cheesy Sausage & Tots Bake 7
Ham 'n' Egg Rollups 16
Hot 'n' Hearty Breakfast Casserole 10
Overstuffed Omelet for Two 6
Sheet Pan Eggs & Corned Beef Hash 2

Fish
Blackened Catfish & Tropical Slaw 145
Greek-Style Salmon in Phyllo 142
Lemon-Butter Parmesan Tilapia 146
Ready-in-20 Baked Fish 144

Fruit
Amish Country Apple Dumplings............... 223
Banana Banana Cream Pie 211
Banana Pancakes with Banana Syrup.......... 13
Banana-Walnut Overnight Oats.................. 19
Bite-Sized Berry Dutch Babies 14
Blackened Catfish & Tropical Slaw 145
Blueberry-Lemon Air Fryer Muffins 18
Cape Cod Cranberry Bundt 207
Cherry-licious Chocolate Cake 199
Christmas Tree Holiday Stuffing................ 182
Cranberry-Herb Glazed Chicken 84
Double Coconut Layer Cake 198
Dreamy Orange Poke Cake....................... 202
Feta & Kale Quick Bread 188
Fruity Chicken Friendship Salad.................. 78
Hearty Harvest Salad 68
Italian-Style Rainbow Cookies 218
Korean Beef Bulgogi................................ 130
Luscious Lemon Cream Puffs................... 224

Make-Your-Own Oatmeal
  Cookie Pizza 20
Naked Velvet Christmas Cake 196
Paradise Pineapple Fritters........................ 24
Peachy-Keen Cinnamon Bun Bake.............. 22
Pink Lemonade Cream Cheese Pie 212
Pistachio Cranberry Biscotti 216
Really Classy Chicken................................ 90
Spatchcocked Greek Chicken 86
Summer-Sweet Strawberry Pie................. 210
Wedge Salad with Chipotle
  Ranch Dressing 70
Weeknight-Easy Blueberry Crisp............... 222
Wrapped-Up Cranberry Brie...................... 48

Grains
Cheddar Cheesy Rice Bake 179
Quick & Hearty Spanish Paella 93
Scallops & Mushroom Risotto................... 153
Tex-Mex Chicken Burritos 97
The Ultimate Chocolate Chip
  Cookies.. 217
Weeknight-Easy Blueberry Crisp............... 222

Nuts
Banana-Walnut Overnight Oats.................. 19
Blueberry-Lemon Air Fryer Muffins 18
Cape Cod Cranberry Bundt 207
Cauliflower Steaks with Romesco 172
Christmas Tree Holiday Stuffing................ 182
Crazy-Good Peanut Toffee 226
Crunchy Cabbage Salad with
  Peanut Dressing 74
Feta & Kale Quick Bread 188
From-Scratch Pecan Brownies.................. 214
Fruity Chicken Friendship Salad.................. 78
Kitchen Sink Chocolate Bark.................... 228
Low-Carb, Keto Margherita Pizza 164
Munch Madness Snack Mix 52
No-Bake Peanut Butter Balls.................... 227
Peachy-Keen Cinnamon Bun Bake.............. 22
Pimiento Cheese Lollipops 34
Pistachio Cranberry Biscotti 216
Pumpkin Pie Cheesecake Squares 206
Salted Caramel Cookie Wedges 208
Simply Nutty Broccoli Toss 176

RECIPES BY CATEGORY

Wilted Bistro Salad 73
Wine & Dine Goat Cheese Bites 42
Wrapped-Up Cranberry Brie 48

Pasta
Asian Chicken Noodle Soup 64
Curried Shrimp Pasta Bowl 148
Easy Cheesy Ravioli Lasagna 157
Heavenly Havarti Orzo Cups 180
Mac 'n' Cheese with Pretzel Confetti 158
Not-Your-Nonna's "Meatballs" 162
Orecchiette with Vodka Sauce 160
Shrimp & Kale Pasta Toss 150
Special Tuscan Tortellini Soup 62
Tuscan-Style Sausage Rigatoni 161
Two-in-One Stuffed Peppers 94

Pies
Banana Banana Cream Pie 211
Pink Lemonade Cream Cheese Pie 212
Summer-Sweet Strawberry Pie 210

Pizza
Barbecue Chicken Flatbread 50
Chicken Caesar Salad Pizza 102
Low-Carb, Keto Margherita Pizza 164
Make-Your-Own Oatmeal
  Cookie Pizza 20

Pork
"Spaghetti" & Pork Chunks 134
All-In Game Day Chili 67
Any Night Soup 58
Bacon-Parmesan Creamy Spinach 174
Cheesy Sausage & Tots Bake 7
Easy Cheesy Ravioli Lasagna 157
Ham 'n' Egg Rollups 16
Hot 'n' Hearty Breakfast Casserole 10
Irish Pub Beef Stew 127
Italian Hoagie Salad 72
Kinda Quiche-y Salad 76
Loaded Potato Bites 39
My Go-To Burgers 126
Old World Sausage 'n' Cabbage 131
Parmesan-Crusted Pork Milanese 132
Pepperoni Pizza Poppers 33
Pimiento Cheese Lollipops 34
Pork Tenderloin with
  Creamy Mustard Sauce 138
Quick & Hearty Spanish Paella 93
Saucy Balsamic Pork Chops 136
Slow Cooker Split Pea Soup 66
Sticky Fingers Spareribs 137
Turkey Cordon Bleu 108
Wedge Salad with Chipotle
  Ranch Dressing 70
Wilted Bistro Salad 73

Potatoes
Buttery Potato Skillet 184
Cheesy Sausage & Tots Bake 7
Farm-Fresh Potato Salad 190
Grandma's Special Mashed Potatoes 186
Irish-American Corned
  Beef & Cabbage 116
Loaded Potato Bites 39
Secret Ingredient Sweet Potato Bake 187
Sheet Pan Eggs & Corned Beef Hash 2
Sheet Pan Root Veggies 178
Skillet Steak & Potato Wedges 119
The Better Brisket Dinner 118

Poultry
10-Minute Turkey Tacos 110
Artichoke Dip Company Chicken 98
Asian Chicken Noodle Soup 64
Barbecue Chicken Flatbread 50
BBQ Chicken Party Ring 105
Bread Bowl Buffalo Chicken Dip 46
Bun-less Egg Sandwich 8
Cheesy Chicken Tortilla Bake 104
Chicken Caesar Salad Pizza 102
Cranberry-Herb Glazed Chicken 84
Creamy Pesto Chicken Rolls 101
Crispy-Crunchy Fried Chicken 89
Fruity Chicken Friendship Salad 78
Garlicky Lemon Chicken Wings 36
Honey Butter Chicken Tenders 96
Maple-Pecan Chicken Breasts 100
Quick & Hearty Spanish Paella 93
Really Classy Chicken 90
Semi-Homemade
  Chicken & Dumplings 106

RECIPES BY CATEGORY

Slow Cooker Italian Chicken 88
Soda Fountain Grilled Chicken 92
Spatchcocked Greek Chicken 86
Tex-Mex Chicken Burritos 97
Turkey Cordon Bleu 108
Tuscan-Style Sausage Rigatoni 161
Two-in-One Stuffed Peppers 94

Rice
Cheddar Cheesy Rice Bake 179
Quick & Hearty Spanish Paella 93
Scallops & Mushroom Risotto 153
Tex-Mex Chicken Burritos 97

Salads
Chicken Caesar Salad Pizza 102
Chopped Greek Salad 79
Crunchy Cabbage Salad with
  Peanut Dressing 74
Farm-Fresh Potato Salad 190
Fruity Chicken Friendship Salad 78
Hearty Harvest Salad 68
Italian Hoagie Salad 72
Kinda Quiche-y Salad 76
Shrimp Scampi Salad with
  Goat Cheese 80
Sweet Pickle Coleslaw 191
Wedge Salad with Chipotle
  Ranch Dressing 70
Wilted Bistro Salad 73

Sandwiches
Bun-less Egg Sandwich 8
My Go-To Burgers 126
New England Lobster Rolls 154
Really Sloppy, Sloppy Joes 122
The Better Veggie Burger 166

Shellfish
"Classy Café" Avocado Toast 4
Curried Shrimp Pasta Bowl 148
Keep-it-Simple Shrimp Scampi 45
N'awlins Shrimp Gumbo 149
New England Lobster Rolls 154
Quick & Hearty Spanish Paella 93
Rustic Steamed Mussels 152
Scallops & Mushroom Risotto 153

Shrimp & Kale Pasta Toss 150
Shrimp Scampi Salad with
  Goat Cheese 80
The Real Deal Crab Cakes 156

Side Dishes
See "Side Dishes" Table of Contents 169

Slow Cooker
Slow Cooker Split Pea Soup 66
"Spaghetti" & Pork Chunks 134
Slow Cooker Italian Chicken 88
The Better Brisket Dinner........................ 118

Soups
All-In Game Day Chili 67
Any Night Soup 58
Asian Chicken Noodle Soup 64
Beefed-Up Cantina Soup 63
Fan-Favorite Mushroom Soup 59
Roasted "Carroflower" Soup 60
Slow Cooker Split Pea Soup 66
Special Tuscan Tortellini Soup 62
Unstuffed Cabbage Soup 56

Spirits / Liquours / Beers
Creamy Swiss Fondue Bread 49
All-In Game Day Chili 67
Irish Cream Cheesecake 204
Irish Pub Beef Stew 127
Irish-American Corned
  Beef & Cabbage 116
Maple-Pecan Chicken Breasts 100
Orecchiette with Vodka Sauce 160
Pork Tenderloin with Creamy
  Mustard Sauce 138
Rustic Steamed Mussels 152
Scallops & Mushroom Risotto 153
Slow Cooker Italian Chicken 88

Vegetables
"Classy Café" Avocado Toast 4
"Spaghetti" & Pork Chunks 134
10-Minute Turkey Tacos 110
All-In Game Day Chili 67
Any Night Soup 58
Artichoke Dip Company Chicken 98
Asian Chicken Noodle Soup 64

INDEX 237

RECIPES BY CATEGORY

Bacon-Parmesan Creamy Spinach............. 174
Barbecue Chicken Flatbread 50
BBQ Chicken Party Ring............................. 105
Beefed-Up Cantina Soup 63
Blackened Catfish & Tropical Slaw 145
Bread Bowl Buffalo Chicken Dip................. 46
Buttery Potato Skillet 184
Cauliflower Steaks with Romesco 172
Cheddar Cheesy Rice Bake 179
Cheesy Chicken Tortilla Bake 104
Cheesy Sausage & Tots Bake 7
Chicken Caesar Salad Pizza...................... 102
Chopped Greek Salad 79
Christmas Tree Holiday Stuffing................ 182
Corn Chip Taco Pie..................................... 124
Creamy Pesto Chicken Rolls..................... 101
Crispy-Crunchy Carrot Pancakes 170
Crunchy Cabbage Salad with
  Peanut Dressing 74
Fan-Favorite Mushroom Soup 59
Fantastic Philly Cheesesteak Dip 30
Farm-Fresh Potato Salad 190
Feta & Kale Quick Bread 188
Fruity Chicken Friendship Salad.................. 78
Grandma's Special Mashed Potatoes 186
Greek-Style Salmon in Phyllo 142
Ham 'n' Egg Rollups 16
Hearty Harvest Salad 68
Heavenly Havarti Orzo Cups 180
Hot 'n' Hearty Breakfast Casserole 10
Irish Pub Beef Stew 127
Irish-American Corned
  Beef & Cabbage...................................... 116
Italian Hoagie Salad 72
Kinda Quiche-y Salad 76
Korean Beef Bulgogi.................................. 130
Loaded Potato Bites 39
Low-Carb, Keto Margherita Pizza 164
N'awlins Shrimp Gumbo 149
New England Lobster Rolls 154
Not-Your-Nonna's "Meatballs" 162
Old World Sausage 'n' Cabbage 131
Overstuffed Omelet for Two 6
Parmesan-Crusted Pork Milanese 132

Pimiento Cheese Lollipops 34
Pumpkin Pie Cheesecake Squares 206
Quick & Hearty Spanish Paella 93
Real Deal Texas Chili 128
Really Sloppy, Sloppy Joes....................... 122
Roasted "Carroflower" Soup 60
Roasted Eggplant Spread 40
Rustic Steamed Mussels 152
Scallops & Mushroom Risotto................... 153
Secret Ingredient Sweet Potato Bake 187
Semi-Homemade
  Chicken & Dumplings............................. 106
Sheet Pan Eggs & Corned Beef Hash 2
Sheet Pan Root Veggies............................ 178
Shrimp & Kale Pasta Toss 150
Shrimp Scampi Salad with Goat Cheese...... 80
Simply Nutty Broccoli Toss 176
Skillet Steak & Potato Wedges.................. 119
Slow Cooker Italian Chicken....................... 88
Slow Cooker Split Pea Soup 66
Special Tuscan Tortellini Soup 62
Sweet Onion Petal Crisps 175
Sweet Pickle Coleslaw.............................. 191
Tex-Mex Chicken Burritos 97
The Better Brisket Dinner.......................... 118
The Better Veggie Burger 166
Tuscan-Style Sausage Rigatoni 161
Two-in-One Stuffed Peppers....................... 94
Unstuffed Cabbage Soup............................ 56
Wedge Salad with Chipotle
  Ranch Dressing 70
Wilted Bistro Salad 73

INDEX

MY FAVORITE RECIPES

RECIPE   **PAGE NUMBER**

NOTES